FRIENDSHIP

FRIENDSHIP

Liberty, Equality, and Utility

JAMES O. GRUNEBAUM

STATE UNIVERSITY OF NEW YORK PRESS

Cover: Small Islands
Lawrence C. Goldsmith
Watercolor, 18 inches x 24 inches

Published by
STATE UNIVERSITY OF NEW YORK PRESS
ALBANY

For information, address
State University of New York Press,
90 State Street, Suite 700, Albany, NY 12207

Production, Laurie Searl
Marketing, Fran Keneston

Library of Congress Cataloging-in-Publication Data

Grunebaum, James O.
Friendship : liberty, equality, and utility / James O. Grunebaum.
p. cm.
Includes bibliographical references and index.
ISBN 0-7914-5717-6 (hardcover : alk. paper) — ISBN 0-7914-5718-4 (pbk. : alk. paper)
1. Friendship—Moral and ethical aspects. I. Title.

BJ1533.F8 G785 2003
177'.62—dc21
2002075883

10   9   8   7   6   5   4   3   2   1

In memory of

Andrew Grunebaum

1945–1987

Brother—Friend

CONTENTS

ACKNOWLEDGMENTS

Portions of this book, in a different form, have been published as "Friendship, Morality, and Special Obligation," *American Philosophical Quarterly* 30, no. 1 (1993); "On Becoming Friends," *Cithara* 38, no. 1 (1998); and "What Is So Good about Friendship?" in *Inherent and Instrumental Value*, edited by John Abbarno, University Press of America, 2002. I would like to thank them for permission to use it here.

I am indebted to Buffalo State College, State University of New York, for a sabbatical leave in 1999 and for its subsequent support of my research that permitted me to bring my thoughts on friendship into final form.

Special thanks to Lawrence C. Goldsmith for the use of his wonderful painting *Small Islands* on the cover.

There are many friendly people who have been generous in reading and commenting on earlier versions of this manuscript, including Cynthia Anthony, John Carbonara, Robert Elmes, George Hole, and Lance Pollock. I thank them for their efforts, and I trust that they will absolve me of my own errors. I thank my wife, Penelope Prentice, for her editorial attempts at making my writing readable, but more importantly, I express my endless gratitude to her for our lifelong intimacy and companion friendship.

ONE

PREFERENCE FOR FRIENDS

INTRODUCTION

A PREFERENCE FOR FRIENDS over nonfriends is at the core of friendship.[1] For example, someone who professes friendship for another person but who acts in no special way toward her in comparison to others or who acts toward her only with what morality requires, but no more, is not considered her friend. Friendship must involve some special preference between friends. Friends preferring each other has been understood as a description of behavior, as a moral prescription, and as a defining characteristic. Two people who treat each other no differently from the way they treat all others would not be considered friends.

Preferring friends to nonfriends is something that friends naturally desire. They prefer spending time together, engaged in the activities of friendship, to spending time with those who are not their friends. Time spent with nonfriends can be boring and a chore. That friends also have an obligation to prefer each other to nonfriends is thought to be morally correct by most individuals and cultures. Not only should friends do more good for each other, but stronger moral prohibitions often exist against harming friends than harming nonfriends. The friendship relation is partial, specific, and particular. By definition, persons who are friends participate in a relationship that they do not and cannot share with everyone else. Friendship, like kinship, marks off a difference and a specialness that differentiates friendship from moral relations that can universally apply to everyone.

Is preferring friends to nonfriends morally justifiable? A number of philosophers, including Michael Stocker, Martha Nussbaum, and Lawrence A. Blum, among others, have noticed a prima facie conflict between friendship and objective, universal, egalitarian, impersonal, or impartial moral principles. They have used this conflict as a reason for questioning not only the legitimacy of friendship but also the justifiability of morality itself and its specific principles. A radically different view is advocated by Jacques Derrida.[2] For friends to benefit each other, either at the expense of, or by ignoring, nonfriends, they claim, is in conflict with these moral principles and the morality they reflect. Other philosophers, such as Bernard Williams, resolve the conflict by claiming that preferring friends is obviously morally right.[3] This "obvious" and perhaps ultimately correct position can obscure many vital philosophical issues. Suppose it is obviously true that friends sometimes should be treated with preference in comparison to nonfriends; it is equally obviously true that at other times friends should not be treated with preference in comparison to nonfriends. Philosophically important questions need to be answered: When is preferential treatment of friends justifiable? When is it not justifiable? Precisely, what kinds of reasons morally justify any preference and set its limit?

There may be reasons internal to the concept of friendship that provide moral justification for preferring friends, perhaps resembling the way that moral obligations are internal to promising. In addition to internal justifications, moral principles external to friendship provide a variety of reasons specifying divergent limits of preferring friends to nonfriends. Yet both internal and external moral justifications of preference in friendship are dependent upon an answer to the most elementary philosophical question: What is friendship? A number of related but nonequivalent conceptions of friendship exist within and without our Western philosophical tradition that give different "obvious" answers to the question, should friends prefer each other to nonfriends, so that a plurality of morally correct answers is possible.

A good deal of philosophical analysis must be undertaken to supply a coherent understanding of preference for friends. Most importantly, a critical schema for comparing and contrasting various different conceptions of friendship needs to be developed. Only through this schema can conceptions of friendship be clearly distinguished and compared, so that it is possible to discover internal justifications for preferring friends to others and to apply external moral principles to determine when and how much preference is justifiable. While conceptions of friendship differ from each other, they all, nevertheless, possess a similar structure that is essential in understanding their resemblances and differences.

The remainder of this chapter sets the stage by refining issues of rights and duties in friendship, by contrasting two of the more important Western conceptions of friendship, Aristotle's and Kant's ideals, and then by briefly introducing other diverse friendship conceptions. Chapter 2 explains the common structure of all conceptions of friendship. Chapter 3 examines moral justifications for preferring friends that are internal to friendship. In chapter 4, preference for friends is justified from three external moral perspectives: liberty, equality, and utility. Chapter 5 defends the value of a "less-than-ideal" conception of friendship and summarizes salient results of earlier chapters.

There has never been a thoroughgoing examination of various conceptions of friendship and the more commonly employed moral principles. Partisan and myopic investigations have reached mixed results. Sometimes supposed conflicts between a vague conception of friendship and some moral principle are used to criticize that moral principle because it conflicts with friendship's demands.[4] Troy A. Jollimore is a recent example. In an otherwise carefully argued book, *Friendship and Agent-Relative Morality*, he employs a much too vague conception of friendship to criticize consequentialist morality.[5] At other times, possible conflicts between friendship and morality are used to criticize what is called foundationalism, that is, any attempt to justify moral institutions or practices by fundamental moral principles.[6] At another extreme, various conceptions of friendship are rejected as being thoroughly immoral, because they appear to conflict with one or another moral principle.

A more general and more neutral approach is worth pursuing. Rather than using friendship merely to criticize one's least favorite moral principle or using one's favorite principle to defend a form of friendship that is not well analyzed, it is more illuminating to explore the complex relationships between various conceptions of friendship and a fairly comprehensive list of plausible moral principles. A more open approach will produce a less biased and more accurate understanding of the complex relations between friendship and moral principles.

PREFERENCE: DUTIES AND RIGHTS

Although analyzing friendship wholly in terms of duties and rights is misleading, because friendship involves caring for and goodwill, as well as duty
or rights, preferring friends to others can still be partially understood in
terms of moral rights and duties. Friends frequently assist and benefit each
other without ever considering any moral rights or duties. Acting with
goodwill and concern for each other is part of what creates or constitutes
happiness for friends. Nevertheless, duties and rights constitute part of many
conceptions of friendship.

That we owe special duties to our friends or that we ought to treat friends
with special preference is a belief held by almost every culture. This belief implies that a special duty to help our friends is stronger than any duty of beneficence owed to humanity in general. Similarly, our duty to refrain from
harming friends is believed to be stronger than any general duty of nonmalef-
icence. For some conceptions of friendship (Aristotle's friendship based on
utility is just one example), friends are to be there when help is needed.
Friends are special relations who can be counted upon for assistance in times
of crisis as well as relations who are sought out to share benefits in good times.
Even though friends may want to help each other without ever thinking of
obligations, obligations do exist. Many conceptions of friendship contain expectations that friends recognize a special duty to assist each other. Certainly
a friend's failing to help in a time of need without having any compelling reason would be subject to specially severe blame and guilt.

Special duties, what W. D. Ross calls "parti-resultant" duties, depend on
certain particular relations such as being a parent, an employer, or a friend,
that constitute one part of a whole situation.[7] Special duties, in Ross's sense,
also are prima facie not duties proper, because they can conflict with and be
overridden by other prima facie duties. Special duties arise in two distinct
ways. For some special duties, only persons who are in the special relations
have the duties in any degree whatsoever. An illustration of this kind of special duty comes from the Old Testament, where a man has a duty to marry his
brother's widow, even if the man is presently married. Nonbrothers have no
duty at all to marry widows, and married men without brothers may not acquire additional wives. Teachers also may have special duties to their students
which nonteachers lack entirely. The second kind of special duties includes
ordinary duties that are magnified, that is, duties that everyone has to some
degree but that are stronger because of a special factor or relation. Everyone

may have a duty to be kind to others, but parents have a greater duty to be kind to their children than to nonkin. Failing to live up to one's duty toward friends in this sense may be a more blameworthy dereliction than is an identical failure toward a nonfriend. Stronger blame may be justified, because of the stronger duty that is violated. Variations exist, however, among different forms of friendship. Some forms would view the dereliction more seriously, while other forms might view it as less blameworthy.[8]

There is an additional way that friends are expected to act specially toward each other. Friendship, as it is sometimes understood, requires that friends treat each other in a morally exemplary way. Failure to live up to all moral expectations is less tolerated between friends than between nonfriends, although there are forms of friendship in which friends are expected to be more forgiving of each other for failing to live up to moral ideals. Nevertheless, for many forms of friendship, friends are supposed to have a special concern for each other that manifests in morally ideal behavior. While it is never morally right to behave toward anyone in an immoral way, there is a greater tolerance of one's moral imperfection if one's failure is directed toward nonfriends rather than friends. Friends are expected to try harder to be good to each other in difficult circumstances. For example, letting down one's friend by failing to behave toward her as she morally deserves is a major shortcoming. Friends should feel greater guilt and embarrassment in behaving badly to each other than to those with whom they are not friends. Behavior between friends exemplifies the very best in human conduct. Later, this moral requirement of friendship, that friends treat each other in a morally exemplary way, plays a major role in understanding whether treating friends better than nonfriends is morally justified.

The preference that friends exhibit toward each other need not take the form of moral duties of assistance or rescue. Special preferential behavior constituting friendship may take the form of a responsibility to receive each friend's personal thoughts and confidences. Friends may be intimate with each other yet feel no duty to be intimate with nonfriends. Some forms of friendship regard intimacy as being essential to friendship, while other forms may only regard it as being permissible. Friends can be intimate with each other, but they also may merely choose to share external interests and activities.

Not all of the ways that friends express preference for each other affect moral duties. Some ways create more while other ways create less potential moral conflict. There are many circumstances, such as choosing someone to go to the cinema with, where no moral considerations normally apply. Certainly it is right to choose to go with one's friend, but it would be equally right to choose to take one's sister, or even to choose to go alone. Preferring friends may be right, that is, morally permissible, because no rights of others are involved, or because preferring friends conflicts with no other duties or obligations.

FRIENDSHIP AND PROMISING

A close parallel exists between preference for friends and promising, which nicely illustrates the moral issue of preferring friends to others. Promising is a rule-constituted social institution that permits coordination of people's activities through voluntarily undertaken moral obligations.[9] Many different social institutions of promising are possible. They are distinguishable from each other by their different constitutive rules. Different forms of promising have constitutive rules that delineate promises: how they are made, when they may be broken, and the strength of the obligation. Within each form of promising, there may be different kinds or degrees of promises (e.g., common agreements, pledges, vows, and oaths). Particular forms of promising differ from each other by rules that, among other things, specify conditions under which a promise may legitimately be broken, for example, if the burden is too great for the promisor or too great for the promisee, if there are unforeseen burdens on third parties, if the promisee changes her mind, and so forth. Different rules will exist for indicating the strength of the duty to keep the promise. Assuming that there are different degrees of obligation within the particular institution, the obligation to return a borrowed book may be less strong than the obligation arising from a pledge to visit a friend in the hospital.

While all forms of promising have in common undertaking some moral obligation or other, the content and strength of the obligation depend on society's rule-constituted form of promising. Since different societies have different institutions of promising, it cannot be assumed that a particular society's institution of promising is morally correct, and that the duties imposed on those who make promises are morally justified duties. For any particular form of promising, it therefore makes sense to ask whether the institution, as well as promises made according to its rules, is morally justified.

Friendship closely resembles promising. Different forms of friendship are constituted by various sets of rules and expectations about who may become friends, how friends should treat each other, what activities typify friendship, the purposes of friendship, and what should attract friends to each other. Different societies may have one or a number of different forms or conceptions of friendship, each with its own specific expectations. Within a society, different forms of friendship are possible, each with its own set of rules and each with its own level of social value. To create a friendship is to undertake certain specific expectations, both moral and nonmoral about each friend's behavior.[10] These expectations are what the participants impose upon themselves when they become friends: how much time they should spend together, how much assistance they owe each other, how much intimacy or self-disclosure is appropriate, and what assets they should share. The kinds of preferences friends exhibit for each other in contrast to nonfriends therefore vary with each particular individual form or conception of friendship.

To discover in what circumstances preferring friends to nonfriends is morally justifiable, different conceptions or forms of friendship must be morally evaluated. By "form" or "conception" of friendship, I mean a specific set of expectations for being friends. Moral justifications for preferring friends to nonfriends depend to a great extent on which conceptions of friendship are morally justifiable, assuming that there may be more than one morally justifiable conception. As with promising, some of the expectations will prove to be immoral (e.g., promises to commit murder). Not every way of preferring friends to nonfriends will be morally justified, nor will every actual instance of preference.

There are, in principle, two different ways of morally evaluating conceptions of friendship. The first, which I call the external justification, evaluates friendship by independent, rationally grounded, moral principles. In an external justification, a conception of friendship, with its constitutive rules and internally defined concepts, is examined in light of some moral principle to see whether its rules and concepts fulfill the justificatory requirements of the principle. According to utilitarian theory, for example, a form of friendship would be studied to see whether it directly or indirectly produces the best overall consequences. A Kantian justification might require that a specific form of friendship should respect all rational beings, both friend and nonfriend, as necessary ends and never treat them merely as means. A libertarian moral principle might permit people to initiate specific kinds of friendships, as long as the rights of others are not violated. Each external justification must include an examination of the basis of friendship, its object, and the nature of friendship, as defined by the particular conception.[11] External justifications should not only be capable of morally evaluating special rights and duties included in the particular form of friendship but also should be capable of determining when, and under what circumstances, friends are justifiably preferred or treated better than nonfriends.

An external justification can have no greater moral cogency than that possessed by its justificatory moral principle. The more firmly grounded any moral principle is then the more confidence there can be in an external justification of a conception of friendship. If, to illustrate, direct-act utilitarianism were firmly grounded by rational argument, then it would be morally right to act with preference toward one's friends in, and only in, those circumstances that produce the best possible consequences. However, to the degree that direct-act utilitarianism is not firmly grounded but is open to criticism or objection, so similarly under suspicion will be an external justification of preferring friends to others based on utilitarianism.

A great deal can be learned by examining various kinds of friendship from a variety of moral perspectives. Some kinds of friendship may turn out to have fewer potential conflicts with rationally plausible moral principles than others. Conflicts can result from any aspect of the structure of friendship, its basis, object, or the nature of the relation, or from them in combination. One important conclusion of this investigation is that Kant's conception of the best achievable friendship is less likely to require the kinds of conflict-producing preferential action toward friends than many other conceptions of friendship. Consequently, conflicts between preferring friends to nonfriends are minimized if friendship is understood according to Kant's best form.

Whatever one's moral allegiances, external justifications illuminate logical relations between moral principles and various conceptions of friendship. Partisans of one of these moral principles will discover what their principle rationally commits them to regarding the moral justifiability of friendship. Chapter 4 discusses external justifications of friendship and preferring friends from the perspectives of liberty, equality, and utility.

The second way of evaluating preference for friends is to see whether conceptions of friendship contain their own moral standards. This I call the "internal justification." If, as some conceptions of friendship require, friends should always act toward each other in the very best possible moral manner, then there may be moral standards internal to the concept of friendship that determine when preferring friends to nonfriends is morally right and when it is morally wrong. Less-than-ideal conceptions of friendship may likewise contain internal prescriptions defining appropriate behavior between friends, but some of their prescriptions may be less than morally ideal.

Internal justifications, discussed in chapter 3, have two primary difficulties to overcome. The first is endemic to both internal and external attempts to justify preferential treatment of friends. Justifications for preferring friends must be sufficiently specific to supply guidance in deciding when friends may rightly receive better treatment and when not. Internal justifications face many difficulties in achieving this precision. The second difficulty that internal justifications face is much more their own. If friendship is regarded as exemplifying the best in human behavior, then it is difficult to see how friendship justifies treating some people better than others. If friendly behavior is morally ideal behavior, then is it only friends to whom such behavior is limited? Internal justifications must explain when the morality internal to friendship legitimates preferring friends to nonfriends.

Great clarity is required to discuss different conceptions of friendship. There are many different conceptions of friendship both within Western culture and in other cultures. The moral implications of these conceptions of friendship are very different from each other. Up until now, discussions of the differences between the various conceptions have remained vague and overly general, because the internal structure of friendship has not been well understood. Of course, it has been known since Aristotle that friendships can have different bases: pleasure, utility, and goodness. The other structural dimensions of friendships that differ from each other (i.e., in their objects and in their natures) have not been well appreciated. Chapter 2 makes all of this clear. But the discussion in that chapter will be clearer if several conceptions of friendship are first sketched out to illustrate the possible range of difference.

TWO IDEALS: ARISTOTLE AND KANT

Aristotle's conception of the best form of friendship has had more influence on Western ideas about friendship than any other. Nancy Sherman calls this friendship "virtue friendship," and John Cooper refers to it as "character friendship."[12] This "best friendship," according to Aristotle, is between equals in virtue who "wish well to each other" and bear each other "goodwill" because of their moral goodness.[13] A friend is "another self," and friends consider all they possess to be common property.[14] More than anything, friends desire to live together, spending as much time as possible with each other helping to promote their virtue.[15] Nancy Sherman sees "virtue friends" sharing a life together, not only in their activities but also in choosing and planning together in ways that take into account not only their commitment to each other but also their separate individuality.[16]

Aristotle's best friendship, unlike his friendships of lesser value, does not depend on external benefits that friends produce for each other. In his lesser friendships, friends love each other because of the utility or pleasure they gain from the relation. Utility-based friendships are friendships where friends count on each other in times of need. Utility friends are "there when you need them," "willing to lend a helping hand," and "someone to be counted on." While it is still true that utility friends have reciprocal goodwill for each other and do not merely use each other as a means, it is the overall benefit of the relationship that creates their mutual love.[17]

Character or virtue friends desire to share their lives together engaging in virtuous activities. Their lives are happy, according to Aristotle, who believes that happiness is an activity of the soul according to right reason or virtue. The activity component of friends' shared virtuous life needs to be emphasized. Friends do things together. Aristotle says virtually nothing about the inner or private mental lives of friends. When friendship is thought about today, it is assumed that friends are intimate and know a great deal about each other's inner or private mental life.[18]

Kant's conception of the best form of friendship is a friendship based on intimacy and communion. In contrast to Aristotle, Kant's intimacy friendship supposes that friends will spend time sharing their feelings or emotions and informing each other about their opinions or sentiments. Friends are thought to be mutual confidants, with their friendship aiming at similar internal mental states or communion. This understanding of Kant's intimacy friendship also is well explained by Lara Denis in her article "From Friendship to Marriage: Revising Kant."[19]

None of this inner mental life is explicitly found in Aristotle's account of character or virtue friendship. It might be assumed that if two character or virtue friends share enough of their lives together, they will become intimate and learn a great deal about each other's inner life, but the exchange of private thoughts need not occur, even if two friends spend a great deal of time together. Their time with each other may be consumed wholly in joint activities, leaving little time for (idle?) intimate chatter. Friends may, nevertheless, learn about each other's private lives, but such knowledge will not be the object of their friendship, and it will arise indirectly and "casually."[20] To argue that character friendships are intimate may be reading back anachronistically more than Aristotle actually says about friendship.[21] David Konstan, in his book, *Friendship in the Classical World*, acknowledges that, "Never in antiquity, so far as I am aware, is the revelation of personal intimacies described as necessary for the formation of friendship."[22] In contrast to Aristotle, Kant's conception of ideal friendship is based on intimacy and communication of private and personal thoughts.

Aristotelian character or virtue friends treat each other in ways that they do not treat nonfriends.[23] First, they will want to spend as much time with each other as they can and share what they own as common property. This is not behavior that they will display to nonfriends. They also will want to do good and avoid doing evil to each other to a greater extent than they will desire to do good and avoid evil for nonfriends. As Aristotle says:

> [I]t is a more terrible thing to defraud a comrade than a fellow citizen, more terrible not to help a brother than a stranger, and more terrible to wound a father than any one else. And the demands of justice also naturally increase with the friendship.[24]

A special duty exists between friends, at least in the sense of a magnification of the ordinary duties of benevolence and nonmalevolence. There are negative duties not to "defraud" or "wound" as well as positive duties to "help" and be "just" that are owed to both friends and nonfriends. Aristotle is saying that with friends, these duties increase in the strength of obligation. Most ways that Aristotle believes friends act with preference to each other are magnifications of duties owed to all, for example, helping to become virtuous,[25] or to better see the truth.[26] These are duties that everyone owes, to some extent, to everyone else. However, at least one special duty exists that is not an ordinary duty magnified. Even though Aristotle believes in a positive duty of benevolence, sharing all property in common is not something that is owed to any degree to nonfriends. Thus to the extent that sharing all in common is a duty of virtue or character friendship, it is a special duty possessed only by friends and not by nonfriends in any degree at all.

Whether Aristotle is right in thinking that friends have special or stronger duties to each other is one of the main questions of this book. A subsidiary, but just as important, question is, will friends act with preference toward each other in situations where it is not justified? Friendship has its darker side. Will feelings of loyalty mislead friends, seducing them away from their legitimate moral responsibilities? Cicero fears that friends will believe that friendship justifies doing something for each other that otherwise would be immoral.[27] The danger always exists that misguided friendships will cause much harm. Aristotle's virtue friends, while equally virtuous, are not perfectly so. They may think that they should assist each other at the expense of nonfriends in situations where preferring each other is not justified. This fear about friendship's darker side is more fully discussed in chapter 4.

While Aristotle's friends of the best kind may benefit each other a great deal as a consequence of their reciprocal goodwill and preferential treatment, they are not friends because of these benefits. Their reason for being attracted to each other is their virtue and goodness, not how they may benefit. Advantage, benefit, and pleasure are bases for Aristotle's less-than-ideal friendships.

Character friends will have many activities with which to occupy their shared life. The basis of character friendship is virtue, that is, for Aristotle, activity of the right kind. Friends will engage in similar daily exercises and gymnastics insofar as exercise is necessary for health and they are roughly equal in body and strength. To the extent that they are similar in knowledge, they will cooperate in learning and contemplation to strengthen their virtue of wisdom. They will assist each other in temperance training to bring their pleasures and pains into the right proportion. There is no shortage of the right kind of activities to engage their time and interest in order to improve their virtue. Character friends are equal in virtue, according to Aristotle, but they are not perfectly virtuous. For them to be perfectly virtuous, they would have to be gods, and unless they both were perfectly virtuous, they could not be friends.[28]

It is not possible to have a large number of virtue friends. Living together in a shared life requires so much time that it is not possible for more than two or three persons to be virtue friends together. There is not sufficient time in a day. For other conceptions of friendship, greater numbers of friends may be possible. One nonmoral criterion for assessing the relevance of various conceptions of friendship will be the number of friends it is possible to have according to each conception.

Aristotle's conception of the best form of friendship, as well as his conception of his two lesser forms, is more fully discussed in chapter 2 as illustrations of the structure of friendship and as a further illustration of the wide variety of possible kinds of friendship.

I now discuss, in somewhat greater detail, Kant's ideal of friendship. My reason for spending more time at this point on Kant's ideal is that it is not nearly as well known as Aristotle's. I want to stress the differences between Kant and Aristotle here rather than the similarities that exist between their two conceptions in order to create a preliminary impression of the range existing in possible kinds of friendship. I end this introductory chapter by briefly discussing some additional, different ideals of friendship.

Kant distinguishes between two different concepts of valuable friendship, one of which is merely an "idea unattainable in practice" and the other of which can be attained, but with difficulty.[29] The unattainable friendship is "the

union of two persons through equal mutual love and respect . . . each participating and sharing sympathetically in the other's well-being through the morally
goodwill that unites them."[30] The love and respect that constitute friendship
Kant carefully differentiates from the love and respect considered feelings. Love
is to be understood neither as a feeling (*asthetischen*) of pleasure in the perfection
of other men nor as a delight in them; instead, it is to be understood as benevolence and practical love.[31] Respect must be understood as the maxim of limiting one's self-esteem by the dignity of humanity in others, not as a mere feeling
of comparing one's worth to others.[32] This friendship is unattainable in practice,
Kant states, because it is impossible to discover whether friends' love and respect
are really equal. Kant's explicit reason for thinking that this friendship is unattainable in practice, namely, not being able to discover whether friends' love and
respect are really equal, is not a reason explaining the failure to attain ideal
friendship, as Kant claims, but only of ever knowing that it is attained.

There is another possible explanation why Kant thinks that this friendship
is unattainable in practice. In his discussion of the duty of gratitude, Kant
points out that being the recipient of a kindness creates an inequality that can
never be removed. One friend who, out of practical love, performs a kindness
for another creates a permanent friendship destroying inequality between
them.[33] So although equality between friends is impossible to achieve, Kant
believes that this ideal friendship serves as a goal for which to aim, a goal that
is equivalent to fulfilling the categorical imperative's morally demanding
injunction to act with benevolence and respect to all rational beings.

Problems surface within Kant's ideal conception of friendship that go beyond his difficulty about the impossibility of ever discovering and maintaining
reciprocally equal love and respect. His equal love and respect conception of
friendship violates an essential characteristic of friendship, that is, that friendship
is partial, specific, and particular, so that a person cannot, by definition, be a
friend to everyone. Friendship requires that friends treat each other in ways that
they do not treat all others. Privileges and obligations in friendship are not extended to nonfriends. Kant's ideal conception of friendship requires behavior
between friends identical to the respect as necessary ends required by the categorical imperative for behavior toward all people. As a result, those requirements
of friendship are no different from the behavior that everyone is expected to extend toward all rational moral beings. Acting on the demands of friendship, according to this conception, is no different from acting on the demands of
impartial (and perhaps impersonal) morality. Kant simply identifies friendship
with ideal moral behavior. Other philosophers make this identification as well;

Neera Kapur Badhwar is one of a number of examples.[34] It is a frequent theme with some philosophers to regard the way friends ought to be treated as manifesting the highest ideal of moral behavior. But there always must be some differentiation between friendship and morally exemplary behavior that is owed to all persons. While it must be possible to treat anyone in the way one behaves toward a friend, and to this extent the behavior must be universalizable, the demands of friendship on friends' behavior toward each other must also illustrate the essentially particular nature of its relation. The love and respect required by Kant's ideal conception of friendship do not show why friends are special. Love and respect are simply the ideal moral behavior required by the categorical imperative toward everyone.

Kant discusses his other and attainable ideal of friendship in both *The Metaphysics of Morals* and *Lectures on Ethics*. In *The Metaphysics of Morals*, he calls it "moral friendship."

> *Moral friendship* (as distinguished from friendship based on feeling [*asthetischen*]) is the complete confidence of two persons in revealing their secret judgments and feelings to each other, as far as such disclosures are consistent with mutual respect.[35] (emphasis in original)

In the *Lectures on Ethics*, this ideal is called "fellowship or disposition friendship."

> But if we can free ourselves of this constraint, if we can unburden our heart to another, we achieve complete communion. That this release may be achieved, each of us needs a friend, one in whom we can confide unreservedly, to whom we can disclose completely all our dispositions and judgments from whom we can and need hide nothing, to whom we can communicate our whole self. On this rests the friendship of dispositions and fellowship.[36]

This same idea also appears in *The Metaphysics of Morals*:

> If he finds someone intelligent—someone who, moreover, shares his general outlook on things—with whom he need not be anxious about this danger but can reveal himself with complete confidence, he can then air his views. He is not completely alone with his thoughts, as in a prison, but enjoys a freedom he cannot have with the masses, among whom he must shut himself up in himself. Every man has his secrets and dare not confide blindly in others, partly because of a base cast of mind in most men to use them to one's disadvantage and partly because many people are indiscreet or incapable of judging and distinguishing what may or may not be repeated. The necessary combination of qualities is seldom found in one person . . . especially since the closest friendship requires that a judicious and trusted friend be also bound not to share the secrets entrusted to him with anyone else, no matter how reliable he thinks him, without explicit permission to do so.[37]

Kant believes that the world is an unfriendly place where people usually cannot trust each other. Disposition friendship arises, Kant believes, because "We all have a strong impulse to disclose ourselves, and enter wholly into fellowship; and such self-revelation is further a human necessity for the correction of our judgment when it is mistaken."[38] This impulse to disclose ourselves, however, need not always aim at self-correction because, Kant adds, people have a strong need to reveal themselves to others "even with no ulterior purpose."[39] Communicating "our whole self" and "complete communion" are the goals of disposition friendship, quite apart from any other effects that friendship produces.[40] Kant's friendship of disposition or fellowship permits friends to unburden themselves, to be frank, to escape contempt, and to achieve complete communion.[41] The term *intimacy* seems to be the most accurate shorthand expression to describe Kant's second ideal conception of friendship.

Kant's intimacy friends believe that they can trust each other with their most personal thoughts, touching upon their ideas, opinions, feelings, hopes, fears, aspirations, doubts, loves, and hates. The complete communion that Kant sees as one goal of intimacy friendship is not communion in the sense of total accord or identity of beliefs but communion in the sense of friends being open and receptive to each other's feelings, hopes, views, aspirations, and so on. Not that each friend would accept the other's ideas without criticism or suggestion. Intimacy friends could offer suggestions, criticism, and assistance; they are more than passive, spongelike receptors. They are willing to regard each other's thoughts sympathetically and compassionately, treating each other's thoughts with the same respect that they would want for their own. Intimacy friends do not expect automatic agreement with everything that they believe or feel; rather, they want sympathetic assistance in evaluating and correcting feelings and judgments. Intimate friends encourage each other to openly discuss each other's concerns.

In their discussion of friendship, Dean Cocking and Jeanette Kennett overlook Kant's point about intimacy friends reaching accord and communion.[42] Kant has more than merely "sharing secrets" in mind as constituting a friendship of intimacy. Reaching communion, understood as being receptive to each other's beliefs, feelings, and aspirations, also is a part of Kant's intimacy friendship. Cocking and Kennett are correct at least that sharing secrets is something patients and therapists do, even though there is no friendship between them, though, for example, a therapist who shared too many of his intimacies might transgress the boundary of professionalism, and if there was a high degree of sharing, one might suppose that a friendship was beginning. Kant's idea of reaching communion closely approximates Cocking's and Kennett's idea about friends being "responsive to the direction and interpretation of one another."[43]

Kant does not expect intimacy friends to spend many hours together. The salient aspect of intimacy friendship is that each knows that the other is trustworthy and reliably willing to receive his or her confidences. Some interval of time is initially required to establish and cement the friend's trust. Learning that another is willing to play the role of a trustworthy confidant is not possible at first. Many false starts and mistakes in judgment about who is reliable most likely will occur. Nevertheless, after an initial, time-consuming period of testing and probation, Kant's intimacy friendship does not require that friends spend much time together monitoring each other. If their mutual feeling of trust can be maintained over time without seeing much of each other, their friendship can be sustained over long periods of absence.

Laurence Thomas argues that "the extent to which a person is willing to reveal to us private information is the most significant measure we can have of that person's willingness to trust us, where the trust in question implies considerably more than that the person takes us to be of unquestionable moral character."[44] In Thomas's view, people signal each other that they want to be friends by seeing if the other reciprocates, through revealing his own intimate thoughts, as a sign that there can be trust between them. Thomas differs from Kant in that intimacy and openness are only the first stages in initiating friendship and are not constitutive components of the friendship itself. Thomas notes that it is not clear to what degree this ritual signaling is culturally determined, or to what degree it is part of the nature of friendship.[45]

Kant's intimacy friends, in contrast to Aristotle's virtue friends, are not expected to assist each other or to spend entire lives with each other. Since the object of intimacy friendship is a disposition to openness and a receptivity of each other's confidences, friends would not expect other mutually engaged in activities. Intimacy friends would not expect to go to football games together, to go skiing together, or to play long chess games with each other. Engaging in these kinds of activities may not be conducive to exchanging intimacies that require the friends to pay attention to each other and to not become engrossed in external diversions. Each friend expects that the other would be available when needed to receive confidences, to listen to problems or other inner-directed thoughts and feelings, but at the same time, and somewhat paradoxically, each friend would be reluctant to burden the other with his own inner pains and problems. For Kant, what is most important is knowing that one's friend would be willing to sympathetically listen, not that he or she frequently listens.

Intimacy friends do not provide each other with services, nor do they count on each other to provide the necessities of life. Friends are not a mutual insurance policy or a close-at-hand crutch in time of need. Kant calls such friendships "need friendship," which is a less-than-ideal form of friendship.[46] Merely knowing that another is willing to share intimacies suffices to ameliorate feelings of isolation and hostility. The benefits of true friendship for Kant are first that "Friendship . . . is an aid in overcoming the constraint and the distrust man feels in his intercourse with others, by revealing himself without reserve,"[47] and second that "it is man's refuge in this world from his distrust of his fellows, in which he can reveal his disposition to another and enter into communion with him."[48] Actual deeds are not required. A perfect intimacy friend's character, for Kant, is composed of "uprightness of disposition, sincerity, trustworthiness, conduct devoid of all falsehood and spite, and a sweet, cheerful and happy temper."[49] These elements are not character traits of someone specially positioned to be helpful in times of need (e.g., someone who is readily available, resourceful, wealthy, and generous). They are, however, precisely the character traits of someone in whom confidences can be safely placed.

In Viglantius's reporting of Kant's lectures on *The Metaphysics of Morals*, five rules of prudence for establishing a perfect friendship are listed:

1. Not to burden our friend with our requirements. This lies quite beyond the bounds of friendship. It is far better to bear evils willingly than to demand relief from them.

2. Intimacy in the mutual disclosure of thoughts calls for *caution*, i.e., that we open our mind to the other only so far that we do not run the risk of thereby forfeiting his respect, by the standard of his judgement and the degree of his practical prudence.

3. In the colloquy and enjoyment of friendship, every degree of modesty, or likewise of delicacy, is needed, in regard to the other's personal self-esteem. . . . If such censure [of moral faults] can be effected without loss of respect, it does not clash with the impulse to friendship, but much caution is needed for this and it always remains a gamble. So that, too, is a duty.

4. To keep sufficiently at a distance from our friend, that the respect which in all circumstances we owe to his personhood is in no way infringed thereby. This happens primarily by incautiously obtruding our goodwill, by rash communication, and by unrestrained love. Too deep an intimacy detracts from worth.

5. It is prudent to engage in a reciprocal development of our principles, and above all to track down those on which we have a need to decide with our friend whether there may be any misunderstandings that hinder agreement.[50] (emphasis in original)

There is something distinctly modern about Kant's intimacy friendship. Friendship understood as intimacy, according to Hanna Arendt, "conforms so well to the basic attitude of the modern individual, who in his alienation from the world can truly reveal himself only in privacy and in the intimacy of face-to-face encounters."[51] Intimacy friends do not have to see each other very often to engage in mutual activities, nor do they have to live close by each other to be available for mutual assistance. Just as long as each knows that the other would be willing to listen and share confidences, then friendship can remain vital and alive. Kant even insists that intimacy friends do not even have to have similar interests. So even if the friends' characters change and they develop divergent interests (e.g., sailing and softball), as long as they remain sincere, trustworthy, and free from falsehood, they could maintain an intimate friendship. They could still count on each other to provide release and communion. Intimacy requires nothing more. It is not as though intimate friends need to know a great deal about the private life of the other. They do not need daily or weekly briefings on the other's mental states.

There is a sense where confidants who frequently or constantly exchange personal thoughts might be considered intimate with each other, while Kant's intimacy friends might not be considered intimate. Constant confidants could have the most in-depth and current information about each other, while Kant's intimacy friends might not. Lack of depth does not undermine Kant's sense of intimacy. While Kant's sense of intimacy has to do with communion between persons and their possessing some knowledge of each other, it need not imply completeness, depth, or breadth of knowledge. Being familiar with someone does imply a great deal of knowledge, but it is possible to be intimate without being familiar. Kant's intimacy friendships are based on the supposition that friends can trust each other with their personal thoughts, and it is such a trust between them that creates the closeness that warrants calling the relationship "intimate."

Intimacy friendships are modern because friends are not required, as are Aristotle's virtue friends, to spend most of their lives together engaging in joint activities. Intimacy friendships, as a result, may be better able to withstand the vagaries of modern life, where friends frequently move from place to place because of school, jobs, or spouses. Intimacy friends do not need to converse regularly with each other or share activities and interests, as do virtue friends. Only a brief time together is required to maintain the friendship. Unlike Aristotle's nonworking, aristocratic virtue friends, busy people with jobs, school, and family can remain friends. They only need to know that their friend remains sincere, trustworthy, and free from falsehood. Intimacy friendship, in Kant's sense, can withstand these modern strains of living.

Because it is not constituted by impossible to detect or maintain equality of love and respect, Kant's intimacy or moral friendship is a possible ideal of friendship. Intimacy friendship does not require acts of beneficence or assistance that undermine equality between friends. Moreover, the behavior constituting intimacy friendship is not the kind of behavior that the categorical imperative requires for all rational beings. No categorical moral requirement exists that people be intimate with one another. While intimacy may be a valuable and laudatory way to relate to others, it is not a moral requirement that is owed to all (or to anyone, for that matter). Thus moral or intimacy friendship fulfills one of the defining characteristics of friendship, that it is a special relation not expected to be shared with everyone. In this important way, intimacy friendship differs from Kant's other ideal of friendship, which requires equal respect, thus only mirroring the behavior that Kant believes is morally owed to all rational beings. Friendship characterized on that other basis is simply equivalent to morally correct behavior. And while it is most certainly true that many conceptions of friendship expect friends to behave toward each other in a morally exemplary way, friendship is not reducible to morally exemplary behavior, especially a morality requiring all persons to be regarded in some basically equal or impersonal way. Friendship, in both conception and practice, is partial and particular.

If intimacy friends do not have to spend a great deal of time together or frequently talk to each other, what prevents people from having many intimacy friends, or even, in the extreme, from being intimate with everyone? If having a great number of friends were possible, supposing Kant's intimacy conception of friendship, then that fact would be a good reason to question whether his intimacy conception is a reasonable understanding of friendship. Intimacy friendship makes only minimal demands on each friend's time, energy, and material resources. Any limitation on those assets is not what keeps the number of possible intimacy friends small, that is, once intimacy is established. Discovering another who is capable of "uprightness of disposition, sincerity, trustworthiness, conduct devoid of all falsehood and spite, and a sweet, cheerful, and happy temper" necessary for intimacy friendship consumes great time and assets. The kind of reciprocal testing that Laurence Thomas discusses, where each potential friend exchanges intimacies of gradually increasing sensitivity to discover the other's trustworthiness, cannot happen quickly or effortlessly. Expenses in discovering intimacy friends are significant factors limiting the number of friends, not the resources and expenses in keeping them. So while maintaining intimacy friendships with a large number might be possible, becoming intimacy friends with many is difficult, time consuming, and expensive.[52]

Intimacy friendship is unlikely to conflict with any moral demands of Kant's categorical imperative. How friends behave toward each other (i.e., being willing to receive each other's confidences) is not likely to place either friend in a position where she would have to act contrary to the categorical imperative. None of the duties prescribed by the categorical imperative—refraining from lying and from suicide, helping others, and perfecting one's virtue—could conflict with the requirements of intimacy friendship—the willingness to be open, trusting, sincere, and free from falsehood. Showing preference for friends over others by being willing to receive their confidences while not receiving confidences from nonfriends cannot conflict with the categorical imperative. As Kant understands this possible ideal friendship, no moral opposition is possible between acting with preference toward one's friend, as required by the intimacy conception of friendship, and acting toward others in a morally exemplary way, as required by the categorical imperative. No moral opposition arises between a willingness to receive confidences and any perfect moral duty. Neither is there any possible conflict between receiving confidences from one's friend and imperfect duties, unless being willing to receive confidences interferes with one's imperfect duty to help nonfriends.

The value of intimacy friendship to friends depends on the value of their being able to find release through disclosing their personal thoughts. One way that release occurs is that intimacy friends meet and disclose their thoughts to each other. Friends do not, however, actually have to meet. According to Kant, knowing that they could disclose their thoughts to each other can suffice for the existence of intimacy friendship. Possession of that knowledge might constitute the friendship's entire value. When friends do actually disclose their intimate thoughts, it might have instrumental value, insofar as they can assist each other in correcting ideas when they are mistaken. If this were the only or primary value of friendship, then intimacy friendship's value would be primarily instrumental and only one among many devices for truth seeking or certification. Were this intimacy friendship's value, then it would be difficult to see the difference between this ideal friendship and the instrumentally useful need friendship that Kant believes exists originally and in primitive circumstances. Moreover, if the disclosure of personal thoughts, quite apart from any correction of erroneous beliefs, has value primarily as a release of some discomforting psychological pressure of a burdened heart then, again, the value of intimacy friendship to the friends appears to be primarily instrumental. It is a way of removing unpleasant psychological discomfort. Not all of its value need be negative. Intimacy friendship could produce positive, though still instrumental, value through pleasures arising from having someone with whom to confide one's thoughts and ideas.

Intimacy friendship need not be rationally undertaken as a means of achieving anything. Intimacy friendship arises not from our reason. Its source, as Kant says, is "a strong impulse to disclose ourselves, and enter wholly into fellowship."[53] Our strong impulses and inclinations give rise to friendship. Though Kant never discusses this issue, it would appear that intimacy friendship is not an essential part of our rational nature. It depends on conditional aspects of our phenomenal, empirical nature. Were humans to lack strong psychological impulses to disclose thoughts, little impetus for intimacy friendship would exist, because humans would have no need for disclosure or for entering into fellowship. According to Kant, inclination has no principles underlying it, thus impulses to disclosure and fellowship might be absent from some individuals who would therefore have no purpose for friends.

Kant's unattainable ideal of friendship, equal love and respect, is not grounded in inclination but arises from our reason. Love and respect are demands of our practical reason as revealed by the categorical imperative. This ideal is unattainable not as a result of the actions required by the friends but, according to Kant, because of the impossibility of discovering the equality of love and respect (just like the impossibility that Kant thinks exists in discovering one's true motives of action). There is no impossibility in everyone acting with love and respect to all. In fact, Kant believes that this is just what morality demands. But universal love and respect is not friendship, because it is universal, not special and particular.

OTHER IDEALS OF FRIENDSHIP

There are three other ideals of friendship that I briefly will mention in this chapter, because they illustrate additional dimensions in the range of friendship ideals that differ from Aristotle's and Kant's. The first to be discussed is that of C. S. Lewis, who defends a strongly interest-based friendship. Montaigne is the second, championing a friendship based on affection. Lastly, to fill out the introduction in greater contrast are ideals of friendship between unequals that originated in India.

C. S. Lewis thinks that two or more people who share some strong, passionate interest in something will become friends:

> Friendship arises out of mere Companionship when two or more of the companions discover that they have in common some insight or interest or even taste which the others do not share and which, till that moment, each believed to be his own unique treasure (or burden).[54]

Lewis conceives of friendship as shared activities focusing on common interests or quests after some truth. He makes several forceful contrasts between sharing interests and sharing intimacies or affection:

> The very condition of having Friends is that we should want something else besides Friends. Where the truthful answer to the question *Do you see the same truth?* would be "I see nothing and I don't care about the truth; I only want a Friend," no Friendship can arise—though Affection of course may. There would be nothing for the Friendship to be *about*; and Friendship must be about something, even if it were only an enthusiasm for dominoes or white mice.[55] (emphasis in original)

Lewis distinguishes friendship from relations of affection or love that are not based on shared interests but on a shared concern for each other:

> Lovers are always talking to one another about their love; Friends hardly ever about their Friendship. Lovers are normally *face to face*, absorbed in each other; Friends, *side by side*, absorbed in some common interest.[56] (emphasis added)

Friends, for Lewis, share interests and external pursuits in the activities of their friendship; they do not share intimacies or sit around discussing their thoughts about each other. Friends want to spend time together, perhaps as much as their lives will allow, pursuing shared interests in much the same way that Aristotle's friends share lives of virtuous activity. Friendship concerns something exterior to friends, some object or interest they care about and wish to achieve together. The interior, the personal, are not primary concerns in friendship:

> For of course we do not want to know our Friend's affairs at all. Friendship, unlike Eros, is uninquisitive. You become a man's friend without knowing or caring whether he is married or single or how he earns his living. What have all these "unconcerning things, matters of fact" to do with the real question, *Do you see the same truth?* . . . No one cares twopence about any one else's family, profession, class, income, race, or previous history. Of course you will get to know about most of these in the end. But casually.[57]

In Lewis's conception of friendship, friends may not care for "the person" if this is understood to mean that friendship focuses on the inner or emotional characteristics of friends that are unessential to any shared interest. This is not to say, however, that a friend is cared for only instrumentally as a means to something else, or that a friend is not cared for because of who he is. A friend is cared for because of what Lewis would consider an important part of the friend's character, the consuming enthusiasm for a shared interest or truth. To this extent, Lewis's conception of friendship resembles Aristotle's character friendship based on virtue. Their two conceptions also are similar, because the common quest, for Lewis, expands and augments each friend's abilities to engage in shared interests in much the same way that Aristotle believes character friends help each other become virtuous.

Montaigne, following an inspiration from Cicero, conceives of friendship as a "perfect union and harmony."[58] Cicero, however, limits complete union and harmony in friendship to "agreement in aims, ambitions, and attitudes,"[59] or "sympathy in all matters of importance, plus goodwill and affection."[60] Montaigne goes well beyond Cicero, considering friendship "the complete fusion of our wills."[61] Montaigne continues:

> In the friendship I speak of, our souls mingle and blend with each other so completely that they efface the seam that joined them, and cannot find it again. If you press me to tell why I love him, I feel that this cannot be expressed, except by answering: Because it was he, because it was I.
>
> Beyond all my understanding, beyond what I can say about this in particular, there was I know not what inexplicable and fateful force that was the mediator of this union.[62]

Montaigne's felicitous choice of the word "fusion" to describe this ideal friendship makes clear the extreme degree to which friends are united compared to ideal friendships of other philosophers. Friends, as Lewis conceives them, are united in their pursuit of interests or truths but still remain separate in many other aspects of their lives. There might be a union of trust and intimacy among friends, as Kant understands friendship, but Kant thinks that friends differ in many ways, only needing to agree on moral principles. Aristotle's ideal friendship requires only an equality in virtue, not complete identity. Montaigne goes the farthest, claiming that friends will entirely lose their individual identities:

> It is not one special consideration, nor two, nor three, nor four, nor a thousand: it is I know not what quintessence of all this mixture, which, having seized my whole will, led it to plunge and lose itself in his; which having seized

his whole will, led it to plunge and lose itself in mine, with equal hunger, equal rivalry. I say lose, in truth, for neither of us reserved anything for himself, nor was anything either his or mine.[63]

None of the other philosophers considers friendship an identity losing fusion. For many contemporary and feminist philosophers, a correct analysis of friendship must be able to explain how each friend maintains her identity within the friendship.

Montaigne agrees with Aristotle and Kant in thinking that the best form of friendship is valued for its own sake and not "forged and nourished by pleasure or profit, by public or private needs . . . and the less friendships, insofar as they mix into friendship another cause and object and reward than friendship itself."[64] It is clear that Montaigne believes that fusion friendship is valued intrinsically. While no reason exists why friendship cannot have both intrinsic and extrinsic value, or be valued by friends both for its own sake and for other goods that it produces, Montaigne rejects this dual valuing:

> In this noble relationship, services and benefits, on which other friendships feed, do not even deserve to be taken into account . . . and banish from between them these words of separation and distinction: benefit, obligation, gratitude, request, thanks, and the like.[65]

This issue, of the kinds of value that friendship has, shall be a recurring theme throughout the remaining chapters of this book.

Montaigne's fusion friendship illustrates an additional issue that will not only recur but that functions as one of the nonmoral differences that will be used to assess the relevance of various conceptions of friendship to our (Western) experience. Montaigne does not believe that it is possible to foretell who will become friends with whom:

> If you press me to tell why I love him, I feel that this cannot be expressed, except by answering: Because it was he, because it was I. Beyond all my understanding, beyond what I can say about this in particular, there was I know not what inexplicable and fateful force that was the mediator of this union.[66]

No characteristics shared by diverse persons can ground predictions about whether or not they will become friends. To this extent, Montaigne agrees with Kant. In contrast, friendship, as understood by both Aristotle and Lewis, may permit fairly accurate predictions in theory about possible friends. To the extent that Aristotle's best form of friendship is between persons of equal virtue, knowing that two people have the same virtue might warrant predicting that they would become friends. In much the same way, assuming Lewis's conception of friendship, knowing that two people possess the same overriding interest or consuming passion for some "truth" also would warrant predicting their becoming friends if their common interests were discovered. These different implications about the possibility of predicting who becomes friends can function to test the relevance of each conception of friendship. To the extent that predicting who will become friends is possible, one set of conceptions is closer to our own experience than the other. More is said about this in later chapters.

There is an additional way that Montaigne's fusion ideal of friendship differs from Aristotle, Kant, and Lewis, showing a possible weakness in Montaigne's conception. Ideal friendships, according to Kant, Aristotle, and Lewis, are possible among more than two friends at a given time. Even though it is very time consuming to discover whether another can be sufficiently trustworthy to be an intimacy friend, as Kant understands his ideal of friendship, it is clearly possible for more than two to be friends. Having equal virtue is possible for more than two, so that, according to Aristotle's ideal, more than two can be friends at one time. Lewis's interest friendship is the ideal most easily shared by several friends who have similar interests. Montaigne believes that fusion friendship permits no "plurality of friends":

> For this perfect friendship I speak of is indivisible: each one gives himself so wholly to his friend that he has nothing left to distribute elsewhere; on the contrary, he is sorry that he is not double, triple, or quadruple, and that he has not several souls and several wills to confer them all on this one object. Common friendships can be divided up: one may love in one man his beauty, in another his easygoing ways, in another liberality, in one paternal love, in another brotherly love, and so forth; but this friendship that possesses the soul and rules it with absolute sovereignty cannot possibly be double. If two called for help at the same time, which one would you run to? If they demanded conflicting services of you, how could [you] arrange it? If one confided to your silence a thing that would be useful for the other to know, how would you extricate yourself? A single dominant friendship dissolves all other obligations.[67]

Despite Montaigne's arguments, there is no conceptual impossibility of more than two becoming friends. If the fusion is as complete as Montaigne maintains, "everything actually being in common between them—wills, thoughts, judgments, goods . . . life—and their relationship being that of one soul in two bodies,"[68] none of Montaigne's possible conflicts might arise. If the union were so complete, no reason could arise for demanding conflicting services. Three friends completely fused together would have no greater difference in thought, diversity in judgment, or divergence in wills than two who are thoroughly fused. The likelihood exists less of finding three or four who could meet the prerequisites of fusion friendship; but if they could be completely fused, then few if any conflicts would arise. If more than one needed assistance at one time, there might be some conflict, but of course if there were more than two friends fused together, assistance for all might be easier to come by.

Bhikhu Parekh discusses three Indian ideals of friendship "that occur in the literature and are thought to cover most relationships of friendship."[69] Unlike Western ideals of friendship, the Indian ideals are not between equals but between a "junior partner" and a "senior partner" who "is a little older, wiser, more mature, better informed about the ways of the world, and more resourceful."[70]

Before discussing the three different Indian ideals, some of the similarities between Indian friendship and the Western conceptions should be highlighted. An Indian friend "gives his heart" where the heart is considered the seat of both feelings and soul.[71]

> The idea of shared feelings and a shared self is central to the Indian conception of friendship. My friend is someone who instinctively feels for and with me, and participates in my joys and sorrows. Our hearts are bonded; our relationship is based on hearts or rather we are related "at the level of heart," and our hearts converge, know, and communicate with each other.[72]

Emotional union between friends is "the closest possible." According to Parekh, friends share a common soul or self and "feel as one."[73] Unlike the fusion that Montaigne believes occurs between friends, which effaces any difference between them, Indian friends "reflect and manifest each other's self, spirit, life-breath, or soul such that each discovers himself in the other."[74] Much like Aristotle's conception of reciprocal goodwill, Indian friends render useful services to each other and make sacrifices of time, money, and energy from a sense of good-heartedness. Also, Indian friends will joke with one another, be playful, and engage in amusing conversations and escapades, and sometimes will disregard social convention; but, as Parekh stresses, unlike in the West, "friendship is the only relationship in which these things are permitted, and those involved released from the stern demands of duty characteristic of other [Indian social] relationships."[75]

A number of additional similarities exist. Friends do not pose a threat to each other, and they can count on each other's affection, support, and loyalty. And, like the Western understanding of loyalty, loyalty is distinguished from flattery, so that Indians expect their friends to be a source of sincere advice and to function as each other's critic and conscience. Further, friends must be open and honest with each other, friends must not gossip about each other, and friends must not harm or demean each other to another.[76] Indian writers also share some of the same concerns as several Western writers about the darker side of friendship. According to Parekh, Indian writers are troubled by the requirement inherent in Indian friendship that a person may be expected to bend rules or violate moral norms to protect a friend in trouble, or that loyalty to a friend might require acquiescing in his misdeeds and even assisting him.[77] An illustration comes from the novel *Train to Pakistan*, by Khushwant Singh:

> The Punjabi's code was even more baffling. For them, truth, honour, financial integrity were "all right," but these were placed lower down the scale of values than being true to one's salt, to one's friends and fellow villagers. For friends, you could lie in court or cheat, and no one would blame you. On the contrary, you became a *nar admi*—a he-man who had defied authority (magistrates and police) and religion (oath on the scripture) but proved true to friendship.[78]

Cicero denies that friends should engage in immoral activities to assist each other, but that the temptation to do so is always present.[79] Indian writers also are troubled by the aspect of friendship that is common in Western thought and is the stimulus for this book. According to Parekh, "they were convinced that friendship, which necessarily involved partiality, was incompatible with justice . . . which involved an impartial application of rules and norms and an equal regard for the well-being of all."[80]

The first of the three kinds of ideal Indian friendship that Parekh distinguishes "is based on genuine affection and fondness, usually built up during childhood and adolescence."[81] This kind of friendship results from familiarity and unity produced by growing up together and sharing formative experiences. Indian writers believe that friendship formed through growing up together can survive many years of separation with little contact between the friends and the length of separation making little difference to the strength of friendship. Such friendship is not based on similarity of character, social status, power, interest, ideals, or goals.[82] Friends' common upbringing forges a bond that creates and maintains their ability to trust each other and to share intimacies, even after years of separation, where their character or interests may have grown in divergent ways. Their childhood experiences continue to support the good-hearted feelings and deep care that they continue to feel for each other.

Early learning permanently forges adult character. An example is the friendship between Binoy-bhusan and Gourmohan in the novel *Gora*, by Rabindranath Tagore.[83] In Charles Dickens's novel *David Copperfield*, Copperfield's and Steerforth's friendship, forged while bonding at boarding school, could be a Western example of this first kind of Indian friendship.

> Unlike the first kind of friendship, which is based on pure feeling, the second kind [of friendship] is based on mutual help and gratitude. Two individuals who render each other valuable services are placed under each other's debt. Such acts over a period of time create a relationship of shared mutual gratitude and pave the way for friendship. Although they have good feelings for each other, not the feelings but the accumulated weight of mutual assistance is the basis for their friendship.[84]

Parekh points out that Indians consider a favor as a sign of goodwill and harm as a sign of hostility. A favor is a sign that a person wants to become one's friend, and it is intended to create a bond that has a deeper moral meaning. Future reciprocal favors are not so much repayments of debts but expressions of the developing friendship.[85] Clearly there are similarities between this Indian friendship and Aristotle's friendship, based on utility, and Kant's conception of primitive, need-based friendship. The similarities are more fully discussed in chapter 2.

In the third and highest form of Indian friendship, which is thought to be rare and divine, "friends . . . share common interests, values, ideals, and lifestyles, are totally at ease in each other's presence, and deeply love and trust each other."[86] Divine friends are practically one, though they retain sufficient individuality to avoid the total fusion that Montaigne values as an ideal. Divine or perfect Indian friendship differs from most Western conceptions of ideal friendship, because the friends are not equal. Even though the friends are totally devoted to each other and love each other equally, there is a senior partner and a junior partner. "Perfect friendship is only possible between individuals who share common interests, temperaments, values, and so on, but one of whom is a little older and wiser and a great source of strength."[87] Unequal relationships are believed to avoid traces of competition, jealousy, and comparison, which are deemed to be characteristic of relations between equals. Parekh uses examples of Gandhi and Jawaharlal Nehru as being typical of perfect friendship and friendships that sometimes arise between teachers and their former pupils. Aristotle's ideal friendship of equals in virtue contrasts with perfect Indian friendship.

There is a final item about Indian friendships that Parekh mentions, which I take note of here because it connects not only to different conceptions of friendship such as Kant's and Aristotle's but also to empirical studies of same-sex friendships, which I discuss in the next chapter. While in many respects Indian friendships between men and between women are alike, "female friendships are generally presented as more intimate, reliable, and durable, more easily made, and less self-conscious than those between men."[88] Parekh points out that the Indian term used to describe female friends involves mutual caring, fondness, support, and, above all, exchanging and keeping confidences.

A wide range exists in how friendship is conceived. While there are many similarities in the conceptions, for otherwise they would not all be recognizable as friendship, the various conceptions differ from each other along several different variables. In the next chapter, I explain those variables and elucidate both their interconnections and independencies.

TWO

THE STRUCTURE OF FRIENDSHIP

THE NATURE OF FRIENDSHIP

THE SEARCH FOR ANSWERS to questions about the moral justifiability of preferring friends to nonfriends and of any special friendship responsibilities must recognize that there are many different conceptions of friendship. In the preceding chapter, five distinct ideal conceptions of friendship were introduced, each of which may have its own explanation about justifications for preferring friends. Additional ideal conceptions of friendship are discussed later on to further illustrate different ways of understanding friendship. Conceptions of friendship other than ideal ones also exist. Both Aristotle and Kant discuss two less-than-ideal friendships: pleasure and utility friendships for Aristotle, and need friendships and friendships of taste for Kant. Each of these less-than-ideal friendships contains reasons for preferring friends to nonfriends. Little has been written about these less-than-ideal friendships, much of it misunderstanding and undervaluing them.

Comprehending the similarities and differences of such a rich abundance of diverse friendship conceptions requires an adequate set of concepts. Three different aspects of friendship must be untangled and separated from each other: the basis of friendship, the object of friendship, and the nature of friendship. They must be distinguished if different conceptions of friendship are to be adequately understood.[1] Many confusions in recent discussions of friendship arise because these three distinct aspects are not well appreciated.

The basis of friendship is the reason friends have for their relationship. Aristotle mentions three different bases: pleasure, utility, and virtue. Kant has his own three: need, taste, and sentiment.

The object of friendship is what friends do together as constitutive of their friendship. It is within the object of friendship that moral issues of preferring friends to nonfriends primarily arise, because the object of friendship establishes how friends are expected to treat each other insofar as they are friends. The word "object" is better to use than either "goal" or "end," because it lacks any instrumental connotation that sometimes is attached to the other two.[2] Aristotle's ideal friendship between friends of equal virtue has as its object a shared life of virtuous activity, while the object of Kant's intimacy friendship is self-revelation and communion. Objects of friendship differ from its basis. The basis of friendship grounds friendship by providing a reason or justification for its object. A friendship might, for example, be based on pleasure and have as its object participation in amateur athletics. Pleasure would be the reason for friends participating together in athletics. Pleasure also can be a basis for friendships with intimacy as their object. Well-defined systematic differences exist between objects of several various conceptions of friendship. Before discussing the ways that conceptions of friendship differ from each other, I first must discuss the nature of the friendship relation, because it is in the nature of the relation that the greatest similarity exists among various friendship conceptions.

The nature of friendship is a characterization of the relationship that distinguishes friendship from other relationships between people. Aristotle believes that a reciprocal goodwill is essential to friendship, and that it is found in friendships grounded on each of his three bases. A reciprocal goodwill between friends is common to friendships, whether they are based on "reasons" of pleasure, utility, or virtue:

> But to those who thus wish good we ascribe only goodwill, if the wish is not reciprocated; goodwill when it is reciprocal being friendship. . . . To be friends, then, they must be mutually recognized as bearing goodwill and wishing well to each other for one of the aforesaid reasons.[3]

To have a friendship, two persons must recognize that they each have goodwill for the other, that is, they do not merely feel kindly toward each other but try to promote the other's good. Aristotle believes that pleasure, virtue, and utility are distinct reasons for having a goodwill. As is seen later in this chapter, when Aristotle's less-than-ideal friendships are discussed, a friendship based on utility is distinguished from commercial or business relationships, because utility friends have reciprocal goodwill, aiming for each other's overall rather than partial good.

Aristotle says that friends consider each other "another self," so that one friend would care for the other as well as she would care for herself. While Aristotle does not believe that friends fuse together to the extent Montaigne believes friends become indistinguishable from each other, bonds of mutual goodwill are strongest between friends.

Bhikhu Parekh characterizes the nature of Indian friendship as goodhearted. Friends help each other with time, energy, and money.[4] To this extent, goodwill is as much a part of Indian friendship as Aristotle's three friendships. Indian friends also identify with each other, acting with "one heart" and sharing joys and sorrows. Parekh continues that Indian friends' hearts are bonded, and that they communicate with each other directly, as though they were one self.

If friends regard each other as "another self," any time, energy, and material assets they consume in assisting or benefitting each other is not lost or thrown away. Because friends identify with each other by adopting each other's goals and ends, they believe that what benefits one of them benefits the other as well. For example, one friend's kindness, such as helping with yard work, is not a loss of time and energy, because she identifies benefits to her friend equally as her own. Any pleasure her friend receives from a beautiful garden is equally her pleasure. It is just as though she labored to improve her own garden rather than her friend's. Because a good for her friend is her own good, a potential exists for achieving much greater good than might be possible if only her own good counted. There are, as it were, two persons whose good counts for each rather than only one. This can double the potential sources and quantity of good. If she were to have more than a single friend, then the quantity of possible good might triple or quadruple. By the same reasoning, however, having friends also increases the risk of suffering greater losses. If her friend is harmed, declines, or loses some good, then her own well-being also will be proportionally diminished. (Perhaps this is why Aristotle believes that a virtuous character is essential in a friend, since a virtuous person is less likely, in Aristotle's understanding, to perform or suffer evil.)

Reason might exist for thinking that friends' apparently selfless behavior toward each other is not all that altruistic. Identifying with a friend's good can be considered an economically efficient means of advancing one's own well-being. In some relations, the participants may only care for each other because of the benefits they expect to receive. Those relations are not relations of friendship, because there is no mutual goodwill. Participants only care for each other out of self-interest or self-advancement.[5] In contrast, friends who identify with each other's good are not egoists in any selfish sense that each maintains the friendship only because of the material advantages that she receives. Selfish egoism would contradict the goodwill that Aristotle and others believe is essential in friendship. The help that friends give to each other, while not egoistic, may not be as selfless or altruistic as all of that. To the extent that friends consider each other "another self," the boundary between them is reduced, if not erased. The good they do for each other duplicates back because of the identification with each other's ends. It is not something that they give up or lose.

Considering friends' goodwill to each other as wholly selfless or altruistic may not be correct for another reason. The identification between friends may create a form of egoism among friends in comparison to nonfriends. This is friendship's darker side. Friends may sometimes selfishly promote their own collective good in preference to the good of nonfriends. The moral limits and legitimacy of friend's preference for each other are fully explored in chapter 4.

Kant, like Aristotle, also considers goodwill the nature of an ideal form of friendship:

> *Friendship* (considered in its perfection) is the union of two persons through equal love and respect. It is easy to see that this is an ideal of each participating and sharing sympathetically in the other's well-being through the morally goodwill that unites them, and even though it does not produce the complete happiness of life, the adoption of this ideal in their disposition toward each other makes them deserving of happiness; hence men have a duty of friendship.[6] (emphasis in original)

As noted in chapter 1, Kant does not believe that this form of friendship is attainable, thus he substitutes intimacy friendship as an attainable ideal. Still, reciprocal goodwill must be a factor in Kant's intimacy friendship and in other forms of friendship Kant discusses, because goodwill is something that his categorical imperative requires in all relations between persons. Goodwill may not be sufficient for friendship as Kant understands it, but goodwill is necessary. Intimacy friendship, as Kant discusses it in *Lectures on Ethics,* substitutes openness and frankness for reciprocal goodwill.[7] The object of the intimacy friendship relation is not sharing a life with friends promoting each other's well-being and developing virtue, as it is in Aristotle's conception of ideal friendship. For Kant, being friends is constituted by the knowledge that friends are willing to be open and frank with each other and willing to divulge their intimate thoughts and feelings. But being frank and open may not always promote a friend's good.

A snapshot of friends' lives on Kant's conception reveals many contrasts with Aristotle. Unlike Aristotle's friends, Kant's friends need not spend a great deal of time together engaged in joint activities. They may provide each other with services or material assistance, but as noted in Vigilantius's compilation of "Kant on the Metaphysics of Morals"

> yet it is prudent, and a sign of much greater and purer friendship, to abstain from those needs which make it necessary to call upon our friend for help. For to demand such support in the way of funds, or the attainment of specific ends, really lies beyond the essential limits of friendship.[8]

Friends need not see each other all that often. The key for Kant is knowledge of each other's disposition to receptiveness and sympathy. Friends can trust each other to be available on those occasions when needed.

Friendship, as C. S. Lewis describes it, involves neither reciprocal goodwill nor reciprocal intimacy. The nature of friendship, for Lewis, is a bond of common interest, goal, or quest. As he says, friendship must be about something beyond the friends themselves.[9] Lewis's friendship resembles Aristotle's, insofar as friends desire to spend time together engaged in activities that express their mutual interests. But it is the interests, not the persons or their virtue, that are the basis of any shared activities. Friends' personal characteristics irrelevant to the shared interests will play no formative part in the friendship. Only their personal characteristics affecting their ability to pursue common interests are relevant to their being friends. In contrast to Kant's conception, friends, for Lewis, are not intimate with each other, and they do not focus on each other's psychology. Those topics are for lovers, not friends.

Lewis might be criticized by some feminist philosophers, because friends, as he understands friendship, do not seem to care for each other; they only care for the shared common interests, goals, or purposes.[10] As long as friends share a common passion for something, it might be thought that they need not even like or have affection for each other. At least it might be logically possible that friends could share a strong common interest but like little else about each other (e.g., I love discussing philosophy with him, but other than that I cannot stand being around him). Lewis, it might be said, omits caring for each other from his conception of friendship or, worse, he might be charged with ignoring the fact that friends must care for each other as the persons they are and not merely for some aspect of the other's interests.

Caring for each other often is thought to be essential to the nature of friendship. Confusions have arisen because of a failure to distinguish between "caring for each other" functioning as a basis, as an object, or as part of the nature of friendship. Sometimes confusion is compounded because of lack of clarity about what could possibly be meant by the more qualified phrase, "caring for each other because of the person he or she is." Illustrations can be found of caring for each other functioning as the basis or object of friendship in addition to functioning as the nature of the relation. I focus here on caring for each other, understood as the nature of the relation, and the subsequent two sections focus on its role as a basis or an object of friendship.

Understood as a part of the nature of friendship conceptions, caring for each other would distinguish friendships from other kinds of relationships. Friends are thought to care for each other, while in other relationships, mutual care may not exist (e.g., employer and employee or professor and student). Students need not necessarily care for their professors nor employees care for their employers. Kim-Chong Chong believes that "care for" can have one of two senses. To care for a friend:

(1) She must have an understanding and an appreciation of his projects, ambitions, and general interests as something separate from her own. She must wish that he achieve them, be glad for him when they are achieved, or be concerned for him and feel sad if and when he fails. She must show a readiness to help him, for his sake.

(2) She must have an affection for [him], and not merely see him as representing something which she desires.[11]

The first sense that Chong lists is equivalent to Aristotle's reciprocal goodwill, where each friend identifies with the other as "another self." Nothing new is added to what Aristotle considers the nature of friendship by Chong's first sense of "care for." Friends simply try to help each other in living their good lives by achieving their individual "projects, ambitions, and general interests." Chong's first sense also is not far from Kant's, "sharing sympathetically in the other's well-being through the morally goodwill that unites them." Thus if the nature of friendship as caring for another person is interpreted in Chong's first sense, then both Aristotle's and Kant's ideal friendships exhibit friends caring for each other.

Later in this chapter I show that even in Aristotle's less-than-ideal friendship based on utility, friends care for each other in Chong's first sense.

Chong's second sense, having an affection for or liking each other, differs from the first sense. Liking or having affection for someone need not be connected to any disposition to help or assist. People who have affection for each other may perhaps be disposed to actions other than assistance or help. Their goal simply may be to enjoy being together or just talking to each other. While in typical cases people who have affection for each other will desire to help and assist if it becomes necessary, conceivably, caring for, understood as merely affection, need not result in any actions at all. Chong's second sense also is independent of any disposition to assistance, because people who have no affection for each other may assist each other by helping to achieve projects, ambitions, or interests. A number of different reasons or bases are possible to explain why they assist. They may get pleasure from assisting people, they may find assisting others useful, or they may believe that they have a moral obligation to assist.

It is possible to think that if mutual assistance is unaccompanied by affection then there is no friendship. Chong's view, however, is that the two senses are each individually sufficient for caring for another, but that they are not jointly necessary. Were they jointly necessary, Aristotle's virtue friendship would not meet the criteria. Marilyn Friedman, like Chong, believes that we care about and for others in various ways:

> To care *about* someone is to take an interest in her, be concerned about her, have regard for her. To care *for* someone is to protect her and attend to her needs, to take responsibility for her well-being, perhaps by providing material sustenance or emotional support and nurturance. Care may involve feelings of affection and solicitude for someone.[12] (emphasis in original)

The difference between caring for and caring about may not be as well defined as she thinks. Both "caring about" and "caring for" have as objects a person's well-being. Friedman seems to distinguish those two from caring that, in addition, "involves feelings of affection." Still, like Chong, Friedman believes that care may involve affection, but that affection is not essential. Mutual assistance, therefore, can be understood as caring for a person, whether or not mutual assistance is accompanied by any affection.

Aristotle says next to nothing about affection between friends. In only two places does he discuss affection in friendship. The first is in Book II of the *Magna Moralia*, where he says that friendships cannot exist between man and inanimate things or gods because there is no possible "return of affection."[13] This seems, however, only to be a stylistic variant of the same point about gods and wine in chapter 2 of *Nicomachean Ethics*, Book VIII, where Aristotle says that no friendship is possible between man and gods or wine, because there can be no reciprocal wishing good to the other.[14] The second place that he discusses affection is in a *Nicomachean Ethics* Book IV discussion of the mean between those who are obsequious and those called "churlish" or "contentious":

> That the states we have named are culpable is plain enough, and that the middle state is laudable—that in virtue of which a man will put up with, and will resent, the right things and in the right way; but no name has been assigned to it, though it most resembles friendship. For the man who corresponds to this middle state is very much what, with affection added, we call a good friend. But the state in question differs from friendship in that it implies no passion or affection for one's associates; since it is not by reason of loving or hating that such a man takes everything in the right way, but by being a man of a certain kind.[15]

Curiously, in *Ethics*, Books VIII and IX, Aristotle does not discuss affection with respect to any of his conceptions of friendship. All three of Aristotle's friendships nevertheless fulfill Chong's first sense of mutual assistance, because they all manifest mutual assistance through reciprocal goodwill. Chong's view is that either sense is sufficient for understanding "caring for a person." Having affection for or liking also can be understood as caring for a person, whether or not the affection is accompanied by any mutual assistance.

If Chong's analysis of "caring for" is correct, then caring for in the second sense as having affection adds a new dimension to understanding Aristotle's friendship relation. Elizabeth Telfer sees affection as a separate essential aspect of the nature of friendship, in addition to reciprocal goodwill.[16] She does not think that having affection for a friend is included in either Aristotle's reciprocal goodwill or Kant's mutual benevolence. C. S. Lewis's common quest or interest friendship also seems to lack what might be considered affection or liking between friends. Lewis's friends may develop affection for each other as a consequence of the quest or common interest, but Lewis would not consider affection an essential part of the nature of their friendship. The first of the three Indian ideal forms of friendship is constituted by "genuine affection and fondness," while the other two ideal forms focus more on mutual assistance and goodwill. While having affection for is not explicitly included in Aristotle's reciprocal goodwill nor Kant's mutual benevolence and thus adds to understanding friendship, it is nevertheless a gross mistake to characterize Kant's and Aristotle's friendships as uncaring. The nature of friendship, as characterized by Aristotle and Kant, encompasses caring for friends in Chong's first goodwill sense.

It is almost impossible to imagine friends, as Aristotle understands them, wanting to spend all of their lives together engaging in joint virtuous activities and failing to like each other or without growing in affection for each other. Much the same affection may develop among Kant's intimacy friendships. That Aristotle and Kant do not explicitly include affection or liking in their definition of friendship relations does not imply that they expect friendships to be cold, lacking in affection, or that friends would not like each other. Liking each other and mutual affection, for Aristotle and Kant, might best be thought of as consequences of friendships arising out of repeated acts of reciprocal goodwill and benevolence. Friends may develop affection for each other, but for Kant and Aristotle, those feelings are not a definitional part of the nature of friendship. Further, it is possible to have affection for nonfriends, though there is no goodwill or desire to promote their good.

Affection and liking also can function as possible bases of friendship. People may become friends because they like or feel affection for each other, but confusions result if the bases of friendship are equated with the nature of the relation.

THE BASES OF FRIENDSHIP

The bases of friendship relations are the various reasons people have for forming friendships; it is the ground or foundation for friendships. Bases differ from the nature of friendship, that is, what the friendship relation is understood to be, and from the object of friendship, that is, what friends do as friends. Ferdinand Schoeman contrasts the basis and nature of friendship:

> We must distinguish *what we like* about a person and *for whose sake we are motivated* in acting. The *what we like* answers to the causal basis of the affection, whereas the *for whose sake* answers to the nature of the relationship, however it is brought into being. Unfortunately, it seems as if Aristotle conflated these vectors of friendship, the "what we like" aspect and the "for whose sake" aspect, promiscuously sliding from one to the other to make the theory seem simultaneously comprehensive and compelling.[17] (emphasis in original)

Schoeman is correct in thinking that Aristotle makes the distinction, but he is mistaken in thinking that Aristotle "conflated these vectors" or is inconsistent in his recognition of the difference. Martha Nussbaum, in *The Fragility of Goodness*, sees similar distinctions in Aristotle:

Here it is important to distinguish three things: the *basis* or *ground* of the relationship (the thing "through (*dia*) which" they love); its *object*; and its *goal* or *end*. Pleasure, advantage, and good character are three different bases or original grounds of *philia*; they are not the goal or final (intentional) end of the relationship. In other words, the two people are friends "through" or "on the basis of" these, but the goal they try to achieve in action will still be some sort of mutual benefit.[18] (emphasis in original)

As noted above, I consider what Nussbaum calls the "goal" or "end" to be better understood (less instrumentally) as the object of friendship, which is discussed more fully in the next section. This tripartite distinction is essential in understanding friendship, not only in Aristotle's senses but in other senses of friendship as well.

Both ideal and less-than-ideal forms of friendship can be distinguished by their having different bases or grounds. Aristotle's ideal friendship is based on the virtuous character of friends. Indian friendships are based on affection, mutual assistance, or common ideals. For C. S. Lewis, the basis is friends' common interests. Kant's ideal attainable form, intimacy friendship, is based on feelings of trust and openness, which in part derive from an individual's nonrational inclination. Montaigne's ideal also is based on nonrational and nonuniversalizable feelings. Pleasure, need, and utility are bases of the less-than-ideal friendships discussed by Aristotle and Kant. These different bases of friendship must be more fully discussed, because the basis of the friendship affects the object and nature of friendships.

The ideal form of friendship for Aristotle is based on the friends' equal virtue, because virtue is the best of the three reasons things are loved.[19] A number of philosophers have mistakenly thought that equal virtue cannot function by itself as a basis of friendship, because it cannot solve the specification or individuation problem—the "why me" or "why her" problem. Why is it that A and B become friends rather than A and C? These philosophers believe that virtue alone must be an incomplete explanation for why someone would choose this equally virtuous person as a friend rather than that equally virtuous person. Douglas Den Uyl and Charles Griswold Jr. illustrate this mistake. They point out, in a discussion of Adam Smith on friendship, which could equally apply to Aristotle, that it does not "seem likely that one would become friends with every person of virtue one encounters simply because he is virtuous," and that Smith fills the lack of specificity of virtue by appealing to the sentiments.[20] Den Uyl and Griswold believe that in choosing between two equally virtuous persons to be friends with, an additional factor is required: that one of them is liked as a result of sharing some nonmoral characteristics or interests. Virtue cannot individuate; so based on their understanding, shared, nonmoral characteristics become decisive in explaining why two people become friends.

Jennifer Whiting also thinks that a person's virtue is not sufficiently specific to individuate choice of friends:

> But even the best sort of Aristotelian *philia*—i.e., friendship based on virtue—is still thought deficient insofar as Aristotle requires not only that the friends be similar in virtue but also that each loves and seeks to benefit the other on account of the other's virtues. For to the extent that the elements of virtue are repeatable—as the conception of the friend as "another self" seems to require—this may be thought to undermine Aristotle's initial achievement: if my friend's virtues are multiply instantiable, concern for her *qua* virtuous seems not really concern for *her*, the unique and irreplaceable individual that she is.[21] (emphasis in original)

Individuating friendships, as Whiting is interpreting Aristotle, becomes a nonmoral rather than a moral decision, because it is assumed that a person's moral virtues do not individuate "the unique and irreplaceable individual that she is." The idea seems to be that in deciding who one will befriend, one begins with a person whose virtue is equal to one's own as a potential friend. Unfortunately, this pool of potential friends is much too large, because the virtues are "multiply instantiable" and therefore not sufficiently specific to individuate choosing one virtuous person rather than another. David O. Brink agrees with Whiting, that it "does not explain why one should single out one's friends, from among the pool of virtuous people, for special treatment."[22] Nonmoral characteristics of pool members must then be examined in order to find someone whose nonmoral tastes, interests, goals, or ends in life are similar to one's own. Whiting's specificity problem may not entirely be solved, since nonmoral characteristics will be "multiply instantiable" as well, though there may be many more diverse characteristics from which to select.

What criteria can be used in selecting the nonmoral characteristics of a potential friend? By definition, the criteria could not be virtue or goodness, because they have already been removed from possible consideration, since they do not individuate from the pool of potential friends. The only criteria remaining in order to make the choice, assuming that Aristotle's premises about why one chooses a friend, are pleasure or utility. Thus choosing one's friend from a pool of persons whose virtue is equal to one's own must be made on either the basis of pleasure or utility. As Aristotle says, there are only three reasons for loving or choosing something: its pleasure, its utility, or its goodness.

This explanation of why people become friends is unsatisfactory, because it undercuts virtue as a basis of friendship. It does accord virtue some role as a necessary condition where only those with virtue equal to one's own are considered potential friends. Yet because virtue is thought to be insufficiently specific to select from the remaining pool of the equally virtuous, only utility or pleasure remains as a sufficient basis for choosing a friend. Aristotle ultimately would have to be understood as failing to escape the idea that either pleasure or utility is a decisive basis upon which people become friends. This surely will be an unacceptable implication for Aristotle, and thus this explanation cannot be the right way of understanding his ideal basis for friendship.

The problem that Whiting, Brink, Den Uyl, and Griswold think they have detected in Aristotle's equal virtue basis of friendship is avoidable by understanding that equality of virtue, if correctly analyzed, can function by itself in individuating friends. Hence, it is not necessary to appeal to nonmoral characteristics in choosing friends. They assume that equal virtue cannot be sufficiently specific to individuate only one or a few potential friends; that, for example, there will be far too many persons to choose from who are equally courageous, temperate, liberal, honest, and truthful. If there are so many equally virtuous people, how then does one choose to become friends with one rather than another?

Their problem arises because they fail to analyze equal virtue in terms of Aristotle's idea of the proportional mean. For Aristotle, virtue is the proportional mean between extremes relative to each individual. For example, the right amount of food, the mean between too much and too little, is not the same for everyone.[23] What is too little food for an athlete might be too much food for a scholar. Two people could be equally virtuous in the sense of having similar amounts, an equal degree, of virtue but achieve their virtue by reaching particular proportional means that are very different, what can be called the "manner of virtue." Both athlete and scholar could have the same degree of virtue, because each consumed an amount right for them, but the particular amount of food each consumed would be very different and so therefore would be the manner of virtue. If friends are to be "other selves," as Aristotle says, then it is plausible to expect that they will resemble each other in the particular means between too much and too little relative to each of them. Because people can be equally virtuous in terms of degree but have very different individually relative proportional means, then the individuation problem can be solved by becoming friends with someone who is equal both in the degree of virtue and in the manner virtue. There would be no reason to appeal to nonmoral characteristics if equal virtue is correctly understood.

The degree of virtue a person has is that proportion of virtue compared to the ideal. John Cooper puts it this way:

> . . . on Aristotle's theory of moral virtue the virtues are essential properties of humankind: a person realizes more or less fully his human nature according as he possesses more or less fully those properties of character which count as moral excellences. And since individual persons are what they essentially are by being human beings, it can be said that a person (any person) realizes his own essential nature more fully the more completely and adequately he possesses the moral excellences.[24]

A very good person, for example, might possess virtues three-quarters of what perfect virtue would be, while a less good person might only possess one-half of perfect virtue, that is, the first person's honesty, courage, truthfulness, liberality, and so on, in combination, would be about three-quarters of what would be the ideal for a person, while the second less good person's would only be one-half of the ideal. A person of perfect virtue or human excellence would lack no degree of any virtue or excellence. Persons who have an equal but less than perfect virtue would have the same percentage of the virtues in combination or individually.

Notice that even in examining only equal degrees of virtue, combinations of particular virtues constituting a person's degree of overall virtue can individuate to some extent. For example, one person might have three-quarters of perfect virtue but might achieve this percentage by having a high degree of honesty with a lesser degree of liberality, while another person might have the same overall percentage of perfect virtue but might achieve that percentage with a high degree of liberality and a lesser degree of honesty. So people could have equal overall degrees of virtue yet achieve this equal degree by having different proportions of particular virtues, such as courage, honesty, liberality, or temperance. Still, in measuring the degree of virtue, the comparison is, in each instance, to the ideal perfection of virtue and human excellence.

Aristotle points out in his discussion of the mean that it is not the same for everyone, but the mean differs from person to person, depending on objective facts about the person. Suppose that a person of perfect courage is a person who always achieves the mean between cowardice and foolhardiness. Two people could be equally perfectly courageous and yet achieve their perfect courage through very different means. As Aristotle points out, the mean between cowardice and foolhardiness is not the same for everyone. In the *Politics*, he says, "For a man would be thought a coward if he had no more courage than a courageous woman."[25] A courageous general, for example, will behave in the face of an armed enemy differently than a courageous unarmed woman facing the same armed enemy. Thus equal degrees of virtue can be achieved by different manners of virtue. The general and the woman can have the same degree of virtue (perfect virtue or three-quarters' virtue) with different manners of virtue: the general may have to stand his ground and fight if he is to be virtuous, while if the woman were to stand her ground and fight, she would be foolhardy, so that for her, retreating might be virtuous. Thus in degree the woman and the general might have equal virtue, but the manner of enacting their virtue would differ.

It is important to notice here, as a brief digression, that different manners of virtue provide a perhaps better explanation for Aristotle's belief that men and women cannot be friends. Aristotle's own notoriously bad explanation, based on his false empirical ideas about female inferiority, appears to explain inequality between men and women as inequality of degree. He implies that women are less close to the ideal of human virtue. Inequality, in the manner of virtue, in contrast, does not imply that one or the other is less close to the ideal. Men and women could be equally virtuous in degree of virtue, in proportion to perfect virtue, and could achieve their degree of perfection by different manners of virtue. Aristotle could then be understood as arguing that friendship is unlikely between men and women not because women are inferior in virtue to men but because of the different manners by which men and women achieve equal degrees of virtue.

While equality of virtue measured only as the degree of virtue might not be sufficiently specific to function as a complete basis for becoming a friend, virtue suffices if equality of virtue additionally includes the manner as a basis for individuating the choice of friends. Two potential friends, choosing each other for their virtue, would look at both similar degree of virtue and similar manner of virtue (i.e., how they resemble each other in what for them is their particular relative mean with respect to courage, honesty, liberality and so forth). If equal virtue is interpreted to include both equality of degree and manner, then sufficient specificity is possible to individuate friendships by singling out only one or a few other selves as potential friends. A nonmoral basis for friendship, such as pleasure or utility, need not be invoked in order to choose friends. Thus there is nothing incomplete using virtue as a basis for selecting friends, as Whiting, Brink, Den Uyl, and Charles Griswold Jr. suggest. Because equal virtue is sufficiently determinate to individuate friendships, there is no need to resort to either utility or pleasure as a basis for becoming friends.

Individuating friends is more of a problem for Aristotle than for others, because the object of his ideal of friendship, where friends share their lives together, severely limits the number of friends it is possible to have. If only one or two friends are possible, a more exclusive selective criterion of choice is necessary to eliminate candidates. A more inclusive criterion can be used where a greater number of friends are possible. For C. S. Lewis, who does not believe that the number of possible friends is so limited, individuation is not as much of a problem.[26] Lewis's basis of friendship is the common interest or quest:

> Friendship arises out of mere Companionship when two or more of the companions discover that they have in common some insight or interest or even taste which the others do not share and which, till that moment, each believed to be his own unique treasure (or burden).[27]

Since many people can share such an interest, there is always the possibility of more than a limited number of friends. His contrasts between sharing interests as a basis for friendship and sharing affection in love deserve repeating:

> The very condition of having Friends is that we should want something else besides Friends. Where the truthful answer to the question *Do you see the same truth?* would be "I see nothing and I don't care about the truth; I only want a Friend," no Friendship can arise—though Affection of course may. There would be nothing for the Friendship to be *about*; and Friendship must be about something, even if it were only an enthusiasm for dominoes or white mice.[28] (emphasis in original)

> Lovers are always talking to one another about their love; Friends hardly ever about their Friendship. Lovers are normally *face to face*, absorbed in each other; Friends, *side by side*, absorbed in some common interest.[29] (emphasis added)

Lewis's distinction in these citations also concerns the object of friendship, that is, the different activities constituting different kinds of friendship, which are more fully discussed later in this chapter. Because a sizable number of people can share the same interest, there can be more than a limited number of friends. Because the object of the friendship is a pursuit of some common interest, there likewise can be more than a few friends who pursue that interest.

The bases for ideal friendships so far discussed in this section have appealed to the rational intellect. Whether the nature of friendship is understood as reciprocal goodwill, mutual benevolence, or partners in the same quest, the basis for friendship is something that appeals to friends' rational intellect. Other bases of ideal friendships do not appeal to friends' rational, intellectual side. Kant's ideal friendship, intimacy friendship, is not based on characteristics such as virtue, utility, need, or taste that appeal to reason or intellect. Its basis is "a strong impulse to disclose ourselves, and enter wholly into fellowship."[30] Friendship is based on inclination or emotion and, as Kant says, ". . . inclination goes its own secret way; indeed it can do no other, because it has no principle," and "emotion is blind in its choice, and after a while it goes up in smoke."[31] Kant's "strong desire to disclose ourselves" functions in his theory of friendship to explain why friendships are formed. Like Aristotle's bases of friendship, it is one of three bases Kant mentions. His other two are need and taste, which are the bases of less-than-ideal friendships. Unlike Aristotle's, and also differing from his own two less-than-ideal bases, Kant's ideal friendship is based on strong desires, emotions, and inclination.

Kant's exclusive dichotomy between reason and inclination or emotion is a rather extreme position. He believes that reason has little or no role in forming emotions or inclinations, and that reason's primary function is to control actions in opposition to capricious inclination and emotion. Aristotle and others would not consider reason and inclination independent and opposed. Emotions may be infused with significant rational components. As bases for friendship, reason and inclination may form more of a continuum by degrees than a dichotomy by opposites.

It may not be possible to predict who will become friends if Kant is right about the basis of his intimacy conception of friendship. Potential friends will be driven by their strong desire to disclose themselves until they fix upon an emotionally compatible and trustworthy partner. Kant supplies no information about how this process would be carried out. His conception of inclination as a force wholly unconnected to reason implies that no rational predictors are possible for who will befriend whom. There is a significant difference in this respect between Kant's and Aristotle's conceptions of ideal friendship. The basis of character or virtue friendship, equality in the degree and manner of virtue, makes possible fairly accurate predictions, at least in principle, about who will become friends with whom. If Aristotle is right in thinking that ideal friendships are based on equal virtue, then, for example, someone who knew that another shared her degree and manner of virtue would have good evidence that they would become friends. Predictions of this kind are impossible according to Kant's understanding of friendship's basis. Inclination, as he says, has no principle, so no functions or norms exist that will ground accurate predictions. Kant is forced to deny that friendships can be predicted because of his view of the totally nonrational, spontaneous nature of desires, emotions, and inclinations. Were Kant to hold a view of emotion that more resembles Aristotle's in having a rational component, predictions about who befriends whom might not be impossible.

Predicting who will become friends is one factor in testing the relevancy of different conceptions of friendship. One conception of friendship may be more adequate to our experiences to the extent that predictions are possible about who will or will not become friends. Kant's and Aristotle's ideal conceptions differ on this point. One conception could be judged more relevant to our experiences, depending on whether friendships can be predicted and on the kind of predictors that evidentially support the prediction. With friendships based on virtue or character, or need, utility, pleasure, or common interests, predictions about who will become friends are possible, at least in principle. For example, if sufficient information were known about the needs of two persons and need friendship were the presupposed conception of friendship, it would be possible to predict their friendship. Predictions also should be possible for friendships based on utility or pleasure. C. S. Lewis's interest-based conception makes predictions more easily than other conceptions, because it has the narrowest, single-factor, rational base.

At the farthest extreme from Lewis is Montaigne's fusion friendship. Montaigne believes "there was I know not what inexplicable and fateful force that was the mediator of this union."[32] Like Kant's intimacy friendship, no predictors are possible, because the basis of friendship is not rational. Neither Kant nor Montaigne gives any indication that they think nonrational predictors are possible.

Before discussing pleasure, utility, and need, which are the bases for Aristotle's and Kant's less-than-ideal friendships, I examine how "caring for a person" is sometimes used as a basis for friendship. In the previous section, I explained how "caring for a person" is considered by some to constitute part of the nature of friendship, and in the next section I discuss caring as part of the object of friendship. Many confusions about friendship can be remedied by keeping clear the different roles that "caring for a person" plays in various conceptions of friendship.

Whiting and others contrast loving someone because she is virtuous with loving the person for who she is: "concern for her *qua* virtuous seems not really concern for *her*, the unique and irreplaceable individual that she is"[33] (emphasis in original). Ferdinand Schoeman draws the contrast between caring for the person and caring for her qualities in slightly different language than Whiting:

> But caring for a person is not the same thing as caring for that person's qualities. We do not care for all of those who have the same moral qualities as our friends any more than we care, typically, for all of a friend's qualities. Except for noting that incidental traits of persons are unlikely to remain the basis of an enduring relationship, Aristotle gives little reason to assent to his line of thinking.[34]

He, like Whiting, is assuming that caring for a person is different from caring for someone because of her qualities, either moral or nonmoral. Is it really possible to care for friends independently of their qualities?

Logically, to care for a person must involve caring either for some, all, or none of the person's qualities or characteristics, even if it is not possible to express in words that those qualities are. What else about a person is there to care for? It is difficult to imagine that someone could care for a person and care for none of her characteristics. Aristotle's thought, that parents love their children, or that siblings love each other, might come close to the idea of caring independently of any personal characteristics, but this is not an example of caring for the person *qua* person, because in these cases it is caring for someone as one's child or as one's sibling.[35] There must be something to individuate friendship, something that does differentiate the unique person. Since neither Whiting nor Schoeman believes that caring for the person involves caring for all of the person's characteristics, the only option logically remaining is that of caring for some but not all of the person's characteristics—those characteristics that are essential for the person being who she is. But those essential characteristics are just what Aristotle would call a person's "virtues."

One common use for the phrase "caring for a person" is in contrast to an instrumental basis for personal relationships where a person is treated well only because of what can be gained from such treatment. "Caring for a person" in this sense is contrasted with using the person merely for one's own purposes. Merely using someone for one's own purposes is definitely not a friendship. Treating someone well can be motivated by self-interest, as Kant notes, but treating someone well from a motive of self-interest is different than using someone merely for one's own purposes—the difference between using someone as a means and using someone merely as a means.

As a basis for friendship, "caring for a person" can be understood as a reason some person is befriended. In this instance, "caring for a person" functions analogously to inclination, utility, or virtue as a basis explaining why two people become friends. Caring for a person, in this instance, might be contrasted with caring for someone because of his virtue, as Whiting and Schoeman stress. Two people might want to become friends not consciously because of each other's virtue but because of some constellation of characteristics that perhaps cannot be explicitly put into words, though this constellation need not conflict with nor exclude the person's virtue. Montaigne's understanding of why two people become friends has just this kind of basis. "Caring for a person" expresses such a basis for friendship. It is in this sense that a contrast can be made between caring for someone as a person and caring for someone on the basis of virtue. Nevertheless, though a distinction can be drawn between caring because of virtue and caring for her as a person, caring as a person must depend on some of her characteristics, for otherwise there would be no reason to care for her rather than for another.

No contradiction has been established within a single concept of friendship. Whiting's and Schoeman's analyses illuminate different bases explaining why people become friends. They could have just as cogently explained the difference between common interests as a basis for friendship in C. S. Lewis's conception of friendship and caring for the person as a basis for friendship as they conceive it. While a contrast can be meaningfully drawn between virtue or common interests as a basis for friendships and caring for a person as a basis, the contrast need not imply a contradiction within one concept of friendship rather than the existence of several different conceptions. Further, no logical incompatibility exists between virtue as a basis of friendship and caring for a person as the object or the nature of friendship.

Pleasure, need, and utility are three additional prominent bases of friendship that I discuss. They are the bases of the less-than-ideal friendships apparently so denigrated by Kant and Aristotle. Later in this chapter, I explain why I think that there is greater worth in these less-than-ideal friendships than is usually thought. In this section, I only want to explain how need, pleasure, and utility function as bases of friendship.

Need-based friendship, Kant believes, is the crudest form, and it arises in the earliest stages of society where friendship is a means of trusting one another for the mutual provision of the needs of life.[36] Kant sees need friendship as a bond among primitive people, permitting them peacefully to satisfy the needs of their existence. "Savages" can cooperate in hunting game that individually they might not consistently be able to kill.[37] This need-based relation is one of friendship, according to Kant, because each has the other's interests at heart (i.e., mutual benevolence for each other). Kant's mutual benevolence friend-ship based on need resembles Aristotle's utility based friendship, where recip-rocal goodwill is grounded on the benefits that each gets from the friendship. As friends they aim at producing benefits for each other or at satisfying each other's needs, just as friends might do whose friendship is based on virtue. The salient difference is not the nature of the friendship, goodwill, or benevolence but its basis. The same nature, goodwill, or benevolence can be grounded on any one of several possible bases (e.g., virtue, interest, pleasure, or need).

Another well-known basis for less-than-ideal friendships is pleasure. In Aristotle, pleasure friendships are the friendships of the young who easily form and easily end their friendships.[38] As a basis for reciprocal goodwill, plea-sure is far less stable or long lasting, Aristotle believes, than is virtue and char-acter, and so the friendships are not as permanent. Good looks or physical beauty will not be as stable a part of a friend as his virtuous character. This lack of stability or permanence seems to be Aristotle's principal reason for thinking that pleasure-based friendships have less value than virtue-based ones. There is no reason to think that pleasure-based friendships have less value because the friends would care less for each other in the sense of pro-moting each other's good than virtue-based friends. Aristotle, at least, never mentions a weaker goodwill as a consequence of pleasure-based friendship. Pleasure-based friends would want to spend as much of their time with each other as would virtue-based friends who share their lives together. A great deal of pleasure can result from the time that friends spend together.

THE OBJECT OF FRIENDSHIP

The object of friendship is what friends do together as friends. The object of friendship differs from the basis of friendship. Consider Aristotle's friendship based on pleasure, where the reason prospective friends have for initiating a friendship is that they expect the friendship will give them pleasure. The object of friendship, as I am using the term, is what the friends do, as friends, that pro-duces their pleasure. Pleasure might be produced by living a shared virtuous life together as Aristotle suggests, or it might be produced by jointly engaging in ex-ternal pursuits, such as football, fishing, and wildflower collecting. Still other ac-tivities might produce pleasure, such as quiet conversations about the friends' feelings and thoughts. Gordon C. Roadarmel points out "that Indians have strongly defined concepts of friendship and hospitality, and to be a friend or guest in India is a less casual matter than is often true in the U. S." He adds that:

[W]hen an Indian feels that friendship has been established . . . he/she is likely to assume what are considered the privileges of a friend—to drop in at any time *without advance notice*, to sit around at length and talk or read your books and magazines, to stay for meals. . . . As a result of differences in customs, Indians may feel that Americans are insincere in their initial friendliness.[39] (emphasis added)

Clearly, what Indians believe that friends may do with each other as the object of friendship is quite different from what Americans believe is appropriate behavior among friends. It has not been widely recognized that the objects of friendship systematically differ from each other as do the bases of friendship. Few philosophers have asked about what friends do as friends as a result of pleasure, utility, virtue, or other bases of friendship.

The object of friendship is crucial in understanding the morality of preferring friends to nonfriends. It is within the object of friendship, activities that friends engage in as friends, where the moral issue of preferring friends to nonfriends primarily, though not exclusively, arises. Friends' preference and partiality for each other expresses itself in activities that constitute the object of their friendship.

Friendships with common interests and external pursuits as objects contrast with friendships that have as their object intimacy or communion and the exchange of private personal information, feelings, and emotions. Objects of friendship are logically independent of the bases, in the sense that objects of friendship (e.g., shared interests or intimate conversations) can have several different bases—pleasure, utility, or virtue. Similarly, one base (e.g., pleasure) can have different objects—intimate conversations or erotic activities. In actuality, practical connections between objects and bases of friendship may exist in that some objects of friendship (e.g., intimacy) may be easier to establish on certain bases.

I am not sure why investigations into the objects of friendship have never really been undertaken. I suspect one reason is that it has just been assumed that activities in friendship simply vary with individual tastes or preferences, and that there were no systematic or focused differences. Another reason may be that no one noticed the extent to which Kant's and Aristotle's (among others) conceptions of friendship differed from each other constituted by different activities.

A striking coincidence exists between the objects of friendship represented by Kant and Montaigne on one side and C. S. Lewis and Aristotle on the other with what Barbara A. Winstead reports about psychological studies in the United States of same-sex friendships.[40] These empirical psychological studies of men's and women's same-sex friendships reveal a close parallel to the different objects of friendship discussed by these philosophers. Kant's intimacy friendship and the fusion friendship of Montaigne closely resemble female same-sex friendships, while Aristotle's virtue friendship and the interest friendship of C. S. Lewis closely resemble male same-sex friendships.

Winstead begins her discussion of same-sex friendships by remarking that female friendships are "face to face," whereas male friendships are "side by side."[41] Male friendships tend to have as their object shared interests or external pursuits. In same-sex female friendships, the friends view intimacy as being essential to their friendship, and they are more likely to talk about their feelings and emotions. Winstead continues, ". . . the factors most central to female friendships are mutual help and support, whereas males emphasize similar interests and shared experiences."[42] Female friends, when they talk to each other, tend to discuss feelings and personal problems, whereas male friends tend to discuss activities.[43] Female friends are more likely to discuss topics involving themselves and their close relationships, while, again, male same-sex friends' in-depth discussions focus on external, activity-oriented topics. Winstead also points out "that female same-sex friends compared to male friends are expected to be more self-disclosing, other-enhancing, and physically affectionate."[44] On the process of becoming friends, she states:

> If male friends *do* things with one another, then it is sensible for them to be concerned at the beginning of the friendship about similarity in activity preference; otherwise, there may be conflict in choosing what to do together. On the other hand, if female friends talk with one another more and talk especially about personal topics, then shared values may make it more likely that they will find themselves able to validate one another's views.[45] (emphasis in original)

If the empirical studies reported in Winstead's article are accurate, then differences in the female and male same-sex friendships closely resemble the different objects of friendship inherent in philosophical conceptions of friendship. The different objects of these philosophers' ideal conceptions of friendship appear to have empirical correlates. Indian same-sex friendships also have similar differences in their objects. Parekh notes that same-sex female friendships are presented as more intimate and less self-conscious than those between men, and that the Indian term used to describe female friends involves mutual caring, fondness, support and, above all, exchanging and keeping confidences.[46]

For Kant, the primary object of ideal friendship is to reach complete intimacy and communion between two friends, so that each believes that he can unburden himself and expose his innermost thoughts. Because intimacy is the object of friendship for Kant, in contrast to Aristotle, friends may not have to spend a great deal of time with each other or engage in many shared activities. Kant even goes so far as to emphasize that friendship is only a disposition to intimacy and communion. Friends do not actually have to get together and exchange confidences or thoughts. What he stresses is that although friends believe that they can be intimate, they need not often engage in intimate conversations. Friendship is conceived of as an unreserved possibility rather than the actuality of exchanging intimate thoughts and feelings.

Objects of friendship, as Kant and Montaigne explain, resemble objects of same-sex female friendships. Neither Kant nor Montaigne emphasizes engaging in external pursuits growing out of common external interests. Friends spend their time in discussions of intimate personal thoughts and feelings. For Montaigne especially, the object may be to move these feelings and thoughts as close to unity as possible. Each friend ultimately desires to possess deep knowledge of the other's inner self and to achieve in inner harmony or identity with the friend.

Lewis's distinction between love and friendship closely parallels what Winstead reports as distinguishing male and female same-sex friendships. Friends, for Lewis, share interests and external pursuits as the object of their friendship; they do not share intimacies or sit around discussing their thoughts focusing on each other. Friends want to spend time together, perhaps as much as their lives will allow, pursuing their shared interests in much the same way that Aristotle's friends share their lives of virtuous activity. The object of friendship for Lewis is something exterior to them, some object or interest that they care about. The interior and the personal are not a primary concern in friendship. To repeat what Lewis has said:

> For of course we do not want to know our Friend's affairs at all. Friendship, unlike Eros, is uninquisitive. You become a man's friend without knowing or caring whether he is married or single or how he earns his living. What have all these "unconcerning things, matters of fact" to do with the real question, *Do you see the same truth?* . . . No one cares twopence about any one else's family, profession, class, income, race, or previous history. Of course you will get to know about most of these in the end. But casually.[47] (emphasis in original)

Aristotle's object of virtue friendship can be called, following Nancy Sherman, a "shared life."[48] A shared life, as an object of friendship, envisions friends inhabiting their lives in common activities both as a means to and a constituent part of the good for each of the friends. Friends, as Aristotle conceives them, would be jointly engaged in sharing day-to-day activities, interests, and pleasures in order to promote each other's good. Most, if not all, of friends' daily undertakings would be engaged in cooperatively. Friends would choose to spend time together and help each other rather than spend time with or help nonfriends.

Friendship, insofar as it can be considered a virtue for Aristotle, is a shared activity between two people according to right reason. As a virtue, friendship would thus require a shared life lived cooperatively with another and is therefore different from other virtues that do not essentially involve common activities. One does not, for example, need to cooperate with others to act courageously in the face of danger.

The ambiguous phrase "caring for a person," which has so far been discussed as both the nature of friendship and as a basis of friendship, also can be understood as expressing differences in objects of friendship. One possible difference is between the objects of same-sex male and same-sex female friendships. According to Winstead, males share external pursuits or interests, while females share intimacies or personal concerns. In same-sex male friendships, the object of friendship is some external pursuit or virtuous activity that resembles the objects of Aristotle's and C. S. Lewis's conceptions of friendship. In contrast, in same-sex female friendships, the object of the friendship tends to be shared feelings, concerns, and emotions resembling the objects of Kant's and Montaigne's friendships. "Caring for a person" as an object of friendship refers to friends' shared thoughts and feelings, in contrast to friends' shared external pursuits or interests. While there is a tendency to add that same-sex female friendships are "deeper and less superficial" because they concern the inner person to a greater extent than do the same-sex male friendships, John Carbonara has pointed out that sharing one's inner feelings about one's hair stylist need not be deeper than a shared pursuit or interest in philosophy.[49]

Thus when Whiting or Schoeman emphasizes caring for a person, they may have in mind the kind of intimacy friendship that has for its object communion and shared feelings, but there is no incompatibility between intimacy as object of friendship and virtue as a basis of friendship. A person's virtue can be the basis for a friendship (the reason for becoming friends), and the object of that friendship can be intimacy and communion. Winstead emphasizes that shared values are an important basis for female friendships whose object is intimacy and communion. In exactly the same way, a friendship where the object is communion and intimacy can be based on pleasure. Friends can have communion and intimacy as an object of friendship based on the reason that they find communion and intimacy pleasurable.

The object of friendship is independent of the basis of friendship (i.e., objects of friendship, either intimacy and communion or virtue and external interest, can rest on any of the possible bases). There is no conflict in caring for someone because of her virtue (the basis of friendship) and caring for someone in the sense of her feelings, emotions, and thoughts in contrast to shared external activities (the object of friendship).

Lastly, caring for a person (as a whole?) is sometimes contrasted to caring for someone because of her qualities. The idea here may be that one person's qualities or virtues can be repeatable in another person, and if this were true, then to care for one person because of those qualities would be a reason to care for any other who possessed those qualities. I am not quite sure why this is a problem. Some forms of friendship so far discussed have implications that one could very well have several similar friends at the same time. While it is most certainly true that each person is unique, the temptation to interpret unique as being totally different must continually be avoided. People resemble each other in more aspects than they differ from each other, and there is nothing incompatible with caring for one's friend and realizing that one could possibly be friends with a number of persons having relevantly similar characteristics.

Concern that friendship is based on the unique person might be better explained not by contrasting caring for a person with caring for her characteristics but by realizing that not all of a person's characteristics can even, in principle, be repeatable in another. My close friend, Lance, for example, has the characteristic that we were great friends while getting our Ph. Ds. Even if it were possible to discover some new person who has many of Lance's best characteristics and fewer of his not so best characteristics, that person could not possibly share the characteristic of being my great friend while we were getting our Ph. Ds. Friends (and lovers) develop a joint history that is unique and, logically, not repeatable in any other person. No incompatibility need therefore exist between caring for a person on the basis of her characteristics and caring for the unique individual, because not all of a person's characteristics are, in principle, repeatable.[50]

If these senses of "caring for a person" are kept distinct, then Whiting's and Schoeman's point reduces to saying that people become friends for reasons other than each other's virtue, that is, that they care for each other for reasons other than their goodness, or to saying that some friendships have as objects the friends' thoughts rather than external pursuits.

Whiting's and Schoeman's confusions arise, I believe, from failing adequately to distinguish the basis of friendship, the object of friendship, and the nature of friendship that constitute various different conceptions of friendship. "Caring for a person" is ambiguous. But in stressing caring for "the unique and irreplaceable person," they may be trying to make a very different point. They may be suggesting that caring for the person (as an object of friendship) can be sustained even if there are significant changes in the person's character (as the basis of friendship). If I care for the person, for example, I would still be his friend were he to do something not at all virtuous, or if our friendship failed to remain pleasant or useful. However, were I to care for the person no matter what changes occur in character or circumstance, that caring would be equivalent to unconditional caring which, if properly understood, cannot be caring for the person because of "the unique and irreplaceable person" he is. It is precisely that property of unconditional caring, caring even if most or all of a person's characteristics change, which implies that it cannot be the particular person who is cared for but some abstract entity compatible with virtually anyone. No specific characteristics of that person are the basis for caring.

Caring for a person as a basis of friendship implies that there is something about the person, even if it cannot be articulated, that functions as a basis for becoming and remaining friends, without which the friendship would not exist. Unconditional friendship, friendship that would exist even if everything about the friend were to change, would have to be a friendship not based on any characteristics of the person.[51] Like Aristotle's parent or sibling friendship, unconditional friendship could not depend on anything about the particular person. In contrast, if "caring for a person" is used in the sense that refers to the object of friendship, then one might continue to share intimate thoughts and feelings, though the basis of the friendship might change.

It might be thought that I have exaggerated the difference between the objects of Kant's and Aristotle's ideal friendships. Philosophers such as Marilyn Friedman, Lawrence A. Blum, and Christine M. Korsgaard consider friendship both as intimacy and as shared active lives.[52] Both objects perhaps could be combined into one possibly more complete ideal conception of friendship without any logical difficulty. While there are no logical obstacles to combining the two objects into one grand ideal conception of friendship, I believe that there are a number of practical reasons for not doing so. First,

Kant's and Aristotle's ideals of friendship individually are attained only with difficulty by a relatively few exceptional persons. Were friendship conceived of as a combination of both objects, then ideal friendship might be even more difficult to achieve. And as a less achievable goal, ideal friendship might be actually less desired, because many potential friends would think that they had little chance of ever achieving it. People might therefore aim for one of the less-than-ideal friendships. If the (swollen or bloated) combined friendship were judged to be ideal, then both Kant and Aristotle would be mistaken about the best friendships.

A second reason for not combining the two different objects of friendship into one greater ideal friendship is that the character traits needed for intimacy may be different from the character traits needed for equality of virtue. Kant believes that for intimacy friendship, each friend must possess, "uprightness of disposition, sincerity, trustworthiness, conduct devoid of all falsehood and spite, and a sweet, cheerful, and happy temper."[53] These traits might not be those of very courageous Aristotelian friends. Many of the friendships that could be considered ideal on Aristotle's conception could not be included in the combined conception because of conflicts with character traits that Kant believes are needed for intimacy. C. S. Lewis's conception of friendship, which does not stress intimacy, also would be excluded from the ideal.

There is a third and, I believe, a decisive reason for avoiding the combination as an ideal. Intimacy and a life of shared activity could be based on pleasure. Persons could want to be intimate and share their lives together because they found doing so pleasurable, and thus virtue is not the only possible basis for a friendship, the object of which is intimacy and shared living together. Neither Kant nor Aristotle would consider any friendship based on pleasure ideal, even if the object of that friendship were a shared activity or an intimate life. This combination of shared activity and intimacy by themselves does not possess ideal value for Aristotle and Kant. Serious thought must be given to whether different bases add to or detract from the value of friendship.

Finally, the combined shared activity and intimacy friendship implies that each person can have only one friend or a few friends. Even fewer friends would be possible for the combined ideal than would be possible for either of the ideals individually. Sharing most of life's activities plus discovering it is safe to share intimacies would consume so much time that more than a few friends would be impossible. I mentioned earlier that the number of possible friends each conception of friendship allows can function as a nonmoral test of adequacy. If a conception of friendship implies that an unlimited number of friends were possible, or if a conception of friendship implies that only one friend were possible, then those would be reasons for doubting the adequacy of these conceptions to our experience. Just as experience shows that it is not possible to be friends with an extremely large number of people, experience also shows that more than one friend is a possibility. C. S. Lewis's and Montaigne's conceptions of friendship are questionable because of their implications about the number of friends it is possible to have.

Before I begin to discuss the much neglected less-than-ideal friendships, I want to emphasize some salient conclusions reached as a result of distinguishing the nature, basis, and object of friendship. Most importantly, becoming clear about the nature, basis, and object of friendship permits understanding relations between different conceptions of friendship. Too often philosophers have either uncritically assumed that there is one single clear conception of friendship about which "commonsense" moral implications obviously follow, or they have found "contradictions" within some set of friendship concepts.[54] There are a variety of ways that conceptions of friendship encompass caring for the person who is one's friend. The truth is that there are a number of related but different conceptions of friendship from our own culture and from others. Different conceptions exist not only about what friendships actually are but about what ideally ought to be aimed at as valuable friendships. The remaining chapters of this book examine friendship's moral implications. Being aware of the difference between the nature, basis, and object provides a much greater clarity about the moral implications of each conception.

LESS-THAN-IDEAL FRIENDSHIPS

Much has been written about what Kant and Aristotle have praised as the ideal or best form of friendship: virtue or character friendship for Aristotle and intimacy friendship for Kant. Too little attention has been focused on the kinds of friendships that they believe possess less-than-ideal value. Not only do Kant and Aristotle think that such friendships have less value, they sometimes write as though some lesser friendships are not really friendships at all. Since Kant and Aristotle believe that few real friendships achieve their ideal, most actual friendships possess this less-than-ideal value. Thus a better understanding of these less-than-ideal friendships will lead to a better understanding of a large number of actual friendships.

Aristotle begins his discussion of friendship by distinguishing between three kinds of friendship based on three reasons for loving, "For not everything seems to be loved but only the lovable, and this is good, pleasant, or useful." Immediately after, he defines friendship as reciprocated goodwill: "To be friends, then, they must be mutually recognized as bearing goodwill and wishing well to each other for one of the aforesaid reasons."[55] This parallels his definition of friendship in the *Rhetoric:*

> Let us now turn to friendship and enmity, and ask towards whom these feelings are entertained, and why. We will begin by defining friendship and friendly feeling. We may describe friendly feeling towards anyone as wishing for him what you believe to be good things, not for your own sake but for his, and being inclined, so far as you can, to bring these things about. . . .Those who think they feel thus towards each other think themselves friends. This being assumed, it follows that your friend is the sort of man who shares your pleasure in what is good and your pain in what is unpleasant, for your sake and for no other reason.[56]

In the *Nicomachean Ethics* Aristotle immediately contrasts the best friendships based on character or virtue with the lesser friendships based on pleasure and utility:

> Now those who love each other for their utility do not love each other for themselves but in virtue of some good which they get from each other. So too with those who love for the sake of pleasure; it is not for their character that men love ready-witted people, but because they find them pleasant. Therefore those who love for the sake of utility love for the sake of what is good *for themselves*, and those who love for the sake of pleasure do so for the sake of what is pleasant to *themselves*, and not in so far as the other is the person loved but in so far as he is useful or pleasant. And thus these friendships are only incidental; for it is not as being the man he is that the loved person is loved, but as providing some good or pleasure. Such friendships, then, are easily dissolved, if the parties do not remain like themselves; for if the one party is no longer pleasant or useful the other ceases to love him.
> Now the useful is not permanent but is always changing. Thus when the motive of the friendship is done away, the friendship is dissolved, inasmuch as it existed only for the ends in question.[57] (emphasis in original)

Aristotle believes that pleasure and utility friendships may not last as long as friendships based on character, because he believes that character is more stable than the circumstances that create pleasure or utility friendships, and thus these two are not as valuable as friendships. In the *Eudemian Ethics*, Aristotle explicitly claims that friendship based on character is the best, simply because it the most stable and lasting.[58]

Aristotle also appears to think that pleasure and utility friendships are less valuable because, unlike character friendships, the friend is not loved for himself but for pleasure or utility. Not loving the friend for himself or herself would appear to contradict both his *Rhetorics'* and *Nicomachean Ethics'* definitions of the nature of friendship.

Aristotle is ambivalent toward the less-than-ideal forms of friendship. In some places he writes as though they were friendships of lesser value, but in other places he seems to regard them not as friendships at all. Aristotle suggests that utility friends or pleasure friends not only have different bases for their friendships, but that they also may fail to have goodwill toward each other:

> But those who exchange not pleasure but utility in their love are both less truly friends and less constant. Those who are friends for the sake of utility part when the advantage is at an end; for they were lovers not of each other but of profit.[59]

> The man who has received a benefit bestows goodwill in return for what has been done to him, and in doing so is doing what is just; while he who wishes some one to prosper because he hopes for enrichment through him seems to have goodwill not to him but rather to himself, just as a man is not a friend to another if he cherishes him for the sake of some use to be made of him.[60]

> But the friendship of utility is full of complaints; for as they use each other for their own interests they always want to get the better of the bargain, and think they have got less than they should, and blame their partners because they do not get all they want and deserve; and those who do well by others cannot help them as much as those whom they benefit want.[61]

> Friendship being divided into these kinds; bad men will be friends for the sake of pleasure or utility, being in this respect like each other, but good men will be friends for their own sake, i.e., in virtue of their goodness. These, then, are friends without qualification; the others are friends incidentally and through a resemblance to these.[62]

Aristotle's words draw a pessimistic picture of less-than-ideal friendships. Some degenerate utility or pleasure friendships can be characterized in ways pictured by these quotations, but there are ways of understanding both pleasure and utility friendships that show that they more closely resemble the ideal friendship by literally fulfilling Aristotle's reciprocal goodwill criterion.

Friends' reciprocal goodwill can arise from any one of the three bases of friendship: pleasure, utility, and goodness. These "motives of the friendship," as Aristotle also calls them,[63] resemble Kant's three motives of action. In the *Grounding for the Metaphysics of Morals*, Kant explains how duty can be performed from the motive of duty or from the motives of self-interest or inclination.[64] Kant believes that all three motives can simultaneously be present on any one occasion, thus making it impossible to discover of anyone, even of oneself, which is the strongest or dominant motive.[65] For Kant, doing one's duty often is pleasurable and in one's own interest; discerning which motive is dominant may be impossible.

While it may be true that bad men will only be friends with each other for pleasure or utility, Aristotle's insistence that good men will only love each other for their goodness is not obviously true. Good men can love each other because of their goodness, but there are no reasons against good men being friends with other good men for the pleasure or the utility that those friendships produce unless, however, Aristotle wants to stipulate that truth by definition. Aristotle argues that things can be loved because they are pleasant, useful, or good, but he never says that good men can only love things because they are good and not love things because they also are useful or pleasant.

When Aristotle says that "the loveable" are loved because they are good, pleasant, or useful, he might be thought to view these motives as being mutually exclusive. As a result, his three forms of friendship would not overlap, because bases for loving someone or something are distinct. While he mentions twice that the best friendship, virtue or character friendship, also will be pleasant and useful in the best sense, Aristotle never explicitly considers the possibility that friendships could arise from more than one of the three bases simultaneously.[66]

One possible way of making sense of Aristotle's omission is to assume that when he discusses utility and pleasure as bases for friendship, he has in mind what is merely useful or pleasant. He may be trying to contrast these lesser bases to the best friendship based on the goodness of friends. Virtue friendships may additionally encompass friends' truly useful and truly pleasant characteristics. Aristotle undoubtedly expects that whatever is good also will be pleasant and useful to those who have a virtuous character. A virtuous person, according to Aristotle, learns to take pleasure in acting according to the commands of right reason, though of course, Aristotle's virtue friends are only equally virtuous then need not be perfectly virtuous. For those who are non-virtuous, however, whatever is useful or pleasant need not be good.

Still, no reason exists why a virtuous person cannot love something, for example, wine, because it is pleasant, or another thing, for example, exercise, because it is useful. Thus a virtuous person might be friends with a useful person or a pleasant person the way a virtuous person could love wine or exercise. It is even possible for a virtuous person to be friends with another virtuous person because it is useful or pleasant rather than friendship based on equality in manner and degree of virtue. Just as long as a friendship requires no compromise of virtue, then a virtuous person can have friends on the basis of what is pleasant or useful. While Aristotle discusses none of these possibilities, these additional species of friendships are logically compatible with his premise that things are lovable only because they are good, pleasant, or useful.

The most troubling critical implication in Aristotle's quotations is his suggestion that friendships based on utility do not exhibit reciprocal goodwill, because they are only based on the desire for profit: "Those who are friends for the sake of utility part when the advantage is at an end; for they were lovers not of each other but of profit."[67] And in the *Eudemian Ethics*, he adds:

> Now kindly feeling is not altogether different from friendship, nor yet the same; for when we distinguish friendship according to its three sorts, kindly feeling is found neither in the friendship of usefulness nor in that of pleasure. For if one wishes well to the other because that is useful to oneself, one would be so wishing not for the object's sake, but for his own; but goodwill seems like . . . to be not goodwill for him who feels the goodwill, but for him towards whom it is felt. Now if goodwill existed in the friendship towards the pleasant, then men would feel goodwill towards things inanimate.[68]

But if there is no reciprocal goodwill between them, then it is difficult to see that the relationship is one of friendship at all, as he defines friendship.

In contrast to the above quotation, it is possible to have both goodwill toward someone and also to base the relationship on utility. The alternatives are not mutually exclusive. Something useful for Aristotle primarily has extrinsic value, though like the pleasant, he believes it may have intrinsic value as well. For a thing to be useful its value has to derive from something else which itself may have extrinsic or intrinsic value and so on, until there is a final intrinsic value that is the source of the whole value sequence. It is important to remember that for Aristotle, things having instrumental value also may be valued intrinsically; there is no reason something extrinsically valuable as a means to something else cannot also be valued for its own sake. Exercise and education are good examples of things that typically have both intrinsic and extrinsic value. Also, to be valued extrinsically need not imply that the thing valued has little value. Intrinsic value is not always greater than extrinsic value. Some bit of trivial information may have some slight intrinsic value as knowledge, assuming that knowledge always has some intrinsic value, but in contrast, learning how to use a computer has primarily instrumental value, yet its value may be much greater. Two people might form relations with each other merely because there is profit to be gained, that is, to value their relationship only instrumentally; they could, in addition, place intrinsic value on each other over and above valuing the relation because of its mutual advantage. There is no impossibility in two friends having goodwill toward each other, that is, valuing each other for his or her own sake, and there being some advantage for them in doing so. Friendships based on utility do not logically exclude goodwill between the friends who are "lovers of each other."

Martha Nussbaum emphasizes one difference between friendship and other instrumental or exploitative relationships where there is no reciprocal goodwill:

> they may think of one another as useful to their other projects (as might be the case between business partners), and still have, again, no deeper mutual knowledge or attachment. Such relationships will not be merely exploitative: for we recall that without mutuality of genuine good well-wishing for the other person's own sake the relationship will not deserve the title of *philia* at all.[69]

She continues on the same page in a footnote:

> Pleasure, advantage, and good character are three different bases or original grounds of *philia*; they are not the goal or final (intentional) end of the relationship. In other words, the two people are friends "through" or "on the basis of" these, but the goal they try to achieve in action will still be some sort of mutual benefit. Pleasure and advantage friendships, while not perfect, are importantly distinct from exploitative relationships, in which the parties aim each at their own pleasure, and not at all at the other's good. The *object* of the relation in all cases is the other person; but the person will be conceived of and known in a way bounded by the basis: as someone who is pleasant to be with, as a person well-placed for useful dealings, as a person of good character. Thus the two inferior types aim at benefit for the other only under a thin and superficial description of the other.[70] (emphasis in original)

Nussbaum thinks that the difference between exploitative relations and friendship where goodwill exists is that friendships will be deep both in knowledge and interest, while the other relationships will be "thin and superficial' in these ways. Her distinction is one based on degrees of knowledge rather than on some qualitative difference in the relationship. There is, however, an additional way of conceiving of the difference that focuses more qualitatively on the good or well-being of those involved.

If Aristotle is saying that utility friends lack goodwill toward each other, aiming only at "profit" rather than each other's good, then there will be no distinguishing utility friendships from commercial or business relationships, what Nussbaum calls "exploitative relationships." In commercial or business relations, participants are motivated by their own self-interest, and in this respect, the relation is thought to resemble utility friendship. Differences nevertheless exist between these relations and friendships that are well expressed, in Aristotle, by associating a goodwill with friendship where friends are concerned with each other's overall well-being.

In business or commercial relations, the participants need not act with goodwill toward each other. Buyers and sellers tend to focus on their own satisfaction with the transaction. Some enlightened sellers may desire the buyer's satisfaction with her purchase so that she may make additional future purchases. More enlightened sellers may desire that the buyer flourish and her well-being advance, so that she will make even greater purchases. Still, even the most enlightened sellers need only be concerned with the well-being of the buyer insofar as it affects her ability to continue to make purchases. Much the same could be said about employer-employee relations. Enlightened employers should be concerned about the well-being of their employees, because that will affect their performance at work. Employees should hope that their employer profits, so that the business survives and they continue to have well-paying jobs. These relations do require some concern for the well-being of the other participants, but only to the degree that it affects the mutual profitability of the relationship. This concern is not equivalent to goodwill; it is only focused on a partial or qualified aspect of others' well-being as it is relevant to their limited self-interested relationship.

In friendship, each friend's goodwill is a desire that the other friend unqualifiedly flourish. To have goodwill toward another is to desire her overall good (i.e., that she flourishes and that her well-being advances). Goodwill in friendship aims at an overall good, not a good qualified or limited by self-interest. Friends desire each other's advantage in areas that do not affect their interest at all. It is this goodwill in friendship that distinguishes it from the other "exploitative relations" that Nussbaum mentions. Unlike her way of expressing the distinction, this is a difference in quality (i.e., the presence or absence of an overall goodwill rather than a partial good, and not a difference in degree, i.e., how much knowledge or interest each possesses).

Utility friends have goodwill toward each other and desire each other's overall well-being. Their reason for having this mutual goodwill is that each finds it advantageous. Utility friends need not be understood as utility maximizers. Michael Slote's concept of a "satisficer" accurately explains how utility friends regard each other.[71] Friends can be satisfied that their friendship produces more benefits than they would receive without their friendship. Their benefits are "good enough." Utility friends do not have to squeeze every drop of advantage out of their relation, thus their goodwill for each other need not be tested or destroyed by an unending quest for ever-greater benefit.

Not all utility-based relations generate mutual goodwill, and thus not all utility-based relations are friendships. Those utility-based relations only generate a concern for the other's well-being in a partial or qualified way, and they are a source of the kinds of conflict and disagreement that Aristotle cites. He may not have clearly separated such exploitative or self-interested relations from utility friendship when he makes his derogatory comments about the motives and aims of utility friendships.

In a friendship based on utility, it is not the character or virtue of the friend that is the reason for the friendship, but its usefulness. When Aristotle says that the friend is not cared for for himself but because the relationship is useful, then he need not be implying that the friend is only cared for instrumentally as a means to promote one's own utility. Instrumental, exploitative relationships, where participants are only concerned with their own good, lack the defining characteristic of friendship: that the friends have goodwill toward each other. Aristotle emphasizes this point not only in the *Nicomachean Ethics* and the *Rhetoric* but also in the *Eudemian Ethics*:

> And the various definitions of friendship that we give in our discourses all belong to friendship in some sense, but not to the same friendship. To the useful friend applies the fact that one wishes what is good for him, and to a benefactor, and in fact to any kind of friend . . . for this definition does not distinguish the class of friendship.[72]

There is one way that friendship motivated by utility is easily made consistent with having goodwill toward one's friend. If friends regard each other as "other selves," then promoting one friend's good augments the other's good because they identify with each other. When something good happens to one friend it is as though it happens equally to the other. Identifying with a friend as "another self"[73] might be very useful, because it promotes utility. Friends could regard each other as another self not in the sense that they possess equal virtue or similar characters, as would be the case in a friendship based on virtue. Rather, they could regard each other as another self in the sense that they identify each other's good as their own good, even if they differ in character or virtue. It is not necessary in order for two people to identify with each other that they share many similar characteristics. "Identify," in this particular instance, need not mean resemble in character or virtue, but "identify" would mean viewing things from the same perspective.

Aristotle may not have had in mind utility as a motive or base for identifying with someone as "another self," but there is no reason to exclude the possibility. Identification with another self based on utility resolves some difficulties faced by the idea that one has goodwill for one's friend because it is useful. An identification between friends seems to remove any possibility that one's own utility will conflict with the utility of one's friend. If friends are not viewed as other selves, then some possibility exists that something beneficial to one will be harmful to the other. In contrast, where there is an identification between the two, then not conflicts but balancing gains and losses from two internal aspects of a single "self" may be the only difficulty. Such balancing may not be easy: trade-offs, even within a single person's life, may require difficult decisions, but individual trade-offs rather than conflicts of interest between two different persons require no questionable interpersonal comparisons of utility.

There may be reasons for thinking that a utility basis for identifying with someone as "another self" contradicts Aristotle. He points out that utility friendships last only as long as circumstances make friendship useful. An objection might be raised that if friends identify with each other as other selves, then no possible change in circumstances would alter the utility of their relationship. Utility friendships would then be as enduring as virtue or character friendships. No reason exists, however, for thinking that changes in circumstances would not affect the utility each receives if utility friends identify with each other as other selves. Suppose that two coworkers are friends, identify with each other's good, and do so because of the utility that each gains at work from the friendship—eating lunch together, engaging in company gossip, developing ideas, helping each other meet deadlines, and so on. Good things that happen at work to one are considered good by the other. Now suppose one is laid off. Both of them would suffer. Many activities they engaged in that produced utility are no longer available to them. Identifying with each other will not produce the same high level of utility. Changed circumstances therefore bring about changes in their utilities that break apart their friendship. Thus friendships where friends identify with each other as other selves because of the utility in doing so need not be more stable than virtue or character friendships and can end because of changed circumstances, just as Aristotle claims.

There is no conceptual incompatibility inherent in utility friends having goodwill toward each other. No contradiction arises between their being motivated to promote each other's good and their being motivated to benefit themselves. They need not view the value of the relation from the perspective of utility maximization but as satisficing utility.

Aristotle is not all that fair in his evaluation of utility friendships in comparison to either virtue or pleasure friendships. In their crassest forms, merely instrumental relationships can dehumanize the participants, reduce people to the status of things, and reinforce unchecked selfishness. Aristotle's argument that life without virtue friendship is not worth living, even if one had all other goods, implies that utility-based friendships have less value in comparison. But compared to crass, narrowly instrumental relations, utility friendships are far more valuable, because utility friends exercise goodwill toward each other. To the extent that having goodwill is ennobling and self-rewarding, utility and virtue friendships share that characteristic in common. Its principal difference in value from virtue friendship is not the absence of mutual goodwill but the less stable basis on which utility goodwill is grounded.

In actuality, utility friendships can be both mutually beneficial and value producing. If concrete experiences of friends are examined, it is clear that utility friends mutually prosper. Utility friendships are the ones where the "friends are there when you need them"; they are the friendships where "you can count on your friend," where friends "lend a helping hand," and where friends "stand by you." Utility friends make life much more comfortable and secure by being willing to help and assist each other (frequently) with no thought of any return. Such friendships may be less stable than virtue-based friendships if Aristotle is right and good character is more stable than chance and circumstance.

An additional difference between utility and virtue friendships is the number of friends it is possible to have. Aristotle believes that one can have only one friend or a few virtue friends, because living together requires so much time and investment. A greater number of utility friends is possible, because utility friends do not spend all of their time together in shared activities. It is not clear whether this difference in the number of friends is relevant to the value of each kind of friendship. Still, the slightly greater number of friends makes utility friendship perhaps more consistent with our contemporary Western experiences.

Aristotle does not say as much about the object of utility friendship as he does about the object of virtue or character friendship. The object of virtue friendship is a shared life of virtuous activity in which the friends hold property in common. Virtue friendships, Aristotle believes, will also be most useful and most pleasant in the best sense of those terms. If utility friends identified with each other as "other selves," would they share their lives in the way that virtuous friends do? Aristotle says that utility friends do not spend a lot of time together.[74] As friends who have reciprocal goodwill for each other, they would want to spend some time together doing good for each other, but unlike virtue friends, whose virtue is equal in degree and manner, utility friends may not possess similar equality or resemblance in character. In virtue friendships, it is the equality in degree and manner of virtue that makes sharing their lives possible, because they are attracted to and engage and excel in similar virtuous activities. Utility friends lack a similar equality of virtuous activities, and thus they may desire to spend less time with each other. Yet, at the end of Book IX, Aristotle does seem to say that all kinds of friends will desire to spend time together:

> For friendship is a partnership, and as a man is to himself, so is he to his friend; now in his own case the perception of his existence is desirable, and so therefore is that of his friend's, and the activity of this perception is produced when they live together, so that it is natural that they aim at this. And whatever existence means for each class of men, whatever it is for whose sake they value life, in that they wish to occupy themselves with their friends; and so some drink together, others dice together, others join in athletic exercises and hunting, or in the study of philosophy, each class spending their days together in whatever they love most in life; for since they wish to live with their friends, they do and share in those things as far as they can.[75]

Utility friends will spend some of their time together engaging in cooperative projects. One of the primary benefits of utility friendship is that two persons can accomplish something that one person alone cannot. There are things both logically and physically that cannot be done by merely one person. A great source of good for friends is this ability to cooperate in activities that cannot be accomplished individually. Utility friends' goodwill enables them to cooperate to a greater extent than nonfriends, who may not recognize each other as potential cooperators. Nonfriends have not established a reciprocal trust with each other, which is a prerequisite for engaging in mutually advantageous activity.

The coworkers who are utility friends would sometimes help each other in meeting deadlines at work, studying for a promotion examination, or spending lunch hours discussing office politics. Such activities are examples of the utility that is the basis of the friendship. Their goodwill for each other, begun as an office friendship, might, for example, extend to helping each other's families by providing child care on occasion, without any calculation that the favor will be repaid. That they are friends implies that they will some-times benefit each other in circumstances where there is little chance that the benefit will be reciprocated.

Aristotle repeatedly asserts that friendship based on utility will be less en-during than friendship based on character or virtue. His reason is that charac-ter, especially a well-formed virtuous character, is much more stable than natural chance and circumstance. Assume for the moment that Aristotle is right and that character friendships are more stable. How much more unsta-ble are friendships based on utility? One reason Aristotle has for thinking that character friendships are more stable is that character is more controllable than natural events are. Even assuming a greater ability to control character, utility friendships affected by fluctuation in circumstances need not be all that frag-ile or precarious. Utility friends can be utility satisficers and not, like utility maximizers, end their friendships for any slight drop in utility. Some of the circumstances that affect utility-based friendships can be controlled by the friends (e.g., coworkers who are friends may choose not to accept jobs else-where). Events are more predictable and controllable than Aristotle would have thought. None of this implies that utility friendships are as stable as char-acter or virtue friendships, but if the primary difference between the two is the alleged greater stability of virtue friendship, then that difference may not be as large as Aristotle imagines.

Aristotle's second less-than-ideal friendship is pleasure friendship. Two people become friends because they find such a relationship pleasurable. Good looks, wit, a sense of humor, similar interests, physical abilities, culinary artistry, or a pleasant-sounding voice can be factors in making people pleasur-able to each other. Aristotle believes that pleasure friendships are spawned and preserved because each friend finds the other pleasurable. Friends will have goodwill for each other and a desire to promote each other's good as a result of pleasure. Just as in friendships based on utility or virtue, in pleasure friend-ships, for Aristotle, those involved must have and recognize goodwill for each other. Aristotle notes that pleasure friendships are most frequently found among the young and least frequently found among the old.[76] Pleasure friend-ships are quickly formed and frequently they are quickly ended by young peo-ple who are constantly finding new sources of pleasure, while the old seek utility rather than pleasure and are less likely to find others pleasurable, according to Aristotle.

It also is unclear why Aristotle thinks pleasure friendships are more per-manent than utility friendships, and why pleasure friends love each other, while utility friends love only profit. Pleasure friends certainly would separate when the pleasure ended, perhaps just as quickly as utility friends would separate when the "profit" ended. Beauty fades, and wit can become stale. Pleasure friendships need not be any more stable than utility friendships, as Aristotle himself points out when he discusses the friendships of young persons that are both based on pleasure and not at all long lasting (changing several times in a day).[77] Nor does it seem that the causes of pleasure are more tightly connected to character than are the causes of utility. When Aristotle says that pleasure friends are more truly lovers of each other, while utility friends are not, he may have in mind the thought that pleasure friends love each other for the pleasure that they derive from each other's personal characteristics (e.g., beauty or wit). He may be thinking that beauty and wit are a part of character, while the causes of utility are external to character, lying entirely in the circumstances. General distinctions between the causes of pleasure and utility are not so easily drawn. A person's character may be what makes him useful (e.g., as an outstanding teacher of philosophy).

The object of friendships based on pleasure is an activity that produces pleasure in the friends. Aristotle thinks that for young people, at least, the object of pleasure friendships is an amorous activity:

> Young people are amorous too; for the greater part of the friendship of love depends on emotion and aims at pleasure; this is why they fall in love and quickly fall out of love, changing often within a single day. But these people do wish to spend their days and lives together; for it is thus that they attain the purpose of their friendship.[78]

Resembling those who engage in virtue friendships, pleasure friends will desire to live together and spend as much time together as possible, because pleasure, like virtue, is frequently desired for its intrinsic value. In addition to amorous activities, pleasure friends engage in activities that depend on emotions and aim at pleasure. Going to the theater, playing cards, gambling, thrill seeking, and drinking would be among the expected activities of pleasure friends, because these create pleasure. As youth age, activities such as reading good books, having quiet conversations, or studying philosophy will come to replace the more frenzied ones as sources of pleasurable emotions.

Pleasure friendships need not be based upon nor productive of virtue. Certain causes of pleasure, according to Aristotle, can be vicious and dehumanizing. Excesses in the pursuit of pleasure may cause intemperance in character. Thus while Aristotle believes that all good friendships will be pleasurable, he also believes that not all pleasure friendships will be good or promote virtue. As a class, pleasure-based friendships are not valuable without exception.

Kant, paralleling Aristotle's reciprocated goodwill, considers caring for each other and promoting each other's happiness a common characteristic of friendship[79]:

> Friendship (considered in its perfection) is the union of two persons through equal mutual love and respect. It is easy to see that this is an ideal of each participating and sharing sympathetically in the other's well-being through the morally good will that unites them.[80] (emphasis in original)

Kant discusses two types of less-than-ideal friendships—friendships based on need and friendships of taste.

> The friendship of need comes about when men can trust one another in the mutual provision for the needs of life. It was the original form of friendship amongst men and is encountered mostly in the crudest social conditions. When savages go hunting, each of them has at heart and endeavours to promote the same interests as his colleagues; they are friends. The simpler the needs of a group of men the more frequent is this kind of friendship amongst them; and in proportion as their needs increase the frequency of such friendships diminishes. When the stage of luxury, with its multiplicity of needs, is reached, man has so many of his own affairs to absorb his attention that he has little time to attend to the affairs of others. At this stage, therefore, such friendship does not exist; it is not even wanted; for if one of the participants knows that the other seeks his friendship as a means for satisfying some of his needs, the friendship becomes interested and ceases.[81]

Need friendship is based on the condition that friends cooperate in benefitting each other, because in simple societies common interests exist, the satisfaction of which requires conflict-free collective action. Because all members of simple society must, for instance, eat, and because only a limited number of different sources of food exists, "savages" must cooperate in supplying food. On his own, each is incapable of killing the game that all require to survive. Thus each works together "to promote the same interests as his colleagues," in providing collective food. Kant calls this relationship "friendship," because participants aim at promoting each other's needs. Need friendship is possible, because actions promoting the needs of one also will promote the needs of others, inasmuch as they possess similar needs that can be achieved only through collective action.

As society becomes more complex and conflicting interests require divergent actions to satisfy them, Kant believes that need friendships will vanish.

First, conflicts of interest require choices between promoting one's own needs and the needs of others. Need friendships, therefore, will be more difficult to initiate. Second, because of different individual interests, overtures to need friendship will be suspect. One will suspect that anyone trying to become a friend will be more interested in what he can get out of it than what he can offer. This is what Kant has in mind by saying, "the friendship becomes interested and ceases." Offers of friendship will become one-sided, aiming only for the happiness of one, not both.

There is a similarity between the utility friendship of Aristotle and the need friendship of Kant. Both relationships are classified as friendships, because in each the participants aim to promote the other's well-being. Kant's need friendship may not be as enduring as his ideal intimacy friendship, just as utility friendship may not be as permanent as Aristotle's friendship based on virtue. Neither less-than-ideal friendship is merely instrumental or exploitative, where each participant essentially aims for his own advantage and only accidentally or indirectly works for the partial advantage of the other. For Kant, instrumental relationships, business or commercial, would not be considered friendships. That need friendships are not exclusively instrumental for Kant can be best appreciated in contrast to what he says about his second lesser friendship: the friendship of taste.

"The friendship of taste is a pseudo-friendship. It consists in the pleasure we derive from each other's company and not from each other's happiness."[82] A newer translation more clearly describes the friendship of taste as "an analogue of friendship."[83] In this "pseudo-friendship," or "analogue," Kant believes opposites attract for the purpose of amusement and entertainment. (One of Kant's longest lasting friendships was with the English merchant, Joseph Green.[84]) People of the same profession who know the same things will not be able, Kant assumes, to engage in informative, amusing, or entertaining conversation, because what one knows the other will know as well. Friendships of taste are not constituted by mutual care and concern for each other's well-being but by how much pleasure each gets from the other. (This would not describe Kant's friendship with Green.) A partial and an indirect concern with each other's well-being might exist insofar as these friends must be sure that they are sufficiently physically vigorous and financially affluent to afford enough leisure time to engage in their mutually pleasurable conversations. To this extent, Kant's analogue or pseudo-friendship resembles commercial or business relations in only aiming at that particular partial fraction of well-being required for commercial or business purposes, and not for each other's unqualified or complete well-being. These "friendships" are therefore purely instrumental, where one is seeking one's own pleasure rather than the other's well-being. Taste friendships could become real friendships if the friends came to care for each other's happiness as well as their own pleasures. Taste friendships would then closely resemble Aristotle's pleasure friendships, where each friend has goodwill toward the other because of the pleasure each receives from the friendship.

The objects of Kant's need friendships are activities that jointly satisfy the needs of the friends—those activities that cannot be accomplished individually and that are necessary for survival. How much time need friends would have to spend engaged in these activities depends on how scarce necessities are and how much time is required for their production. The objects of taste friendship are pleasurable and entertaining conversations. It is not clear from what Kant says how often pleasurable conversation could be pursued. For Kant, even the ideal form of friendship does not require that friends spend a great deal of time with each other.

Aristotle's and Kant's less-than-ideal friendships, the kinds of friendships that may be the most common, are neither merely self-interested nor without value. In many respects, they closely resemble ideal forms. Each friend has goodwill toward the other. Both aim at more than their own immediate advantage, thus creating a socially important anti-egoistic impulse, which is more fully discussed in later chapters.

In this chapter I have discussed a number of different conceptions of friendship, both ideal and less-than-ideal, which have been advocated and endorsed as possessing value and as being a worthy, if not the most worthy, form of interpersonal relationship. Even less-than-ideal friendships are more valuable than many other possible but potentially exploitive relationships and more valuable than living in isolation without any human relationships at all. These conceptions of friendship are marked by bases, objects, and natures that, though similar, are different in important respects. Not only do different reasons exist for forming friendships but also diverse activities exist that constitute what friends do as friends. Because of these inherent diverse activities, no single approach is possible to the moral justification of preferring friends to nonfriends. The remainder of this book explains why and when preferring friends to nonfriends is morally justifiable.

Distinguishing between the nature, object, and basis of friendship also clarifies how friendship involves caring for a friend as a person. Understanding how caring for a friend sometimes is a basis and sometimes an object of friendship removes the ground for several unfounded objections to various conceptions of friendship.

I have introduced three nonmoral criteria of relevancy for conceptions of friendship. The first criterion is the number of friends it is possible to have. One conception of friendship limits the number of friends to one, where some conceptions limit the number to a few, and other conceptions imply that many friends are possible. The second nonmoral criterion is predicting who will become friends. Some conceptions permit predictions about who will become friends and for what reasons, while other conceptions imply that predictions are impossible, because friendships are based on nonrational considerations. The last criterion is whether friends should fuse into one indistinguishable persona rather than each friend maintaining her identity as many contemporary understandings of friendship maintain. Differences within these three criteria need to be assessed. If some philosopher's conception of friendship fails to connect to some reasonable experiences of actual friendships, then perhaps it should be ignored. In discussing possible moral justifications for preferring friends to nonfriends, only the more relevant conceptions shall be included.

THREE

INTERNAL JUSTIFICATIONS

THE MORALITY WITHIN FRIENDSHIP

SHOWING PREFERENCE for friends is something internal to friendship. Friends care for each other, wanting their "other self" to thrive and flourish.[1] Moreover, friends desire to be the one who promotes the other's well-being.[2] Friendship is one of the few human relationships where individuals care for each other's intrinsic value and try to promote each other's well-being without constantly considering what they may gain for themselves by doing so. Reciprocal goodwill, following Aristotle, is considered the "highest" form of friendship. Friendship exemplifies what is deemed best in human behavior.[3] Acting out of friendship promotes goodness in others and suggests that the world would be greatly improved if everyone treated each other as though they were friends.[4] These values in friendship provide powerful reasons for encouraging friendship formation. If people developed and extended friendships, then they would learn to care about others besides themselves and would desire to treat others in a morally exemplary way.[5]

But friendship has its darker side. Friendship incorporates partiality, exclusivity, and inherent inequality. Friends are tempted to prefer each other even when such preference is not morally correct. Special behavior expected by friends creates moral problems. Because friendship is essentially particular, requiring that friends behave toward each other in ways that they do not behave toward nonfriends, forms of friendship are in prima facie conflict with egalitarian, impartial, impersonal, and universal morality. Conflict arises, in part, because friends show each other preference in their intentions and actions rather than treating all persons equally. Conflict also arises from a belief that it is right to do something for a friend that would not be morally right if done for a nonfriend. Because different conceptions of friendship exist with different objects and bases, not all conceptions of friendship have equivalent potential conflicts with morality.

Two questions about this darker side need to be addressed: Does doing something for a friend alter the moral quality of the action, that is, make an act right that would otherwise be wrong? Is it morally permissible to prefer a friend to others, simply because he or she is a friend?

I pointed out in chapter 1 that friendship resembles promising as a social institution by creating expectations, some of them moral, among its participants. This morality in friendship specifies how friends ought to behave toward each other. Just as institutions of promising specify when promises must be kept or may legitimately be broken, and for what kinds of reasons, so friendships specify how individuals must treat each other if their relationship is to be understood as a friendship. Individuals who treat each other no differently from the way they treat all others would not be considered friends. Friendship is a special relation that implies different behavior from the ways nonfriends are treated. Forms of friendship differ from each other because of differences in the special ways that friends are expected to treat each other—what, in chapter 2, I called the "object of friendship."

Moral justifications for treating friends differently from nonfriends can be approached from two perspectives: the internal and the external. External justifications, considered in chapter 4, employ moral principles, such as egalitarian, utilitarian, and libertarian, to try resolving the prima facie conflicts with friendship. Internal justifications examine different conceptions of friendship to determine whether their internal reasons implying special treatment for friends successfully justify friends preferring each other to nonfriends.

Cicero asks whether "the laws of friendship" permit doing something for a friend that would otherwise be immoral to do.[6] Is it morally right to tell a lie to save the life of one's friend because the life saved is the life of one's friend? He replies that friendship does not justify performing an action that would be immoral, except that it is done to benefit a friend. Cicero's question cannot be answered in the abstract. To answer his question about the morality internal to friendship, it is necessary to specify a conception of friendship. Friendship understood as reciprocal goodwill seems to be presupposed by Cicero's question, because it is the very strong desire to promote a friend's well-being that functions as a possible justification for lying. Other forms of friendship might not contain reasons that give rise to life-saving lies. C. S. Lewis's shared interest conception of friendship does not contain any imperative to promote a friend's well-being, so that lying to save a friend's life might not be an issue internal to friendship, as he conceives it.

For most philosophers, telling a lie to save a life is not always wrong; perhaps Kant is the only exception. Sometimes lying is the right thing to do. Its rightness depends on morally relevant circumstances. Usual and common justifications for lying are that by lying, a great deal of good will be produced or a great deal of harm prevented. A duty not to lie may sometimes be overridden by additional duties, such as gratitude or justice. Parallel arguments might be made supporting the moral rightness of stealing, assaulting, or other commonly immoral actions if they are performed for the sake of a friend.

Cicero is right, nevertheless. Benefitting a friend is not the kind of reason that would, by itself, justify performing an act that otherwise would be immoral. Consider the well-known "Jean Valjean" example from Les Miserables, but substitute a young friend for Jean Valjean's child. Is Jean Valjean morally justified in stealing a loaf of bread to save the life of his starving young friend? While many people, including Victor Hugo, would answer that Jean Valjean is morally justified, the question remains whether the justifiability of stealing bread depends on its being stolen to save the life of his friend rather than to save the life of any starving child. Does the special relation of being a friend of the starving child alter the moral quality of the action? Either stealing food to save the life of a starving person can sometimes be justified, or such stealing violates the rights of others and is never justified.

Assuming that it is never morally justifiable to steal food to save the life of any starving person, no special relation, not kinship or friendship, changes the moral quality of the action. If there were an absolute prohibition against stealing food to feed any starving person (because of inviolable property rights, for example), it is difficult to understand how the morality of stealing would change solely because the theft were motivated to save the life of a friend. Jean Valjean may feel an obligation to provide food for his young friend because of his goodwill toward his friend. No doubt desperate friends would contemplate stealing because of their strong mutual goodwill. Perhaps only friends with a most vigorous moral upbringing would be capable of respecting an inviolable moral imperative against stealing. Something may even be perverse about moral prohibitions that give priority to property rights over innocently starving young people. In such circumstances it is entirely understandable that friends might violate prohibitions against stealing. Yet understanding what motivates an immoral act is not equivalent to acknowledging that the act is morally right or morally justifiable. If stealing to save the life of any starving young person were wrong, then stealing to save the life of one's friend would not make stealing right.

Suppose this assumption about the immorality of stealing were relaxed. Instead of a universal prohibition against stealing, suppose stealing usually is wrong, or wrong in most cases, except where stealing is absolutely necessary to save lives.[7] Accordingly, stealing a loaf of bread to save the life of a starving person would not be morally wrong if it were the only means of saving the life. In this hypothetical situation, stealing would be right if it were necessary to save the life of an innocently starving person. (I am assuming that only those too poor to buy bread would be among the group justified in stealing. Those who could afford bread should buy it and donate it to the starving.) In practice, however, chaos might result if anyone too poor to buy bread stole it to save some other starving person. Too many people could be justified in stealing if the number of starving persons were sufficiently large. Thus a practical rule of thumb might warrant legitimatizing stealing only by those who have kinship or friendship relations to the starving young person.[8] Restricting the right to steal bread to friends of those who are starving limits the number of persons who would be justified in stealing and thus avoids chaos. Friendship or kinship would make a practical difference about who may steal but not about the moral rightness of stealing itself. Permitting friends to steal while prohibiting stealing by others functions merely as a practical rule of thumb to avoid the chaos resulting from too many people stealing. Thus while stealing may sometimes be right for friends as a practical restriction, stealing is justified only because the action itself is independently right. Restricting its performance to those with special relationships is solely a practical moral compromise. Cicero is correct in thinking that friendship does not, in this case, convert what is morally wrong into what is morally right.

Cicero discusses two other examples that appear to reach different conclusions. In trying to prove that people desire friendship for its own sake and not because of any "feebleness" and "inadequacy," or because friendship fulfills some need, Cicero notices that friends often are strongly inclined to do things for the sake of a friend that they would be unwilling to do for themselves. For example, a friend sometimes desires to do favors for his friend that he would not do for himself and would refuse to have his friend do for him.[9] A friend also is willing to lower and humiliate himself by asking others to help his friend in circumstances where he would never consider asking for himself.[10] Cicero concludes that if friendship were only to have extrinsic value because friends valued friendship for what they got out of the friendship, then friends would be unlikely to perform either of these self-sacrificial acts. He believes that the correct explanation of why friends are willing to perform such inexpedient actions is that the intrinsic value of friendship covers the cost.

While friendship supplies reasons in Cicero's two examples for a friend to behave in ways that she otherwise would not behave, the moral quality of her behavior is not altered. Cicero is not imagining that receiving assistance or favors from others is immoral. Nor does he seem to think that asking others for favors or assistance usually is immoral. Asking for or receiving favors, in Cicero's value system, may be humiliating and degrading but it is not immoral.

Dean Cocking and Jeanette Kennett, in their article, "Friendship and Moral Danger," appear to disagree with Cicero's assessment of the laws of friendship.[11] They believe that too much emphasis has been placed on a "highly moralized" view of "true and good" friendship where good friends cannot lead each other to acting badly.[12] They contend that "much of the good of friendship itself has little, if anything, to do with morality. Indeed, the reasons that arise out of friendship may well conflict with moral considerations and may at times override such considerations."[13] They define what they call "close" or "companion" friendship, which they maintain is partially constituted by five features, the first three of which are necessary: (1) mutual affection; (2) the disposition to promote the other's serious interests and well-being; (3) the desire for shared experiences; (4) exhibiting receptivity to being directed and interpreted, and so in these ways being drawn to each other; and (5) making contributions to each other's self-conception.[14] The connection between morality and their conception of "close" or "companion" friendship is, they argue, importantly contingent. Friends may direct each other toward well-being promoting actions that conflict with morality as it is commonly understood.

Cocking and Kennett are right about the relation of their conception of friendship and morality. Their conception differs from Aristotle's virtue friendship and Cicero's friendship just in its contingent connection to morality. For Aristotle and Cicero, the basis of friendship is the moral goodness or virtue of the friends' characters. Cocking and Kennett are silent about the basis of their friendship conception. Still, to this extent, there need not be any incompatibility between Cocking and Kennett, on the one hand, and Cicero and Aristotle, on the other hand. Each pair has a different conception of friendship in mind.

Cocking and Kennett, however, push farther. They wish to claim that their conception of friendship also reflects what they call a "good and true" friendship.[15] In defense of their claim they argue, "It would be foolish to suggest of those cases where friendship moves us against competing moral reasons that we thereby exhibit a lesser friendship or realize less of the good of friendship."[16] Both Aristotle and Cicero would disagree. Certainly Cocking's and Kennett's conception of friendship is less of a moral ideal, and thereby perhaps more easily achieved by more people. But obviously it is not as good. Relationships in which people lead each other to immorality are not as good as relationships which lead people to virtue. Would society have any interest in encouraging friendships that frequently lead to immorality? "Close" or "companion" friendships, as Cocking and Kennett understand them, may have value, but nevertheless a lesser value than virtue friendships.

It is difficult to know what Cocking and Kennett mean when they call their conception of friendship "true" in addition to its being "good." If they mean that there are actual friendships that fit the constitutive criteria they outline, then there is no quarrel that friendships such as the ones they describe exist. A variety of different conceptions of friendship is actually practiced in different cultures. As discussed in the third section of chapter 1, there is an analogy between friendship and promising, in that different conceptions of each are actually practiced. As a result, there might be a sizable number of "true" forms of friendship that differ significantly from each other. This sense of "true," however, only means actually being practiced. It should not be surprising that some people actually call relations of this sort "friendships."

Capable of being practiced is very different from worthy of being practiced. Not all of the actual forms of promising or friendship are good or valuable. Some actual forms may be morally more valuable than others, while there may be forms with little moral value at all. From the fact that friendship, as they understand it, is actually practiced, Cocking and Kennett cannot conclude that that is good or valuable. They must, additionally, argue that its basis, nature, or object either is intrinsically valuable or will lead to value.

In a recent *Ethics* article, in contrast, Neera Kapur Badhwar explains that friendship contains the moral ideals of benevolence and justice:

> Benevolence, the disposition to be generous in good times, helpful in bad times, and forgiving in the face of injury, is the characteristic of friends. So is justice, the disposition not to cause injury, to be honest, and to judge fairly. Someone who lacked these dispositions to another could hardly be said to be her friend.[17]

Badhwar believes that these moral values constitute part of friendship, and that they also justify special treatment of friends. Two issues need to be separately addressed concerning Badhwar's analysis of this internal morality of friendship: first, the extent to which these values are successful in defining both the internal and preferential morality of friendship; and second, the extent to which these values are successful in explaining why friends ought to be treated in such special, preferential ways.

Badhwar's definition of the internal morality of friendship appears to be on strong ground. The values that she believes are internal to friendship well express Aristotle's idea that the common nature of friendship is reciprocal goodwill. Virtues of benevolence and justice are certainly components of goodwill friendship as an ideal of human relationships, that is, as magnifications of ordinary duties owed to all persons. Kant's ideal but unattainable friendship, "the union of two persons through equal mutual love and respect . . . each participating and sharing sympathetically in the other's well-being through the morally good will that unites them," also contains justice and benevolence as values internal to friendship which, for Kant, also are duties owed to all persons.[18]

Badhwar's suggestion that benevolence and justice also define the limits of preferential treatment is worth pursuing. She believes that the internal morality of friendship—justice and benevolence—can be used to decide when it is morally right to treat one's friend preferentially.[19] As examples, Badhwar quotes from E. M. Forster, "if I had to choose between betraying my country and betraying my friend, I hope I should have the guts to betray my country," and from R. Lovelace, "I could not love thee (Deare) so much,/ Lov'd I not Honour more.."[20] Badhwar thinks that the morality internal to friendship shows that Forster is right in the first case choosing his friend and that there could be reasons Lovelace is right choosing his country in the second case. She does not, however, offer detailed reasons explaining why Forster's and Lovelace's choices are correct. Her problem is explaining how to weigh the different strengths of benevolence, or any virtue internal to friendship, toward friends and nonfriends. Do equal quantities of good or harm count equally, or does a unit of harm to a friend, for example, count for twice as much as a unit of harm to a nonfriend? If other values external to friend-ship become involved, as Badhwar suggests that they sometimes do, then how are the weights of those values calculated?[21]

Benevolence to one's friend might not be considered a virtue but an immoral selfish action if, as Aristotle suggests, giving to one's friend is equivalent to giving to oneself. To the extent that there is an identity with one's friend, acting with benevolence toward a friend may not be an exam-ple of a morally virtuous act but an instance of an action that is self-cen-tered. In one sense, this would explain why friends may not regard their behavior toward each other as duty bound or duty constituted, because it is sometimes thought that there are no duties to oneself. In another sense, identifying with one's friend raises questions about the justification of spe-cial treatment of friends because of the parallel between such special treat-ment and morally suspect self-centered egoism. Whether special treatment is virtuous, vicious, or neutral depends on the specific basis of each friend-ship, and on whether each friend's whole, unqualified, or partial good is the object of favoritism and how nonfriends are affected.[22]

In contrast, Badhwar's idea of justice, of judging fairly and being honest, does not seem to lose its moral quality through self-reference created by an identity with one's friend. There is nothing morally suspect in an increased honesty with oneself, nor in treating oneself fairly. In many instances and for many individuals, an increase in the quantity of these virtues would be a wel-come correction.

It makes good sense to think that justice and benevolence are part of a goodwill conception of friendship. Persons who fail to act toward one an-other in these ways could hardly be friends. Even based on C. S. Lewis's shared interest conception of friendship, friends would act toward each other at least with benevolence and justice, as required by morality.

What is not obvious and is in need of explanation is how Badhwar's in-ternal morality of friendship justifies preferential treatment of or special duties to friends. Applying Kant's categorical imperative as an example, it is always a duty to act so as to respect others, both those who are and those who are not friends, as an end and to never use them merely as a means, that is, to respect their rational wants and desires as having a value equal to one's own wants and desires. But if someone always acted in this moral way toward nonfriends, as Kant believes, then according to Badhwar's account of how friends treat one another, these are actions of friendship, although in this instance, friendly actions may be only one-sided and not reciprocated.

Friends are mutually benevolent and mutually just toward one another, so at least this much seems plausible: while a person without friends may not have the goodwill of others, since not everyone lives up to his or her moral duties, if she acts toward others in a morally correct way, which manifests goodwill, she nevertheless acts as a friend would act. If others also fulfilled their moral duty toward her, then mutual goodwill would exist, and everyone would act toward others in a friendly way. Based on Badhwar's analysis, it is because nonfriends fail to fulfill their universal moral duties that friends, who do not fail, treat each other better than nonfriends. If people lived up to their moral responsibilities, then little difference would arise between how friends and nonfriends behave toward each other.

Thus while Badhwar is successful in explaining the internal moral content of friendship, she is less successful in explaining how this internal morality defines the preferential behavior that she believes ought to be shown toward friends. She needs to say more about how it is possible to know when to treat friends in the same or in different ways from nonfriends.

Addressing the second issue, whether the inherent morality of friendship, as Badhwar defines it, justifies preferential treatment of friends compared to nonfriends, there is nothing in Badhwar's list of virtues inherent in friendship that provides any reason for behaving with greater justice or benevolence toward friends. Similarly, respecting people as an end is a moral duty that Kant believes applies to all persons. What additional premises does the special treatment of friends require?

Badhwar discusses what she calls "end-friendship," which she clearly intends to correspond to Aristotle's best friendship. Badhwar believes that in end-friendships, the friends are not replaceable.[23] A similar argument is made by Martha Nussbaum:

> Friendship does not supply a commodity that we can get elsewhere; it is that very thing, in its own peculiar nature, that is the bearer of value. This is what it means to judge that something is an end, not simply a means to an end: there are no trade-offs without loss.[24]

By itself, however, irreplaceability does not entail preferential treatment; there is no moral reason why what is not replaceable ought to be treated any differently from what is replaceable.

What is replaceable if destroyed can be replaced by an equivalent without any loss whatever, whereas what is irreplaceable cannot. Nevertheless, it is unclear how this fact is a reason for morally behaving one way or another. If a friend does not want to lose what is irreplaceable, then she must be sure not to destroy or lose it. But how does this translate into special moral preference for friends?

Assuming that it is always wrong to treat someone merely as a means, and assuming that it is always right to respect a person's ends as equivalent to one's own, a third option is left: to treat people as a means as well as to respect them as an end. This third option is morally permissible based on Kant's view. Does friendship, as Badhwar conceives of it, demand a different standard—that friends always should be treated as ends and never treated as a means in any way at all? If she were right, would it provide a good reason for the preferential treatment of friends?

The connection first must be made between being irreplaceable and being treated only as an end, never in any way as a means. Kant himself does not argue that being irreplaceable has anything to do with treating something either as a means or as an end. His argument for treating rational beings as necessary ends and not merely as a means does not appeal to the fact that humans are unique and cannot be replaced. For one thing, humans are not the only creatures in the universe who are unique: every cow, toad, and tadpole is unique, as perhaps are snowflakes. Their uniqueness is no reason for treating them as ends in themselves, any more than it is a reason for treating a human as an end in itself.

Kant's explanation why a rational being must treat other rational beings as ends in themselves is premised on how each rational being must regard herself. A rational being logically must regard herself as having intrinsic value. Because, as Kant believes, things in the world have value only insofar as they are the means of satisfying the wants and desires of a rational being, then the value of things is dependent on the value of the rational wants and desires they satisfy. This explains what Kant means by the idea that rational beings are the source of all value. But, as Aristotle points out, there cannot be an infinite chain of means–ends valuation without something that is valued for its own sake. What explains the value of satisfying the ends of a rational being? Rational beings must logically regard themselves as an end with intrinsic value in order to judge that things are valuable because they are a means to satisfying their own ends. Kant's argument is that each rational being must logically regard herself as possessing an intrinsic value, since unless she assumed her own intrinsic worth, she would have no reason to think that the satisfaction of her wants or desires is something valuable.[25] This argument can be called Kant's "Transcendental Deduction of Human Dignity."

Universalizability requires that each rational being must recognize that every other rational being also has intrinsic value and therefore ought not to be used as a means only. Thus for Kant, being unique and irreplaceable has nothing to do with why rational beings must be valued as ends and never merely as a means.[26]

Badhwar cannot rely upon uniqueness or irreplaceability as reasons friends must value each other as ends. She must supply other reasons to justify preferential valuing among friends. The virtues that Badhwar argues are inherent in friendship are none other than the virtues inherent in morality itself (i.e., in how we ought to treat all persons, whether friend or nonfriend).

To the degree that goodwill friendship is considered an ideal of human relations, as Kant and Aristotle clearly believe, it is not at all unexpected to find that moral virtues toward all people are idealized in friendship. If it were concluded that there should be no preferential treatment of friends, what might be inferred is that the benevolence and justice that friends more intensely feel toward each other are only morally ideal or exemplary behavior owed to all persons. If friends were morally stronger or wiser, if there were no scarcity of material resources, then they would feel the same benevolence and justice for friend and nonfriend. Were this true, being a friend would not be a good reason for preferential treatment. All people would have to be treated with the same benevolence and justice with which friends feel they should treat each other.

Another alternative would be to deny that friendship is a moral ideal of interpersonal relations for all individuals in the way that Kant's intimacy friendship, Montaigne's fusion friendship, and C. S. Lewis's shared interest friendship are not considered moral ideals, even if they are considered valuable. This alternative would, however, entail denying what Badhwar argues to establish, that the values inherent in friendship are among the basic values of morality. Such denial might imply that friendship has value and that friends ought to be preferred, but that the values that justify preferential treatment are external to friendship. Thus values internal to friendship would not be an idealization of values fundamental to morality, and friendship would not be considered a moral ideal. That friendship is not a moral ideal does not imply that the institution of friendship or the social practice of friendship cannot be morally justified. Making promises may not in itself be a moral ideal: a person who makes no promises is not failing to be moral, yet the institution or social practice of promising can be justified by appeals to external moral principles. Only friendships that are believed to embody ideals of moral behavior support internal justifications for preferring friends to nonfriends.

THE IMPERSONAL PULL OF FRIENDSHIP

Within all forms of friendship, there is a personal pull to prefer friends to nonfriends. In this section, I argue that there also is a second impersonal pull within friendship. The personal pull of Aristotle's shared life friendship is to prefer the well-being of one's friends to the well-being of others. It is a pull toward partiality, personality, and inequality. A similar personal pull is believed to exist in the second Indian friendship, where the object of the friendship is mutual assistance. Even in Kant's intimacy friendship, which I show in the next section to have few possible conflicts with egalitarian, utilitarian, and libertarian morality, friends prefer receiving their friend's confidences to the confidences of nonfriends.

An impersonal pull exists in friendship that stretches beyond preference for friends and attaches to the well-being of others. This impersonal pull is found in ideal friendships exemplifying what is best in human behavior, and it is additionally found in less-than-ideal but still valuable forms of friendship. The values inherent in any goodwill friendship, for instance, require friends to behave with mutual goodwill by promoting each other's ends. This is true of both Aristotle's best goodwill friendship based on virtue and his less-than-ideal forms of goodwill friendship based on utility and pleasure. In an ideal Indian friendship, the superior tries to mentor and develop the character of the inferior. As Badhwar points out, friends desire to treat each other in ways that closely resemble the way people ideally ought to treat each other (i.e., they try to do what is benevolent and just for each other).

Not all friendships contain a significant goodwill component. Goodwill in friendship may be limited, as in Kant's intimacy friendship, to a willingness to be open and sufficiently trustworthy to receive communion-enhancing confidences. C. S. Lewis's conception of friendship as a shared interest or quest has the least goodwill component. While objects of Kant's and Lewis's forms of friendship are not activities aimed at promoting friends' well-being, their friendships are nevertheless activities that are considered good for the friends. Lewis believes that it is good to share a common interest or quest, even if promoting each other's well-being is not friendship's object. For Kant, promoting others' well-being is an imperfect moral duty implied by the categorical imperative, and thus promoting well-being is not specially required between friends. Reaching communion and intimacy as objects of friendship is considered a good for the friends, but a good that is not morally required. Thus friendship, whether limited or broad in extent, implies that friends desire to promote what they believe is objectively good for each other.

An additional insight about the good that friends try to promote is offered in Jennifer Whiting's article, "Impersonal Friends":

> If I value my own good and the activities in which it consists not as mine but rather as that of *a* person of a certain *sort*, then I can value my friend's good and the activities in which *it* consists in the same way that I value my own *without* having to value them *as* mine. This allows me to grant independence to the value of another's good in a way in which the egocentric reading does not. And this seems to me *morally desirable*. The good of my friends is good—and good for *them*—independently of their relation to me and of whether or not I happen to care; that's why I *should* care.
>
> Moreover, it seems plausible to say that I must value their goods as independent if I am to value them in the same way that I value my own: I do not take the value of my ends to depend on my friends having endorsed them and made them parts of their own (though I will expect my true character friends to do so). So I should not take the value of *their* ends to depend on my having endorsed them and made them *parts* of my own (though I will of course do so). I can aim at my friends' ends in the same way that I aim at my own only if I aim at them as independent goods and not as parts of my own. This, I submit, is what is demanded by Aristotle's requirement that we care for our friends for *their* sakes (as distinct from our own).[27] (emphasis in original)

Whiting explains that we desire our own and our friend's good, because it is good and not either simply because it is our friend's or simply because we desire it. Friends desire to promote what they believe is objectively good for each other. It is its goodness that supplies the reason for desiring it either for our friend or for our self. It is desired because it is good rather than being good because desired. This good need not be a universal good; it need only be thought to be a good for our friend or our self. Whiting's point is that friends desire certain things for each other, because those things are thought to be objectively good for the kind of persons friends believe they are.

The personal pull for friends takes different forms in each conception of friendship. In conceptions of friendship regarded as ideal forms of human relationship, friends' preference for each other takes as objects of friendship what friends regard as expressing moral exemplary behavior. In Aristotle's ideal, the object is a shared life of virtue. In the Indian ideal, the object is guiding and being a mentor. For other conceptions, friends still aim at objects of friendship that they consider good; in Kant, it is shared intimacies, and in C. S. Lewis, the object is shared interests. No one would ever desire, out of friendship, something evil or hurtful for her friend.[28] Friends who have goodwill for each other in less-than-ideal friendships, such as Aristotle's utility or pleasure friendships, express that personal pull in trying to promote each other's overall good ends and purposes.

Objective good is how the impersonal pull is contained in friendship. Because friends desire to promote what is objectively good for each other, they have a reason to promote similar goods for persons who are relevantly similar to themselves. If something is good for one's friend because of the kind of person she is, then that same thing also would be good for any other relevantly similar person. And, in this context, "relevantly similar" means more than merely she is my friend. In conceptions of friendship that consider themselves to exemplify what is best in human relationships, the objects of friendship are constituted by activities considered morally good, whatever the particular differences are that distinguish one conception from another. The reason something is desired for one's friend is that it is good. It therefore also must be judged good for any nonfriend who is relevantly similar.

Friendship contains an impersonal pull toward good for nonfriends. The impersonal pull is only prima facie, one reason for acting that can be overridden by other stronger reasons. It is one of a number of possible conflicting reasons, and its strength cannot be assessed in the abstract apart from specific circumstances. Still, where the impersonal pull is the only reason, and where there are no countervailing reasons, then similar goods should be promoted for nonfriends as for friends. This impersonal pull is not externally imposed on friendship by any (alien) libertarian, egalitarian, or utilitarian morality; rather the impersonal pull is contained implicitly within friendship itself because of the good that friends desire for each other. Whether friendship is understood as an ideal of human relationships or as a less-than-ideal but valuable form of human relationship containing reciprocal goodwill, friends aim at what is good for each other. Both ideal forms of friendship and some less-than-ideal friendships contain a reason for nonfriends being treated as favorably as friends.

That friendship contains both a personal and an impersonal pull does not constitute a contradiction within friendship. There is no contradiction in friendship's demand that the good of nonfriends be advanced along with the good of a friend. If having enough to eat is good, then the personal pull of friendship implies that friends have reason to secure sufficient food for each other. By the same reasoning, if having enough to eat is good, the impersonal pull of friendship implies that friends also have reason to secure sufficient food for nonfriends. It is the goodness of food that supplies a reason to see that everyone possesses it in sufficient quantities.

If friendship contains a reason for treating nonfriends similarly to friends, an explanation is required why nonfriends are not generally treated in the same good way as friends are. Two possible reasons must be considered explaining this failure. First, limitations exist on the external assets of energy, time, and material wealth. Second, limitations may exist on feelings of affection.

People may not possess sufficient energy to fulfill moral requirements for both friends and all nonfriends. With the exception of some libertarians who believe that our only moral duty is noninterference, morality requires positive duties of assistance that often cannot be fulfilled for both friends and nonfriends. Aristotle's shared life of virtue friendship consumes great quantities of friends' energy, leaving little energy to devote to any nonfriends. Initiating a Kantian intimacy friendship can consume a good deal of energy, although less energy is consumed in maintaining it. So while Kant's intimacy friendships may release more energy for treating some nonfriends as they morally deserve, insufficient energy might be available for treating all nonfriends as favorably as friends.

Material wealth may be more limited than people's energy. Most people's material assets are insufficient to disburse to everyone as they morally deserve. Even where some people desire to treat both friends and nonfriends in the same morally ideal way, virtually no one has sufficient material assets to do so if literally all nonfriends must be taken into consideration.[29]

Time constraints are the most limiting. Time affects the number of possible friends who can be treated well in each of the different forms of friendship. Time limits the ability to maintain Aristotle's shared lives friendships where so much day-to-day time is spent with friends to the exclusion of nonfriends. For Montaigne's fusion friendship, there appears to be no time at all for any friend but one. The great amount of time it takes to test others to determine their trustworthiness limits the number of Kantian intimacy friendships that it is possible to undertake. C. S. Lewis's interest friendships are the least affected by time constraints. Lewis, in fact, not only believes that a fairly sizable number of different friends are possible but that increasing the number of friends can frequently strengthen interest friendships.

If there is hardly enough time to go around for treating more than a few friends well, then there is even less time to devote to nonfriends. Even where the number of possible friends is small and demands little of friends' time, so many needy nonfriends exist that there is not enough time to meet their moral demands in addition to the moral demands of friends.

It is most interesting to note, as a parallel, that a scarcity of time, energy, and material resources is precisely what Thomas Hobbes, David Hume, and John Rawls believe creates the need for moral rules of justice.[30] They argue that were it not for the scarcity of these resources, no rules of justice would be required. In exactly the same way, without scarcity, no resource impediments would exist against promoting the good of nonfriends along with the good of friends. It is only scarcity that creates reasons conflicting with friendship's impersonal pull. The personal pull of friendship, preferring friends to nonfriends, may even contribute to overall scarcity.

Hume and Rawls add to scarcity of resources what they call "limited benevolence" as a reason for rules of justice. They do not believe that most people feel affection or care for persons beyond a narrowly circumscribed circle of friends and kin. This is the second reason for not treating everyone as favorably as our friends. It is thought to derive from a limited capacity to have affection for others.

The quantity of affection available to be bestowed on others, however, does not have the same limiting constraints as the other scarce resources. There does not seem to be any empirical evidence that parents who have more than one child have less affection for their additional children just because there are more of them, although additional children strain their time, energy, and material resources. Nor do parents love each other less after they have children. Brothers and sisters need not ration their love for each other simply because there are more of them. Affection also can be felt toward people who are not friends or kin. There does not seem to be a limit on the number of persons for whom one can have affection. Chong's two senses of "care for," one of goodwill and the other of affection, discussed in chapter 2, only seem to be limited by resources and not by quantities of affection or concern.[31] Goodwill and affection can be felt for many, but acting on them requires resources that may not be abundantly available.

Montaigne argues that only one fusion friend is possible at a time:

> For this perfect friendship I speak of is indivisible: each one gives himself so wholly to his friend that he has nothing left to distribute elsewhere; on the contrary, he is sorry that he is not double, triple, or quadruple, and that he has not several souls and several wills to confer them all on this one object. Common friendships can be divided up: one may love in one man his beauty, in another his easygoing ways, in another liberality, in one paternal love, in another

brotherly love, and so forth; but this friendship that possesses the soul and rules it with absolute sovereignty cannot possibly be double. If two called for help at the same time, which one would you run to? If they demanded conflicting services of you, how could arrange it? If one confided to your silence a thing that would be useful for the other to know, how would you extricate yourself?[32]

It is not quite clear what Montaigne believes to be limited with "nothing to distribute elsewhere." He at least believes that resources limit the number of friends, because if two friends asked for assistance, there might be resources to help only one. Reserves of affection are another matter. Were Montaigne to have said that fusion friendship excludes all other relationships involving affection, such as parent–child or sibling love, then he might be interpreted as holding affection to exist in a limited quantity that is exhausted by fusion friendship. But he does not say that fusion friendship dominates these other relationships to the point of extinction. He thinks that other affectionate relationships exist at the same time as does a fusion friendship. A fusion friendship would not exhaust affection for one's wife or children. So even Montaigne, who believes that friendship is most exclusive, does not base his argument on affection being limited or fixed in quantity the same way that time, energy, and material resources are.

C. S. Lewis's common interest friendship is the form of friendship that permits the greatest number of friends. Lewis does not think that the number of friends is limited because of limits in the quantity of affection people can feel. Additional friends may simply engender additional affection. He believes that even erotic love's strongly exclusive affection can be amplified by friendships:

> But you will have no jealousy at all about sharing the Friendship. Nothing so enriches an erotic love as the discovery that the Beloved can deeply, truly and spontaneously enter into Friendship with the Friends you already had: to feel that not only are we two united by erotic love but we three or four or five are all travellers on the same quest, have all a common vision.[33]

There is no reason to doubt that people possess more than enough affection to go around for both friend and nonfriend, though its supply is not infinite. Adequate quantities of affection exist to fulfill friendship's demands, even if friendship is understood to contain both personal and impersonal pulls that are owed to friend and nonfriend in appropriate ways. The quantity of affection that people possess supplies no excuse for neglecting friendship's impersonal pull to act in an equally friendly way by promoting well-being in nonfriend and friend.

An important distinction exists between the quantity of affection that can be felt for others and having any affection at all for others in the first place. This is where I think that Hume and Rawls believe that benevolence is limited. Believing that everyone can feel affection for everyone else is naive. Absence of affection for others results from personal differences in tastes, temperament, and character. People feel affection for their relatives, for those they resemble, or for those with whom they share interests. It is not common to find people who feel affection for others in the abstract; some concrete knowledge, connection, or identification with another is needed to generate affection. Friends' felt affection for each other provides them with a strong motive to promote each other's well-being. Without affection, the same strong motive to assist each other is absent, and where disliking or negative feeling actually occurs, malevolent motives to harm others may arise. These feelings toward nonfriends, either positive or negative, are, nevertheless, irrelevant to any justification for treating nonfriends less well than friends.

Just as lack of affection does not excuse treating nonfriends less well, disliking someone is, by itself, an insufficient reason for morally substandard treatment. Although no intense desire arises to promote the well-being of someone who is disliked, universal moral duties of justice and benevolence that are external to friendship remain owed to nonfriends to the same extent as friends. These obligations exist independently of any limits on our affection. People may not feel friendly to everyone, but lack of feeling does not diminish their obligation and capacity to do what reason and morality require. This also is true as a reason for ignoring friendship's impersonal pull.

The only legitimate excuse for treating nonfriends less favorably than friends is the first reason deriving from scarcity of time, energy, and material resources. Limited quantities of affection do not imply that friends must ration affection toward nonfriends. Limited quantities of affection, by itself, cannot justify treating nonfriends morally less well than friends.

Friends desire to promote each other's good. This is the point that Badhwar makes about justice and benevolence constituting friendship. Justice and benevolence also are duties owed to everyone. Because friends desire to act justly and benevolently to each other, since they believe such action to be valuable, then they must logically acknowledge that equivalent benevolent and just actions are valuable to any relevantly similar nonfriends.[34]

If my friend is in the hospital, I probably will visit him because I know that he wants company. His having company and avoiding boredom is a good thing for him (and of course for anyone resembling him). I therefore visit him because I want to do good for my friend. Were I not to regard his having company good, then I would not desire to visit him. Moreover, I must logically acknowledge that it would be equally good for me to visit any similar person in the hospital who is in need of company. None of this implies that I will have equally strong affection for everyone in the hospital, nor that I will desire to visit them all. But if my reason for visiting my friend is that it is a good thing to do, then I also have a reason for visiting any of the others if that also is good. My friend may receive a greater benefit from a visit from me as a consequence of our friendship than some nonfriend would, therefore, utilitarian reasons might require that I visit my friend rather than someone else. Nevertheless, the better consequences for my friend are a contingent matter, and there always is a possibility that some other extremely lonely person in the hospital might benefit a great deal more as a result of my visiting him. The goodness of visits supplies a reason to go: were visits not good, then there would be no reason to visit either a nonfriend or my friend.

Reasons for failing to treat everyone as favorably as friends derive from causes extraneous to forms of friendship or moral values. Were resources less scarce, including time and energy, then no reason would exist for treating nonfriends less favorably than friends. Treating friends better than nonfriends arises because insufficient resources are available to behave equally well toward everyone. Were resources unconstrained, no morally sufficient reason would arise for treating some people less favorably than others, either friend or nonfriend. Human capacity for generating affection would not be limited in the way that material resources, time, or energy would be. (Is this why an eternal, omnipotent being who has unlimited time, energy, and resources can allegedly love all living beings equally?)

Reciprocal goodwill friendship presupposes that promoting a friend's good would be a good for any relevantly similar nonfriend. Only practically constrained resources limit treating everyone with justice and benevolence required by goodwill. Thus practical constraints aside, reason exists for respecting others in the same exemplary way that friends are treated. Preference for friends does not explain exemplary behavior toward friends, but rather the value of the exemplary treatment explains why friends, those who are cared for and loved, are treated in the best possible way. The object of friendship should not be confused with the reasons for valuing friends (i.e., the basis of friendship). Because friendship requires that friends treat each other well, then friends must logically acknowledge that it is right to treat all others as they treat their friends.

The good that one tries to promote for a friend need not be a general good (i.e., a good that would benefit many individuals). It may benefit only one's friend. Nevertheless, a good for a friend is implicitly universal, in that it would be a good for anyone who resembled one's friend in the relevant particulars. Universality is implied, even though few people exist who possess just those characteristics. My friend, for example, may help me by critiquing rough drafts of my philosophy articles. That is a good for me or anyone like me who writes philosophy, but it would not be a good for most other people who do not write philosophy for publication.

Whether friends realize it or not, they have a prima facie reason for treating nonfriends in the same way that they treat each other. This reason does not derive from preference for friends but from the good that friends hope to promote for each other. The reason for desiring this good for a friend is the same reason one would have, all things being equal, for desiring it for anyone else who is relevantly similar to one's friend.

Friendship appears to have an inner tension. The personal pull is to prefer the good of friends to the good of nonfriends, and to promote friends' good. The impersonal pull is the well-being promoting behavior that constitutes some forms of friendship. In goodwill friendships, friends try to promote each other's objective well-being. Because what friends try to promote is thought to be objectively good, then they must logically recognize that such goods are reasonable to promote for friend and nonfriend alike. In other words, friendship has both a universal component, doing what would benefit anyone, and a particular component, doing what is good for a friend in preference to others. This internal tension pulls friends in opposite directions. On the personal pull, friends want to benefit each other, because they care for each other and they desire to be the cause of each other's flourishing. On the impersonal pull, friends must acknowledge a prima facie reason to promote similar flourishing in nonfriends. Insofar as friends want to treat each other in an exemplary way, they have equivalent reasons to treat nonfriends in the same exemplary manner. Only the inescapable scarcity of time, energy, and material resources makes treating both nonfriend and friend alike difficult or even impossible.

JUSTIFIED PREFERENCE AND MORAL CONFLICT

In this section I discuss the implications of various forms of friendship for conflicts with morality. Each of the various forms of friendship has its own implications about morally justified preference for friends. Forms of friendship, such as Montaigne's fusion friendship, the second mutual assistance ideal of Indian friendship, and Aristotle's shared life virtue friendship, are in greatest potential conflict with egalitarian and impersonal morality. Other forms of friendship, C. S. Lewis's interest friendship and Kant's intimacy friendship, have as objects of friendship acts of preference for friends that raise fewer possible conflicts with morality. These other friendships do exhibit partiality, which I take to be a principal defining characteristic of friendship, but the way that partiality in the objects of friendship manifests itself does not create significant moral conflicts.

Conflicts with morality arise because forms of friendship have as objects actions that tend to conflict with moral requirements. If friendship requires sharing one's time and material resources with one's friend, then few resources may be available to fulfill duties of beneficence. If, in contrast, actions constituting the object of friendship are confined to exchanging intimacies, then few conflicts with morality may arise. While I am concerned in this section with kinds of conflicts that essentially follow from how friendships are conceived, there also is always the possibility of accidental conflict. Accidental conflicts can result, for example, from an affection for a friend arising out of shared interests that may cause preference for the friend in ways having nothing to do with the shared interests. The conflict with morality is accidental because it is caused by an affection that is not part of the specific form of friendship. Essential conflict arises from actions considered to constitute each of the various forms of friendship.

There is a parallel between friendship and promising in this respect. An essential conflict between promising and morality would arise from a promise to do a favor for one person that makes impossible living up to one's duty of benevolence toward another. Similarly, a promise to do something immoral creates an essential conflict. An accidental conflict would arise not as a result of any special obligations incurred through promising but out of habits created by an institution of promising. One might rely on someone to keep a promise and thereby ignore a duty of benevolence that one otherwise would have fulfilled.

In Aristotle's shared life virtue friendship, equally virtuous friends share goods and lives together, promoting each other's well-being. Aristotle clearly believes that friends have a greater responsibility to benefit from each other and avoid any evil. There is no question that their behavior as it affects the two of them is morally correct, at least, that is, if only the two friends are considered. The benefits that they supply to each other might, however, occur at the expense of third parties. This again is the darker side of virtue friendship. Virtue friends might promote each other's well-being with assets that would benefit nonfriends, for example, by going out to dinner with each other rather than donating money to assist the starving. Insofar as friends identify with each other as "other selves," benefitting each other at the expense of nonfriends might be considered selfish and unjust.

Aristotle might be defended by arguing that virtuous friends, who as virtuous are just, would not promote their own well-being unjustly at the expense of nonfriends. Friends would not promote their own well-being at the expense of anyone else because, as Aristotle's defender thinks, the friends are perfectly just. However, virtue friends, according to Aristotle, need not be perfectly virtuous but only equally virtuous. Virtue friends choose each other because they are equal both in their manner and quality of virtue. Equality in manner and quality of virtue are not, however, equivalent to perfection of virtue. It is possible that equally but not perfectly virtuous friends will promote each other's well-being unjustly at the expense of nonfriends.

Even if virtue friends are perfectly just, conflict with egalitarian or impersonal universal morality still arises. Aristotle says:

> There is a difference, therefore, also between the acts that are unjust towards each of these classes of associates, and the injustice increases by being exhibited towards those who are friends in a fuller sense; e.g., it is a more terrible thing to defraud a comrade than a fellow citizen, more terrible not to help a brother than a stranger, and more terrible to wound a father than any one else. And the demands of justice also naturally increase with the friendship, which implies that friendship and justice exist between the same persons and have an equal extension.[35]

Aristotle faces the same problem as Badhwar, who tries to show that greater justice and benevolence are owed to friends. In calculating the justification in promoting a friend's well-being rather than the well-being of some non-friend, there must be a way of measuring the value of each option. Aristotle seems to be saying that helping a friend is more valuable than helping a stranger or nonfriend, and that the closer the friend, the more valuable the assistance. Friendship must be thought to confer extra value on friends that justifies their preferential treatment. Aristotle's judgment that friends are more valuable than nonfriends is in prima facie conflict with egalitarian and impersonal morality. Is a unit of well-being in a friend worth two or three units of well-being in a nonfriend? There must be some way of measuring the extra value in assisting friends compared to assisting nonfriends. If a choice has to be made between saving the life of a nonfriend and some trivial increase in a friend's well-being, to justify a friend's small gain over a nonfriend's life implies that the friend's well-being must have much greater value than the life of the nonfriend.

Identification between friends as "another oneself" creates an additional prima facie conflict with the various moral principles that obligate persons to respect others equally, impersonally, or impartially. One way of understanding the conflict is by an analogy to morally suspect egoism. If advancing the good of one's friend is at the same time regarded as advancing one's own good (since friends have common property, or that a good to one's friend is a good to oneself), then when friends act generously to one another, they are ultimately acting to benefit themselves.

This analogy to egoism should not be confused with egoistic motivation that is sometimes mistakenly associated with friendships based on pleasure or utility.[36] It would be egoistic to benefit a friend only for the pleasure or utility that may be returned. This analogy to egoism arises even in friendships where friends care for each other for their own sakes, that is, even where the object of friendship is promoting each friend's whole or unqualified well-being. Neither friend need be guilty of caring for the other only for calculated returns to himself at some future time. Identification with each other as "another oneself" (in the sense of an extension of the self) is what grounds this analogy to egoism. Helping a friend for his own sake is helping oneself, because the two make "no distinction between them." Borrowing a distinction from Paul Schollmeier, egoism based on the identification between friends could be called "essential egoism" to distinguish it from "accidental egoism," which would be the egoism in caring for a friend merely because of an expectation of pleasure or utility.[37] Schollmeier says, "Aristotle assumes that we act essentially for the sake of an end and accidentally for the sake of a means."[38] Acting for the sake of a friend is to promote her well-being as an end for her own benefit. But because of the identification with a friend, the benefits produced will be one's own as well inasmuch as a friend is "another oneself."

Montaigne's fusion friendships, with their union so complete "that they efface the seam that joined them," produce an even greater identification between friends than Aristotle's.[39] Montaigne states that "each one gives himself so wholly to his friend that he has nothing left to distribute elsewhere. . . . A single dominant friendship dissolves all other obligations."[40] Fusion friends may likely ignore their obligations to nonfriends.

Pressing this analogy to egoism, fusion friends may logically lose any ability to act generously toward or to make sacrifices for each other. Because of their very close identification, any good that one friend does for the other is ultimately a good for himself. When Pylades tends to Orestes during Orestes's illness, he is not acting with "selfless devotion."[41] What appears virtuous or supererogatory is not. If Pylades and Orestes are closely fused together to efface the seam that joins them, then Pylades could legitimately be judged not as sacrificing himself with selfless devotion to Orestes but only to be tending to himself. Much of what is considered noble or virtuous behavior between friends evaporates once the strong identification in friendships resembling Montaigne's fusion friendship is fully understood.

Potential conflict arises between Aristotle's and Montaigne's forms of friendship and egalitarian, impersonal, and impartial morality, because their objects are activities where preference for friends may conflict with moral demands. Aristotle must believe that friends have more value than nonfriends, because he believes that it is just to treat friends better than nonfriends for no other reason than they are friends. Additional conflicts arise because identifying friends as "another self" not only undercuts much moral value in behaving well toward one's friend but increases immoral temptations to benefit one's friends.

Indian friendships, too, can possibly conflict with morality. As I discussed in chapter 1, part of the internal morality of Indian friendship is an expectation that friends sometimes bend rules or violate moral norms to protect each other when they are in trouble. Loyalty to a friend might require acquiescing in his immoral misdeeds or perhaps even assisting him.[42] Again, it is the object of Indian friendship that comes into conflict because of the kinds of actions that friends are expected to perform for each other. Were different actions to express preference for friends, there might be less potential conflict.

Kant may have been aware of a potential conflict between the internal morality of friendship and the demands of morality entailed by his categorical imperative. In his *Lectures on Ethics*, he explains intimacy friendship, which has few, if any, possible conflicts with morality.[43] This friendship, according to Kant, is "the friendship of disposition or sentiment. There is no question here of any service, or of any demand. The friendship is one of pure, genuine disposition, and is friendship in the absolute sense."[44] It is constituted by fellowship, self-disclosure, and perfect, complete intimacy that permits friends to unburden themselves, be frank, escape contempt, and achieve complete communion.[45]

Kant's intimacy friendship satisfies the principal characteristic of friendship, that friends treat each other in ways that they do not treat nonfriends.

Friendship identifies a special relation between persons that distinguishes friendship from other relations, such as collegiality or moral rectitude.[46] For Kant, self-disclosure and intimacy are not dispositions that people possess toward others in general. One cannot be friends with more than two or three people, even if it is a friendship of disposition, because the intimacy required in friendship requires much testing to get established. Intimacy friendship, for Kant, is a disposition that need not manifest itself in actions that generate moral conflicts with nonfriends' well-being or rights. As Kant says, friendship requires no demand or service. It is a feeling of openness and trust, that is, a disposition to intimacy, but not a disposition to promoting the good of one's friend (except insofar as the categorical imperative would require promoting the good of others, whether friend or not).

It might be objected that when Kant says that friendship requires no demand or service, what he finds out of place is merely demanding proof of friendship rather than separating friendship from actions. Relationships that constantly require proof or demonstration are clearly not relationships of friendship (at least in our culture). But I do not think that Kant is merely voicing this obvious but narrow truth. He does say that friends should "abstain from abusing [friendship] by making calls upon it."[47] Kant also explicitly separates intimacy friendship from external action; he classifies the disposition of friendship as a "disposition of feelings," which he explicitly contrasts to "dispositions of actual service."[48] He must be taken at his word, that intimacy friendship is not bound up with external, benevolent actions but only with an intimacy or a feeling of mutual trust and confidence. What is essential, from Kant's perspective, is only a disposition to be intimate, trusting, and sympathetic toward one's friend.

Benevolent actions by one friend can actually destroy friendship. As Kant remarks in *The Metaphysical Principles of Virtue*, benevolence creates an obligation on the part of the recipient that can never be repaid and that unbalances the equality and mutuality needed for friendship.[49] A debt of gratitude is created in a recipient of benevolence which, having to be repaid, places the recipient on a lower level. Kant seems to believe that such an inequality is more or less permanent, because even if the debt of gratitude were to be repaid by some equivalent or other, complete equality could never be reestablished since the initial benefactor was the first to provide assistance unsoiled by any duty of gratitude.

Kant's intimacy friendship results in few conflicts with morality, because as a disposition, it is very different from Aristotle's virtue friendship. For Kant, friendship as a form of intimacy need not manifest itself in time- and asset-consuming activities of a shared life. Nor does Kant believe that friends must have many interests in common; too many shared interests may make friendship more difficult, because friends will have little to talk about. What is essential is that they share moral principles or a moral outlook on life, so they agree on the bases by which to judge actions and events. Friends must be concerned about one another and wish each other well, but quite unlike Aristotle, for Kant, friendship does not require that friends spend a great deal of time together or engage in many shared activities. Friends can feel an openness toward each other, but Kant thinks that they will not "make calls upon it" by actually confiding in each other all that often. The importance of friendship, for Kant, is that friends know that they can confide in each other if necessary and can receive a sympathetic, compassionate hearing.

Intimacy friendship does not command actions that would favor friends at the expense of nonfriends or treat others merely as means. The internal morality of intimacy friendship, being willing to listen to a friend, being honest and open, and being trustworthy are not dispositions that lead to actions that violate duties to nonfriends. Thus intimacy friendship is morally compatible with the requirements of the categorical imperative.

Additional evidence for this compatibility is Kant's belief that violations of the categorical imperative reduce to heteronomy of the will: yielding to desire, egoism, or self-interest. The reasons for entering into Kant's less-than-ideal friendships are need satisfaction and pleasure. Thus acting from less-than-ideal friendships are clear examples of heteronomy, inclination, or self-interest, which might require actions incompatible with goodwill.

Kant's reasons for entering intimacy friendship offer confirming evidence for the absence of moral conflict. For Kant, the benefits of intimacy friendship are first that "Friendship . . . is an aid in overcoming the constraint and the distrust man feels in his intercourse with others, by revealing himself without reserve,"[50] and, second, that "it is man's refuge in this world from his distrust of his fellows, in which he can reveal his disposition to another and enter into communion with him."[51] These are not benefits likely to create violations of the categorical imperative. Finding refuge from distrust would not require actions that use others as a means only.

Kant's intimacy friendship minimizes potential conflicts with the categorical imperative, not because of the small number of friends that one has but rather because of the narrow range of actions that intimacy friendship requires. It would be extremely rare for any requirements of intimacy friendship (e.g., self-revelation and communion) to contradict duties imposed by the categorical imperative. Duties to help those in need or the duty not to lie could be virtuously fulfilled without at all affecting what is required between friends by intimacy friendship. Further, maintaining an intimacy friendship need not compel friends to perform actions violating those duties to others.

Kant's intimacy friendship thus succeeds in avoiding many conflicts with morality. Unlike Aristotle's idea, that friendship requires promoting a friend's good for its own sake through a shared life, little likelihood exists that Kant's intimacy friendship would imply preferring the good of one's friend to the good of others. Intimacy friendship is not threatened or diminished because one friend acts from moral imperatives in a way that benefits some nonfriend over her friend. If, indeed, equality or impartiality is what morality requires, then no loss of fellowship, self-disclosure, or intimacy need arise between friends.

Same-sex female friendships, surveyed by Winstead, whose objects are self-revelation and intimate conversation, likewise create few possible conflicts with morality. Female friendships resemble Kant's intimacy friendship in this respect. Because female friendships require few external activities and material resources, they are less likely to place friends in situations where they must make moral choices between friends and nonfriends. While it is possible that one female friend may request sensitive, intimate information about another friend, unless there is a moral imperative to divulge all that one knows, her request raises no moral conflict, though there may be conflicting loyalties.

Same-sex male friendships, as Winstead reports them, resemble C. S. Lewis's interest friendships. These friendships are based on common interests and external pursuits. Lewis does not regard promoting friends' well-being to constitute part of the object of friendship. Friendship, as he understands it, supplies little reason for preferring a friend's well-being to the well-being of nonfriends. Few conflicts with libertarian, egalitarian, or utilitarian morality would arise simply from pursuing common interests or quests. While it is most certainly possible to pursue interests and quests with a fanaticism or fervor that neglects morality, shared interest friendship is neutral, neither increasing nor decreasing the likelihood of affecting morality. For example, a fervent collector might sacrifice his family to spend money on collectibles. Friends who shared in his interests might encourage him, or they might restrain him from neglecting his moral family responsibilities. Nothing in the nature of friendship, as Lewis understands it, would dispose friends one way or another. Accidental conflict with morality is, however, always possible. Shared interest friendship has no internal moral imperative to promote friends' interests or to treat them with preference to nonfriends. Shared interest friendship, according to Lewis, is inclusive, not exclusive, in that more friends are better than less.

INTERNAL MORALITY AND MORAL JUSTIFICATION

I have shown that forms of friendship contain an internal morality prescribing how friends ought to treat each other. There are reasons justifying friends' preference for each other, and there are reasons for treating others with the same benevolence as friends. A morality internal to friendship presupposes that friendship is a fairly well-defined, normative concept. Friendship resembles promising, in that undertaking a friendship presupposes some particular set of expectations, what I have called "forms of friendship," similar to the way that making a promise presupposes some particular set of rules about promise keeping. Confusion results if the existence of several different forms of friendship (or of promising) is not clearly kept in mind.

It is possible for two people to mistakenly believe that they are friends when they are not, and it is possible for two people to misunderstand the nature, basis, or object of their friendship. Similar mistakes can occur with promises. One person may think that another has made a promise because she misunderstands the spoken words, or she may misunderstand the strength of the duty imposed on the promisor, believing it to be a vow when the promisor takes it to be only an ordinary promise that can be legitimately broken for cause. Differences exist from culture to culture about both promises and friendships, which can lead to misunderstandings, and as I have shown, even within our own Western culture, differences also exist. Aristotle points out that misunderstandings arise because of different beliefs about the basis of friendship, whether virtue, utility, or pleasure.[52] Misunderstandings also are possible about the nature and object of friendships in much the same way people can confuse friendship and romantic love. Two people believing that they are friends is not sufficient for their being friends.

Morality and friendship come into conflict on a number of different levels. One is that friends exhibit a preference for each other. Some forms of friendship contain reasons that supposedly justify preferential treatment for friends. The premise seems to be that because friends either have each other's best interest at heart or because friends treat each other in morally exemplary ways, then they are justified in treating each other better than they treat nonfriends. Aristotle and Badhwar hold this position. For their argument to succeed, they either must assume that friends have more value than nonfriends, or that acts of benefitting friends have intrinsically more value than acts of benefitting non-friends. Neither assumption seems obviously true. Other ways of exhibiting preference, such as sharing intimacies, spark different and fewer conflicts.

Montaigne's fusion friendship and Aristotle's "other self" might be thought to include an inner morality that answers questions about when friends should be preferred and when it is wrong to prefer them. An identity between friends as the basis of friendship might justify treating one's friends better than nonfriends in circumstances where it is justified to prefer oneself to others. A parallel could be said to exist between when it is right to treat friends better than nonfriends and when it is right to treat oneself better than others. John Cottingham also notices this parallel in a discussion of self-concern.[53] For example, circumstances that would justify a person treating himself better than others also would justify treating his friends, those with whom he identifies, better than others. Connecting justifiable preference for friends to justifiable preference for oneself is a plausible line of inquiry. Libertarian, egalitarian, and utilitarian moralities sometimes justify treating oneself better than others. In those instances, treating friends better than nonfriends also might be justified according to Montaigne's and Aristotle's friendships. Of course, sometimes morality does not justify preferring oneself, and in those cases, conflicts arise if self or friend is preferred.

Goodwill friendships require actions that cause many moral conflicts, even though they also implicitly contain reasons for promoting the well-being of nonfriends. Intimacy and common interest friendships require actions that cause the least potential conflict with libertarian, egalitarian, and utilitarian moralities because of the limited range of actions constituting the objects of these friendships.

A second category of conflict between friendship and morality does not depend on the kinds of actions that friendship requires among friends. This category of conflict arises because of moral requirements on the motives and intentions of action rather than because of action required by friendship and morality. Kant, for example, believes that actions have moral worth only if they are performed from a sense of duty as their primary motive rather than being primarily motivated by self-interest or inclination. Were this true, then promoting one's friend's well-being out of friendship might have less moral worth than promoting a nonfriend's well-being from a sense of duty. Another possible motivational conflict arises between the idea that one ought to care for one's friend for her own sake and utilitarianism, which sometimes is thought to require that friends only be cared for as a means to advancing some greatest overall good. Conflicts within this category are believed to be independent of the diverse actions constituting objects of friendship, so that most forms of friendship are susceptible to a motivational conflict with morality. This category of conflict is more fully discussed in the next chapter.

It might be asked whether intimacy and interest friendships, which minimally conflict with these particular moralities, nevertheless conflict with morality itself. Is there some generic primordial conflict between morality in itself and friendship in any of its conceptions, conflicts that arise either from actions or from intentions and motives of friendship? It is not at all clear what is being asked by this question. First, there are many different conceptions of friendship. Second, it is not clear what sense can be made of "morality in itself" as a concept. Morality, as it affects human life, is always some particular morality with specific rights, duties, or obligations, whether it is a philosophical moral theory, such as utilitarianism, or a culture's practiced mores, such as Hinduism or Buddhism. Great differences exist between various moralities, and if any aspects exist in common, it is difficult to know whether these are essentially or accidentally common. People try to act morally according to some particular morality, even if they only unthinkingly conform to the morality in which they were raised. No sense can be made in asking about friendship conflicting with morality itself, apart from some specific conception of morality. So-called "commonsense morality" is only a set of moral rules that appeals to the intuitions of persons who share some common upbringing, socialization, or acculturation. What is "common sense" in Varanasi most likely would not be "common sense" in Vienna (e.g., in the treatment of widows).

Friendship's internal morality entails preferring friends to nonfriends. Preference for friends is part of the nature of all specific forms of friendship. Friendship is not a relationship that can be shared with everyone (though everyone can be treated in a friendly way). Goodwill, caring for, and feeling affection create imperatives defining how friends are to behave toward each other. I have argued that friendship also entails a reason for pursuing the same good for nonfriends that is pursued for friends. In the absence of scarcity, there is as strong of a reason to assist and benefit nonfriends as there is to benefit and assist friends. Of course, in the absence of scarcity, many philosophers believe that there would be little reason for moral rules at all.

The remainder of this book is an examination of the relation between distinct forms of friendship and various moral theories defending a variety of different moral principles. The examination is necessary in order to better understand conflicts between the internal morality of various friendships and external moral theories. An awareness of these conflicts has prompted a number of attempts at reconciliation, which will be examined as well. Reconciliations are attempts to demonstrate that conflicts are only apparent, and that preference for friends is compatible with a particular morality. Both utilitarians and libertarians attempt this kind of reconciliation. Egalitarian moral theories are least likely to dissolve conflicts.

A final word is needed about the relationship between friendship's internal moralities and moral theories that are external to friendship. Some philosophers take morality to be, by definition, overriding, supremely authoritative, or equivalent to practical rationality. For them, conflicts between morality and friendship inevitably should be resolved in morality's favor. Other philosophers view morality as one practical consideration among a number of comparable reasons for action. Morality, as one of many practical considerations, may not always trump or overrule friendship. My examination in the following chapter is intended to be neutral between these two different views of morality. My discussion is useful in understanding the conflicts in whichever way that morality's authority is ultimately understood. Knowing where conflicts lie is an essential first step.

FOUR

EXTERNAL JUSTIFICATIONS

THE EXAMPLE

THE CLASSIC EXAMPLE of preference for friends dates back to the Stoics, was revived in the eighteenth century by William Godwin, and was recently made popular by Bernard Williams.[1] Its skeleton reads like this: If two people are in mortal danger and it is only possible to save one, is it morally permitted to save a friend, a beloved, or relative rather than someone about whom one does not care as much? Godwin complicates the example by stipulating that the nonfriend is capable of greatly benefitting many people, while the friend, beloved, or relative is not. Godwin's complication is especially troublesome for utilitarians who judge the rightness of actions by their consequences on the well-being of all affected. In Williams's example, it is one's wife who is in mortal danger. Williams argues that if someone has to think whether it is morally right to save his wife, then he has "one thought too many." The classic mortal danger example is the most dramatic illustration of the choice of whether to promote a friend's well-being or the well-being of nonfriends. Most everyday choices between friends and nonfriends do not normally involve as much drama and do not entail as tragic consequences for nonfriends not chosen. Typically, choices have to be made between visiting friends or nonfriends, sharing resources, sending presents, receiving confidences, or pursuing common interests.

This chapter examines three moral answers to the question of when friends may be preferred to nonfriends: libertarian, egalitarian, and utilitarian. Answers are complicated, because each moral perspective contains several variant theories. Within the utilitarian perspective, there are a number of related versions of the theory that will have to be discussed (e.g., act, rule, direct, indirect, and so on). Similarly, egalitarian perspectives contain a number of theories besides Kant's. There are versions of impartialism or impartiality by Marcia Baron and Susan Wolf that warrant discussion in addition to Alan Gewirth's attempt to bridge the gap between universal and particular egalitarian morality. Answers also are complicated because each moral theory must be responsive to different conceptions of friendship, each with its own internal set of expectations about how friends are to behave. Actions that Aristotelian virtue friends would expect from each other as expressions of their friendship are significantly different from actions that Kantian intimacy friends would expect. Similarly, expectations between friends based on Lewis's conception, on Montaigne's conception, on the three Indian conceptions, and also on Kant's and Aristotle's less-than-ideal friendships each have their own implications for each moral theory.

The conflicts with various moralities considered here arise from different objects of friendship, that is, the kinds of actions understood as constituting each form of friendship. It is because friendships imply diverse types of preference between friends that different forms of friendship will have different potential conflicts. Where friends are expected to share all of their property in common, as they are expected to do in Aristotle's virtue friendship, there may be conflicts with a moral requirement to produce the best overall consequences, but sharing property in common may not conflict with a libertarian duty of noninterference.

It is important to remember that not every way friends behave toward each other is behavior required by their specific form of friendship. Two people who maintain an Aristotelian, utility-based friendship may decide to share intimacies with each other, even though neither gets anything of value in doing so.[2] Not all of the actions between friends are ones "out of" friendship or expressive of the friendship. Shared intimacies could be said to exceed the requirements of Aristotle's utility friendship. In much the same way, Lewis's shared interest friends may come to feel affection for each other as a result of pursuing their common interest. Shared intimacies and affection do not arise as a result of those friendships' internal requirements. It might be said, without misleading, that they are caused by those friendships but are not implied by the forms of friendship. Chapter 3 distinguished between essential conflict and accidental conflict. Primarily essential conflicts will be discussed here.

Goodwill friendships contain two pulls, the personal and the impersonal. Because the two pulls have not been widely recognized, no discussion exists of their role in morally justifying preference for friends. I shall explain what each of the moral theories implies about friendship's impersonal pull. Of the two pulls, the personal is most likely to come into conflict with egalitarian, impersonal, and impartial moralities. The personal pull is friends' desire to promote each other's well-being instead of the well-being of nonfriends. The impersonal pull of friendship supplies a reason for promoting nonfriends' well-being and to that extent is unlikely to conflict with the egalitarian, impersonal, or impartial. It might be thought that the impersonal pull also is less likely to conflict with utilitarian requirements to produce the best overall consequences but, surprisingly, acting on the personal pull is what several utilitarians believe to be "optimific."

A second category of conflict between friendship and morality must be discussed. This conflict arises not from actions required by friendship that potentially conflict with various moral requirements; rather, it arises from motives and intentions. Lawrence A. Blum, for example, suggests that Kant's equal dignity morality conflicts with preference for friends. Blum interprets Kant's conception of morality as embodying the notion that "[e]very human being, simply in virtue of being human, is worthy of equal consideration, and his good is equally worthy of being promoted."[3] Friendship, as Blum conceives of it, contradicts Kant's conception of equal consideration. "In friendship one desires and acts for the good of the friend, not simply because he is another human being but precisely because he is one's friend."[4] Blum argues that just as Kant views acting out of our own interest where we make exceptions for ourselves to be immoral, Kant also believes that it is immoral to benefit our friend out of our own interest in him. Kantian morality, for Blum, requires impartiality as a reason for acting toward beings who possess equal dignity and worth. Blum is not arguing that only where actual conflicts arise between helping a friend and helping a nonfriend would Kant consider it immoral automatically to prefer the friend. Blum's primary point is that acting on motives of friendship is incompatible with Kant's demand that we act impartially from the motive of duty. This is a conflict that arises even in circumstances where acting to benefit a friend has no effect at all on nonfriends. This conflict arises between the motive of duty and motives of friendship.

Motives of friendship may not conflict with the requirements of other moral theories to the extent that Blum thinks that they conflict with Kant's. Certain forms of utilitarianism, for example, place no value on the motives of action independently of their consequences. Motives have value or disvalue only because of the consequences that they produce.[5] Acting from motives of friendship might pose no special conflict for an act utilitarian, as long as acting from them is optimific. Libertarians, unlike Kant but resembling act utilitarians, tend to ignore motives and focus on acts of noninterference.

There are, however, other alleged conflicts between moral theories and motives and intentions. Motives of friendship are thought to be adversely affected by utilitarianism. In the section on utilitarianism, I discuss a claim by two philosophers that utilitarianism fails to account for motives to care for a friend for her own sake.

Focusing exclusively on the mortal danger Classic Example of preferring friends to nonfriends exaggerates and distorts conflicts with morality. The Classic Example will be discussed for each theory and various forms of friendship, but the results are not all that morally illuminating, although there are some interesting surprises. It remains true that hard cases make bad precedent. Less extreme examples are needed to better understand the underlying reasons for why friends are or are not to be preferred to nonfriends for each moral theory. It might be convenient to pick one or two simple but interesting examples to use throughout the following sections. Unfortunately, doing so is impractical. So many different conceptions of friendship exist, each having its own possible conflicts with morality, that limiting discussion to one or two precious examples is not a stylistic option.

LIBERTARIANISM

The moral theory appearing to have fewest conflicts with friendship is libertarianism. Though drawing the limits of liberty in different places, all libertarians hold individual liberty to be fundamental. Lansing Pollock writes:

> The libertarian view that I am defending maintains that persons have one fundamental right, the equal right to be free. This libertarian view is incompatible with other egalitarian views that focus on different fundamental values.
>
> I have proposed that our freedom should be limited by the equal right of others to be free. This constraint can be stated more formally by what I call the *freedom principle*: Each person ought to grant other persons an equal right to be free. The underlying idea is that interactions should (ideally) be based on mutual consent.[6] (emphasis in original)

Coercion and deception are two paradigmatic ways that cause persons to be-have involuntarily. Coercion as an actual use of force or as a threat of force against someone causes her actions not to be free, because she most likely would not consent to what she is being forced or threatened with force to do. Similarly, deceiving someone makes her actions involuntary, because she would not consent to what she does, were it not for the misinformation by which she is deceived. Pollock believes that, "The basic moral rules (it is usu-ally wrong to lie, it is usually wrong to steal, it is usually wrong to attack oth-ers) can be deduced from the freedom principle."[7] Unlike Rawls's principle of equal liberty, which applies only to the basic structure of society, the libertar-ianism defined by Pollock's freedom principle applies to relations between in-dividuals.[8] Libertarians maintain only the most limited role for government because of its potential for unjustifiable limitations on people's right to be free.

Some libertarians believe that there are no positive duties to assist those who are in need. Jan Narveson characterizes libertarianism as

> the doctrine that the only relevant consideration in political matters is individ-ual liberty: that there is a delimitable sphere of action for each person, the per-son's "rightful liberty," such that one may be forced to do or refrain from what one wants to do only if what one would do or not do would violate, or at least infringe, the rightful liberty of some other person(s). No other reasons for compelling people are allowable: other actions touching on the life of that individual require his or her consent.[9]

A person's rightful liberty, for Narveson, extends from his person and body to any material objects that he rightfully acquires. No duties exist to promote "positive liberty" or to minimize interferences by others.[10] Narveson limits libertarianism to prohibiting interferences with another person's rightful lib-erty. According to Narveson, libertarianism requires only one duty, a duty of noninterference with the liberty of others. No positive duties exist involun-tarily creating obligations to assist others in avoiding harm or in advancing well-being. He believes that rational persons would not agree to positive du-ties because of the potentially high cost to each person, were such positive du-ties coercively enforced.

One primary way that moral theories, both libertarian and nonlibertar-ian, differ is in characterizing morally salient ways that people can possibly af-fect each other. One source of disagreement is whether intentional omissions, that is, failures to act, are morally relevant. People might affect each other not only by the acts that they perform, but some philosophers argue that people can be affected by what others choose not to do. For example, a starving child who cannot feed himself will die if others choose not to feed him. While failing to feed a starving child (who is not one's own child) might not be infringing on his liberty, in Narveson's understanding of libertarianism, it is not as clear that failing to feed a starving child "grants" the child's equal liberty in Pollock's understanding.

Not only is there disagreement about the moral relevance of intentional omissions, but there also is disagreement about whether both "positive acts" and "negative acts" are relevant, about the foreseen but unintended consequences of one's acts or omissions, and about whether there is symmetry in moral relevance between the good that could be caused and the evil that could be prevented. Libertarians tend to adopt a view on these issues that holds each person morally responsible for a narrow range. Libertarians would be least likely, for example, to hold persons morally responsible for any unintended consequences of their omissions. The mythical Dutch boy, for example, would not be responsible, according to many libertarians, for flooding caused by a dyke collapsing if he bypassed the leaky dyke to hurry to the store to buy some candy. By rushing to the store, he intentionally omitted putting his finger in the leak, but he did not intend to flood his neighborhood. Also, by rushing, he omitted warning his neighborhood, saving his parents, and performing a myriad of other acts, all of which had consequences potentially good or bad. Egalitarian, impartial, and utilitarian theories have different ideas about relevance in this area, discussed fully in the next section.

Libertarians also disagree about what it is a person ought to be free to do. Narveson's noninterference might variously refer to not interfering with a person's performing exactly the same action, similar actions, classes of action, or actions in general. For example, if a man picks an apple off of a tree and eats it, he takes away others' freedom to pick and eat that particular apple, though he may leave enough apples on that tree for anyone else who wants apples to pick and eat them. Even if he were to pick all of the apples on that tree, if others had trees elsewhere from which they could pick apples (how far away?), their equal freedom might be undiminished. Would their equal freedom be reduced if they could not pick apples because all of the apples had been picked but there were still ample unpicked pears to eat if they wanted fruit? If they could not pick fruit but could appropriate some other food sources, would they still have equal freedom? Some libertarians are clear about which position they are defending; my point here is that there are a variety of different perspectives libertarians have advocated.

Libertarians such as Narveson and Robert Nozick use ownership rights to refine their understanding of the area of legitimate individual liberty.[11] They argue that people are free to use land and material objects that they have legitimately acquired so that others have a duty not to interfere with owners' legitimate use of what they own.[12] What friends legitimately own will affect how they may treat each other in comparison to their treatment of nonfriends. Wealthy friends are able to confer benefits on each other that poor friends are not. For libertarians such as Narveson and Nozick, no duties are violated by Aristotle's virtue friends sharing in common with each other all that they "legitimately" own, even if nonfriends might go without something that they desperately needed.

Libertarians also differ in their definitions of duty. This is an important difference for friendship, because preferring friends to nonfriends typically involves moral but not enforceable legal duties. Libertarians such as Pollock sometimes use the word "duty" to refer to enforceable obligations, so he does not consider moral obligations unenforced by threats of punishment to be duties. Other libertarians might argue that some moral obligations are duties, even though they ought not be enforced by threats of punishment (e.g., I may have a legally unenforceable moral duty to go fishing tomorrow, because I promised to go). Such an obligation can be reasonably considered a duty, even though it is a duty that ought not be enforced by threats of punishment. Positive moral obligations (e.g., to feed children who cannot feed themselves) also might be considered unenforceable duties, though many libertarians only recognize positive moral obligations that are voluntarily undertaken.

I will use the word "duty" to refer to actions that are right to do and wrong not to do, that is, obligations either moral or legal. Some duties may be legitimately enforced by threats of punishment, and other duties may not be so enforced.[13] Nothing substantive is decided by using "duty" in this way about when friends may morally prefer each other to nonfriends. I find it more natural to use "duty" in this way, and as long as I am consistent, no moral questions should be begged by my choice.

Libertarian solutions to the choice posed in the Classic Example are fairly straightforward. If two persons are in mortal danger and it is possible to save only one, then libertarians would agree that it is morally justified to save a friend simply because she is a friend. Libertarians deny the existence of any positive duties to help others, unless those duties are voluntarily self-imposed. So if a friend and a nonfriend are in need of assistance and it is only possible to help one, then without a voluntarily undertaken special positive duty to help the nonfriend, helping one's friend is morally right.[14] If no contracts or promises have been made to save a nonfriend's life, then there is no duty to save him, and saving one's friend is perfectly permissible. By similar reasoning, libertarians acknowledge that it would be equally right, if one chose, to save a nonfriend. It is permissible, according to libertarians, in the Classic Example to save whomever one chooses.

The equal freedom of the person who drowns has not been violated, even if he has not voiced consent to his being left to drown. Pollock could argue that neither the drowned person's equal freedom has been violated nor that his consent been ignored by the "interaction." There is no interaction. In Narveson's terms, even though the person who drowns is dead, and therefore not free to do anything, his "rightful liberty" is not interfered with, because there has been no interference. Both Pollock and Narveson would claim that no action has been carried out against the person who has drowned. He has not been interfered with, and he has not been interacted with. Were the lifesaver not to have been present in the area, the unlucky nonfriend nonswimmer would have drowned anyway. By choosing to save his friend, the lifesaver neither interacts nor interferes with the nonfriend. Neither intentional omissions, which have consequences that affect others, nor simply doing nothing, which also may have consequences that affect others, is considered by Pollock and Narveson an interaction or interference and as such morally blameworthy. Their reason is that were the lifesaver not to have been present in the first place, both friend and nonfriend would have drowned.

Libertarians believe that it is not wrong to save one's friend because she is one's friend and to let the other swimmer drown. Godwin's complication that the nonfriend is capable of greatly benefitting humanity does not alter this libertarian conclusion. Because there are no positive duties to assist others unless they are voluntarily undertaken, no duty is violated in letting a great potential benefactor but poor swimming nonfriend drown. Also, for libertarians, there are no involuntary general positive duties to produce benefits for humanity, so the benefactor's potential benefits to humanity are not a sufficient reason to generate a duty for saving him rather than one's friend. The great benefactor would drown anyway if the lifesaver were not present, therefore, he is not interfered with or treated unequally by any interaction.

One way of interpreting the libertarian position is that it is right to save one's friend in preference to a nonfriend, because there are no positive duties to help anyone unless voluntarily self-imposed. Based on this interpretation, it is permissible to let a nonfriend drown by saving one's friend, because it would be equally permissible to let both drown. In the absence of any positive duties of assistance, letting both friend and nonfriend drown violates no duty. For utilitarians and egalitarians, this libertarian position is unacceptably cold, inhumane, lacking in compassion, or insensitive to fundamental human equality. A degree of absurdity exists in believing that it is morally permissible to save one's friend in preference to a nonfriend, because it is morally permissible to save neither friend nor nonfriend.

Some conceptions of friendship can show that libertarians need not be committed to an absurd interpretation that it is right to save one's friend because it is right to let both drown. In Aristotle's friendships based on virtue, utility, or pleasure, in Indian friendships, and in Kant's need friendship, where the nature of friendship is understood as reciprocal goodwill, friends are expected to promote each other's well-being. Being friends based on one of these conceptions of friendship is understood as voluntarily undertaking duties to promote each other's well-being. Two people would not be considered friends unless they promoted each other's well-being. Like making promises, undertaking goodwill friendships voluntarily imposes positive duties on friends to advance their well-being.

Goodwill friendships understood in this way rescue libertarians from the absurd view that it is right to save a friend rather than a nonfriend, because letting both drown would be right. In goodwill friendships, friends voluntarily undertake special duties to promote each other's well-being. Like breaking a promise, failing to save a friend violates a self-imposed, positive, special duty or obligation.

Libertarians' rescue from absurdity comes at a price. Goodwill friendships contain an impersonal pull over and above the pull to prefer one's friend. Because saving the life of one's friend is good, there is a reason to save her that also is a reason for saving anyone else for whom life is good.[15] Goodwill friendships contain reasons for saving one's friend that also are reasons for saving other similar persons. In the Classic Example, goodwill friendship that supplies a voluntarily imposed special duty to save one's friend also supplies a reason to save nonfriends. If libertarians are rescued from absurdity (that it is right to save one's friend, because it is right to let both friend and nonfriend drown) by goodwill friendship providing a special obligation to save one's friend—they now must explain how to decide between friendship's personal and impersonal pulls. Libertarians might conclude that it is right, after all, to override friendship's impersonal pull and sometimes to save one's friend. They might arrive at their conclusion by a variety of different arguments, namely, that omissions are not culpable, or that there is an asymmetry between doing good and avoiding evil. Whatever their particular conclusions, libertarians must nevertheless acknowledge the presence of friendship's impersonal pull and the possibility that sometimes it may be right to save a nonfriend in preference to a friend.

Not all conceptions of friendship contain both impersonal and personal pulls. C. S. Lewis's shared interest friendship contains no requirement to promote a friend's well-being. If the Classic Example were approached with Lewis's conception in mind, then there would be no reason, arising out of the nature and object of friendship, to choose to save a friend rather than a nonfriend. To the extent that affection might have arisen between two shared interest friends as a result of their friendship, affection might be a reason for choosing one's friend. But affection would be an accidental and not an essential aspect of friendship, as understood by Lewis. The reason for saving one's friend would be affection, not friendship, something that might be felt for a nonfriend too.

In much the same way, Kant's intimacy friendship does not require that friends promote each other's well-being to a greater extent than nonfriends. Kant's categorical imperative creates an imperfect duty of beneficence to promote the well-being of others, but intimacy friendship does not strengthen Kantian duties of beneficence between friends compared to nonfriends. No impersonal pull exists within these forms of friendship that libertarians need consider in deciding whom to save. The absence of impersonal pulls derives from the absence of any reason inherent in these forms of friendship to promote friends' well-being to a greater extent than nonfriends. And while decisions that libertarians confront, whether to save friend or nonfriend, are simplified by the absence of any impersonal pull, they are forced back into the absurd position where it is right to save one's friend because no wrong is done by letting both drown.

In situations other than the Classic Example of preferring friends, libertarians believe that friends are free to prefer each other, except where they interfere with the freedom of others. It is important to stress this. Consenting acts of preference between friends may affect the freedom of others, but the affecting relation may not be morally relevant for many libertarians. A group of friends may form a philosophy club within their department. They may decide, for reasons of their own, not to admit any nonfriends into their club. Nonfriends may not be permitted to join the club if they want to. Their freedom may be affected, but it is not interfered with. They are free to form a club of their own if they wish and to engage in philosophical activities, even though they are not free to join the friends' club. It might even be thought that these nonfriends are not made worse off by the friends forming their exclusive club, because before the club had been formed, there was no club for the nonfriends to join anyway. So not being able to join does not erode their level of well-being from where it was before the club was created. They also are just as free after the friends' club was formed as they were before to form a club of their own.

Suppose that the friends who form their club are tenured members of the department and that the nonfriends are untenured. Might the club's existence interfere with their freedom to get tenure by making it more difficult for them to impress tenured faculty with their philosophical abilities? Untenured faculty could form their own club and invite tenured faculty to join or to attend meetings where their papers are discussed. Still, untenured faculty might regard an exclusive club of tenured faculty as interfering with their freedom to pursue tenure.[16]

Fully resolving these issues involves more analysis of the nuances of affecting, interfering, respecting, and granting freedom than I want to pursue here. While libertarians engage in intraterritorial squabbles about differences in nuance, their principles imply the largest area for friends preferring each other to nonfriends. Egalitarian and utilitarian theories imply a more narrow range of legitimate preference.

Most daily activities where friends act with preference for each other—by sending holiday cards, visiting homes, going to dinner, helping with yardwork, caring for each other's children, listening to problems, sharing confidences, and pursuing pleasurable interests—lie within the range of legitimate freedom as understood by many libertarians. Only in special atypical circumstances created as counterexamples by gifted philosophers would any of the above expressions of preference by friends for each other be understood as possibly morally suspicious.

EQUALITY

The greatest potential conflict with friendship comes from egalitarian moral theories. Egalitarian moral theories ground primary rules for action on an assumption of a fundamental equality of all human beings. Kant's categorical imperative, the Golden Rule, and Alan Gewirth's principle of generic consistency are examples of egalitarian theories.[17] Impartial and impersonal moral theories by Marcia Baron and Susan Wolf attempt to accommodate friendship yet do not make as rigid an assumption of fundamental human equality. They must be separately discussed.

Neither utilitarians nor libertarians is egalitarian. Utilitarianism is not an egalitarian moral theory in the relevant sense, because it makes no assumptions about fundamental human equality. Utilitarians at best assume only that equal units of well-being have the same value in all sentient beings. Many libertarian theories are agnostic about fundamental human equality. Libertarians such as Nozick defend equal rights to be free or rights of noninterference without trying to ground these rights in human equality.[18] Pollock, however, does claim that his libertarianism is the only defensible form of egalitarianism.

The extent of conflict with egalitarian moral theories depends in part on the objects of friendship. Some ways that friends express their preference for each other conflict less with egalitarian moral requirements. Kant's intimacy friendship, which only requires that friends be willing to receive confidences from each other, is not likely to also require actions that conflict with any egalitarian demands of the categorical imperative. Similarly, C. S. Lewis's shared interest friendships and Montaigne's fusion friendship, which "abjures advantage," also may create few conflicts. It is the goodwill friendships of Aristotle, the Indian ideals, and Kant's need friendship that cause the greatest potential conflict. Because the object of these forms of friendship is to promote friends' well-being, friends may fail to respect morality based on equality or impartiality. To a similar extent, this is true also of Aristotle's less-than-ideal friendships. I begin with the forms of friendship that are in the greatest potential conflict with egalitarianism to see whether any of the attempted resolutions are successful.

As a first example of an egalitarian moral principle, consider the Golden Rule, which not only obligates everyone to love his neighbor as himself but also to consider everyone, including enemies, his neighbor. This fundamental principle of "Christian" morality is thoroughly egalitarian. All people are believed to be created equal, and as a consequence they ought to be treated equally. To act with special beneficence to one's friends, to love them more than others, violates the Golden Rule. Because of the Golden Rule's strong commandment to equality, there appears to be no justification for special treatment of friends by promoting their well-being more than nonfriends' well-being. Loving one's friends more strongly than loving one's other neighbors is precisely the kind of nepotistic behavior that the Golden Rule is designed to exclude.

Kierkegaard is aware of this conflict and tries to resolve it through Christian love of God.[19] He believes that friends who try to benefit each other more than they try to benefit their neighbors violate the Golden Rule. But

Kierkegaard believes that if self-renouncing Christian love replaces preferential love, then the conflict with the Golden Rule is resolved through loving God, who loves all humans equally.[20] Friends will be loved for the same reason that nonfriends are loved, namely, the love of a Christian God. Kierkegaard sees differences in reasons for action as a way of resolving the conflict. His way of trying to solve the conflict between friendship and equality, however, depends on beliefs that are perhaps more difficult to ground than are beliefs about friendship and equality themselves.

Kant's categorical imperative has implications for friendship similar to the Golden Rule. Kant's moral theory, like the Golden Rule, assumes the fundamental equal dignity of all persons.[21] Equal human dignity creates a conflict between the categorical imperative and special preference for friends that takes the form of advancing friends' well-being ahead of nonfriends'. Consider the first formula of the categorical imperative: act so that it is possible to will that the maxim of one's act can become a universal law. Could a rational being will a universal law that permits friends to show special beneficence toward one another? Kant never directly addresses this question; still, there are discussions in *The Grounding for the Metaphysics of Morals* that shed light on a possible answer.

Kant's explanation of an imperfect duty to help others acknowledges that the world could go on, as would human life, even if no law required a duty to help those in need. But a rational being could not will such a universal law because, in circumstances where he needed help, it would be irrational to count upon help merely from those who would offer it from inclination or self-interest, since there may not always be enough of those people for the needed help to be rationally and reliably counted upon.[22] If this is Kant's argument, then a special overriding duty to help friends rather than nonfriends could not rationally be willed, for much the same reasons. If a rational being realizes that he might need help at some point in his life, it would not be rational to will a law that would permit others to ignore his need and help only their friends, since this would reduce the number of people who could be counted upon for help. Therefore, if others are treated according to rules willed by rational beings, they would not will a rule that might deprive them of the help they urgently need. A lowest-caste Indian might not will such a universal law, because in all likelihood, his friends lack the capacity to substantially assist him.

While this interpretation may stretch Kant's meaning to cover an example that he has not considered, and while his argument concerning a duty to help others may itself stretch the concept of rationality, his commitment to equal human dignity conflicts with acts of special beneficence toward friends. The object of Kant's own best form of friendship, intimacy friendship constituted by exchanges of confidences and personal information, does not conflict with the categorical imperative's imperfect duty to benefit others.

As mentioned at the beginning of this chapter, Blum stresses a second reason for believing that Kant's equal dignity morality conflicts with special preference toward friends. He believes that Kant's categorical imperative is grounded on the idea that "[e]very human being, simply in virtue of being human, is worthy of equal consideration, and his good is equally worthy of being promoted."[23] Friendship, as Blum is conceiving it, is an Aristotelian goodwill friendship that does contradict Kant's equal consideration. "In friendship one desires and acts for the good of the friend, not simply because he is another human being but precisely because he is one's friend."[24] Blum's point is that just as Kant views acting out of our own interest in cases where we make exceptions for ourselves as immoral, Kant also would condemn our benefitting our friends out of our own interest in them. Morality for Kant is based on impartiality among beings who possess equal dignity and worth.

Blum is not arguing that only where there is a conflict between helping a friend and helping a nonfriend would Kant consider it immoral to automatically prefer the friend. Michael Stocker calls those conflicts "external" rather than internal.[25] The internal conflict that Blum's argument documents is a theoretical one between acting impartially from the motive of duty and the belief that one should prefer to benefit one's friends. Blum contends that acting on the motive of friendship is always incompatible with Kant's demand that one act impartially from the objective motive of duty. The fundamental human equality, which grounds the categorical imperative, according to Blum, inevitably conflicts with preferential motives that underwrite (for goodwill friendships) special beneficence to friends.

Kant, however, does not believe that only one motive for action can be operative at a time. He believes that inclination, self-interest, and a sense of duty are simultaneously capable of motivating the same action. Further, Kant argues that it may never be known with certainty which of the three motives of duty is strongest in any situation.[26] Since the three motives—inclination, self-interest, and a sense of duty—all may operate at the same time and in the same direction, Kant does not "demand we act impartially from the objective motive of duty," as Blum suggests. Kant believes that genuine moral worth comes from acting from a sense of duty, but he does not believe that it is possible to command acting from that motive. Acting from the motive of duty cannot be commanded, and it is impossible to know whether or not duty is actually the strongest motive in any particular case. Moreover, Kant never argues that acting from the motives of inclination or self-interest is immoral. Duty can be performed from these motives, though the person may lack genuine moral worth.

There is a second difficulty for Blum's argument. Kant's intimacy friendship does not require that a friend "desires and acts for the good of the friend," which would conflict with Kant's categorical imperative. Aristotelian goodwill conceptions of friendship, requiring friends to promote each other's well-being in preference to the well-being of nonfriends, might conflict with the notion that "[e]very human being, simply in virtue of being human, is worthy of equal consideration, and his good is equally worthy of being promoted."[27] Kant's intimacy friendship has a different object from Aristotle's goodwill conceptions and thus does not raise conflicts with imperfect duties to equally promote the good of others. The conflict that Blum recognizes between actions motivated by respect for human equality and actions motivated by friendship arises for some forms of friendship and not for others. Intimacy friends who receive each other's confidences do not disrespect the equal worth of others in the way that others' equal worth may be disrespected by goodwill friends who promote their own well-being while ignoring greater needs in others.

It is difficult to see how accommodation is possible between a belief in fundamental human equality and conceptions of friendship whose objects are actions to promote each friend's well-being. To the extent that fundamental human equality grounds a universal moral principle, little justification exists for advancing friends' well-being instead of nonfriends' well-being.

In "Ethical Universalism and Particularism," Alan Gewirth argues that his Principle of Generic Consistency (PGC) provides a compelling justification for preferential treatment of friends. Gewirth's article is important, because he discusses the justification from a perspective of reconciling his universalist moral principle based on what he believes to be fundamental human equality with a particularist position that

> one ought to give preferential consideration to the interests of some persons against others, including not only oneself but also other persons with whom one has special relationships, such as, for example, the members of one's own family or friendship circle.[28]

Though not directly addressing specific forms of friendship, by his characterization of the problem, Gewirth can be understood as assuming forms of friendship resembling Aristotle's goodwill friendships, the Indian ideals, Kant's need friendship and, in some cases, Aristotle's less-than-ideal friendships.

Gewirth criticizes other attempts to justify preference toward friends because the justifications are "extrinsic," that is, "the particularist goods are not valued for their own sakes but only as a causal, calculated means to the universalist end of maximizing the total amount of utility."[29] Forms of rule utilitarianism, discussed in the next section, are Gewirth's target. Yet his criticism does not apply to all forms of utilitarianism in the way that he thinks it does. When Gewirth says that any justification must show that particularist preferences are justified as being good or right in themselves, his argument only applies to forms of utilitarianism with an unnecessarily impoverished value scheme.[30]

Gewirth's PGC implies that all persons have equal rights to freedom and well-being. The freedom component is crucial to his justification of preference toward one's friends:

> The universal right to freedom entails the universal right to form voluntary groups or associations whereby persons freely band together for various purposes, so that all their members voluntarily consent to the various groups and obey their rules. Such groups are justified, i.e., morally permitted insofar as their purposes do not involve violating the human rights of other persons by adversely affecting their general freedom or well-being in ways not derived from the rights themselves. Since such voluntary groups are morally permitted so noninterference with them is morally mandatory.[31]

While his PGC does not directly justify special beneficence to friends, having friends and acting with preference toward them are things people ought to be free to do, according to Gewirth, just as long as friendship does not violate others' equal rights to freedom and well-being. The PGC directly justifies freedom conferring rules that then permit preferential beneficence toward friends. Thus any interference with legitimate preference toward friends would be an unjustified interference with freedom.

In this respect, Gewirth's justification resembles a rule utilitarian justification. His single moral principle, the PGC, justifies a "subprinciple" that voluntary associations may be established for special purposes. It is the subprinciple that warrants preferring friends and, perhaps, ignoring nonfriends. Since making friends is something the PGC implies that people should be free to do, it follows, according to Gewirth, that to restrict this freedom or to interfere with it would not be morally justifiable. And since Gewirth seems to assume that making friends is essentially to show preference for friends over others, acting with preference toward friends is a morally justified expression of freedom. Gewirth extends this argument to include favoring one's local community and one's nation as well.

Gewirth also draws an analogy between making friends and making promises as social practices, the rules of which are justified by some moral principle.[32] Friendship and promising are activities that moral agents may legitimately engage in. They create rational grounds for special treatment, and both activities have moral limitations. And just as some types of promises are morally illegitimate, so are some kinds of special treatment of friends.

The rights to freedom and well-being of others who might be affected, according to Gewirth, limit special treatment between friends, just as the freedom and well-being of others limit the legitimacy of promises. A problem exists for Gewirth's argument. How can it be determined which aspects of another's freedom a friendship may legitimately interfere with or how much well-being friendship may legitimately reduce? Gewirth's answer is that friendship cannot interfere with or adversely affect others' equal right to freedom and well-being, but he does not supply any method for discovering in specific instances what constitutes an unjustified or illegitimate interference. Gewirth must concede that preference toward friends is justified, even if it causes some small harm to others or places some small limit on their freedom, otherwise few acts of preference would ever be morally permitted. But how much?

Gewirth tries to answer this question by an appeal to "human rights" or "general freedom."[33] These concepts are not sufficiently clear or well defined in Gewirth's theory to give precise guidance. Does a homeless beggar on the streets of New York City have a human right that I give him a dollar he can use for food rather than give it to my friend who will buy some candy? The beggar's general well-being certainly will improve from a good meal. Or suppose that tenured faculty form a philosophy discussion club but do not admit untenured faculty who themselves are free to form their own group: has the untenured faculty's right to general freedom been limited, or has their general well-being been diminished?[34] Untenured faculty, even though they are free to form their own parallel philosophy discussion club, might nevertheless be less free to pursue tenure and to feel less well off because they are excluded from the tenured faculty club.

In his most recent book, Gewirth tries to show how preference for one's friends is justified by his PGC through an understanding of self-fulfillment.[35] The PGC is based on the necessity of freedom and well-being for all action:

As we have seen, freedom and well-being are the necessary goods of action and generally successful action, and universalist morality requires that every person's rights to these goods be respected as an essential part of self-fulfillment. But because freedom and well-being are thus necessary goods, their development for each person is also an essential part of personalist morality concerned with the good life. If persons are to fulfill themselves by making the best of themselves, they must have good lives that are based on these necessary goods.[36]

Self-fulfillment requires freedom and well-being in the first instance as necessary conditions of any actions by which agents attempt to attain things they regard as good. Gewirth also believes that freedom and well-being in the second instance become components of every kind of life agents regard as good.[37] Gewirth concludes that the good life for each person is "achieving the best that it is in one to become, what is best here is whatever is found by reason to lead to or consist in the fullest development of freedom and well-being, within the limits set by the universalist morality of human rights."[38]

Friendship, according to Gewirth, "as one of the strongest objects of human aspirations, would seem to be a prime example of the autonomy of aspirations-fulfillment as neither needing nor allowing any justification by universalist morality."[39] He is well aware that friendship "seems to conflict with the egalitarian universalist morality according to which all persons ought to be treated with equal and impartial positive consideration for their respective goods or interests."[40] Like the resolution he offers in his earlier article, Gewirth again argues here that partial and unequal treatment is justified indirectly by the PGC through the application of a subprinciple to the practice of friendship. Also, like his earlier article, Gewirth seems to be presupposing a reciprocal goodwill conception of friendship. Where Gewirth seems to have changed is how he sets limits to friends preferring each other compared to nonfriends. Instead of "general freedom" and "human rights," Gewirth now employs arguments against nepotism, as defined by legitimate institutional roles and by what could be called "importance":

> In addition, whenever objects of distribution (such as academic grades, prison sentences, and so forth) are sufficiently important, their distribution should be determined by general official or institutional rules that prescribe corresponding rights and duties, and these set limits to justified, particularistically preferential actions.[41]

It is possible that these two criteria may be more determinate and as a result easier to apply than his more nebulous earlier concepts, although there is still considerable room for disagreement about what are, for example, appropriate standards for awarding academic grades. There is more determinacy at least in society's official rules that can serve as a beginning place for moral evaluation.

Gewirth's arguments decide the Classic Example in favor of saving friends.[42] He emphasizes, however that priority is not equivalent to exclusivity; duties also are owed to nonfriends. Gewirth is silent on Godwin's complication that the unsaved other is a great potential benefactor of humankind. While saving friends in dire and exceptional circumstances is justified, obligations to promote freedom and well-being still exist toward others. Gewirth does not actually say why he believes it is right to save one's friend. What can be inferred from his arguments is that friends are such a valuable component of self-fulfillment arising from freedom and caring that friendships constitute part of "the best that it is in one to become."[43] Saving friends in these circumstances, according to Gewirth, is an exercise of one's freedom and promotes one's well-being. While duties certainly are owed to others, Gewirth is claiming that in circumstances resembling the Classic Example, it is right, everything considered, to save friends.

While it could be wished that Gewirth gave a more detailed explanation justifying preference for friends in the Classic Example, he is right on target in his answer to Williams's objection that a person who in saving her friend also thinks that it is morally permissible to do so, has "one thought too many."[44] Preference for friends, Gewirth believes, both needs and allows for justification by universalist morality. The purposes implicit in friendship

> because they further the purposes of universalist morality, do reflect what is best in the self in the context of personal relationships; they are therefore intrinsic parts of self-fulfillment as capacity-fulfillment. The personal, emotional capacity that motivates these relationships is, of course, distinct from the rational capacity that serves both to justify them through the PGC and to trace their impacts on other parts of the participants' lives. The argument for the PGC is not intended to remove or subordinate the felt compellingness of these aspirations, if for no other reason than that psychological motivation is distinct from rational justification.[45]

Gewirth is agreeing with Williams that the existence of strong emotional ties to one's friend as a motive to save her life may not need justification, because those ties are intrinsic to the relationship. But Gewirth nevertheless believes that moral justification remains relevant in deciding to save one's friend.

The parallel between friendship and promising illuminates how motive and justification function here. If I borrow money from a friend and promise to pay it back in a week, then at week's end I repay the loan, because I promised to do so. Williams might say that if, in addition to my thinking of repaying the loan because I promised to do so, I also had the thought that it is a duty to keep promises, then I would have one thought too many. My motive is keeping my promise, but my justification is that it is right to keep promises. Both motive and justification are relevant, though the justification need not be in my mind when I repay the loan. Justification lies in the background of promising. Gewirth is correct in criticizing Williams for confusing the two. Though I need not think of the justification when I repay the money I owe, it is because keeping promises is justified that I am right in repaying the money. In saving my friend's life, my motive is that she is my friend, and I need not have any additional conscious thoughts. Still, as Gewirth correctly insists, moral justification lies in the background, and the rightness of saving my friend depends, inescapably, on its being morally justified to save her.

Susan Wolf's way of explaining who to save in the Classic Example reinterprets human equality as impartiality: "the idea of acting from a position that acknowledges and appreciates the fact that all persons . . . are in an important sense equal, and that correspondingly, all are equally entitled to fundamental conditions of well-being and respect."[46] Wolf distinguishes between "Extreme Impartialism" and a "Moderate Impartialism," which she advocates.

> A moral person, on this view, does act only in ways that she believes any reasonable person would allow. She does hold herself to the same standards that she expects of others.
>
> First and most obviously, Moderate Impartialism allows the existence of deep friendships and love without apology. Consequently, many, if not all, of the preferences for loved ones most of us express in our daily lives will turn out to be unequivocally permissible. Since Moderate Impartialism never asks a person to value every human or sentient being as much as every other, there is no problem about coaching *one's own* daughter's soccer team or taking *one's own* friend out to dinner, or loving *one's own* spouse more than the equally deserving but much less interesting man across the street.[47] (emphasis in original)

Unlike Extreme Impartialism, which requires taking seriously all people's well-being and working hard to secure their rights, Wolf believes that showing preference for one's friend in taking her out to dinner is morally permissible, because it is a preference that all rational people would allow.[48] Saving the life of one's friend would be morally permissible, according to Wolf, only if all other rational persons would accept that preference as a "reasonable standard." Each person is permitted to show preference for "her circle of friends and loved ones" in situations where others would equally select the same rational standard.

Wolf's Moderate Impartialism does not imply equality of treatment. Her theory is nevertheless egalitarian, because her two justificatory criteria, she believes, reflect "people's basic moral equality."[49] One formal and more moderate interpretation of impartialism, according to Wolf, is "to act only in ways that one thinks any reasonable person would accept." Her second interpretation is that "one must hold oneself to whatever standards one expects of others."[50] She believes that her first interpretation counts as impartialism, because it treats all persons as having an equal say in setting the standards that all will follow, and her second counts as impartialism, because in setting the standards oneself, one sets them is such a way as to avoid granting oneself or one's friends special privileges.[51] Wolf is attempting to find a middle compromise between the extremes of strict equality and excessive partiality.

Wolf's idea is a promising way of reconciling preferring friends to nonfriends with fundamental human equality, but there are problems in deciding what Moderate Impartialism permits in the examples discussed so far. Moderate Impartialism is supposed to help decide when preferring a friend is a "reasonable standard." All reasonable persons, however, might not agree on one standard for preferring friends. For example, would some impoverished, lowest-caste Indian agree to a standard that friends should help each other rather than helping nonfriends? His extreme poverty severely limits his ability to care for his friends and loved ones. He might reasonably prefer that the more affluent assist in caring for his friends and loved ones, insofar as they are more economically capable of doing so. Wolf supplies no reasons for believing that the Indian's standard is not rational. She supplies no method for testing standards to discover whether all rational persons agree with the Indian's preferences about preferring friends.

Wolf's second criterion, holding ourselves to standards we expect of others, may not help decide this case either. Could she reasonably expect a poverty-stricken, lowest-caste Indian to hold himself to the standards that she holds for herself? To hold him to the standards of affluent Americans hardly "acknowledges and appreciates" his equal "fundamental conditions of well-being and respect."

Moreover, Wolf's Moderate Impartialism is incapable of deciding the Classic Example with Godwin's complication, whether saving the life of a friend or saving the life of some great benefactor of humankind is reasonable. Not all rational persons agree that it is justifiable to save the life of a friend, or that it is justifiable to save some benefactor who can do so much good. Libertarians argue that there is no duty to save the benefactor, because there are no positive duties to help others unless they are voluntarily undertaken. Libertarians' reasonable standard is to save a friend if that is what one wants. Some utilitarians (see the next section) would argue that saving the benefactor is justified because of its good consequences. The good consequences for humanity might outweigh whatever pain and sadness one feels as a result of a friend's death. Utilitarians argue in one direction, and libertarians argue in the other. Both appear rational. Wolf's Moderate Impartialism is therefore an incomplete compromise between strict equality and unfettered partiality, because she has not presented arguments demonstrating which standards reflect rational preferences and which only reflect personal biases.

Wolf might reply that Godwin's complication illustrates the limits of Moderate Impartialism. No "reasonable standard" might exist in this case with which all rational persons could agree. Wolf might argue that rationality is indeterminate in Godwin's complication. Saving a friend and saving a benefactor in these circumstances are rationally undecidable. To defend this reply, she must present arguments to explain why reason is not capable of reaching a conclusion in such a case.

Wolf also might reply that Moderate Impartialism only creates imperfect duties that need not always require action. What is more interesting, however, is Wolf's idea that Moderate Impartialism and preference for friends sometimes permit possibly immoral actions. Her own example is letting friends slip into a concert without paying. Wolf believes that where to draw the line about how much one can do on behalf of a friend is open to "reasonable moral disagreement."[52] While Wolf does acknowledge that reasonable disagreement complicates Moderate Impartialism, she does not seem to appreciate how it undercuts its usefulness.

Marcia Baron also argues that special treatment of friends does not violate the equality implicit in impartiality.[53] Like Gewirth's indirect application of the PGC, which justifies a subprinciple permitting preference for friends, Baron believes that impartiality applies at "the level of rules or principles. . . . It tells us, for instance, that in formulating rules of distribution we are not, as individuals, to give any special weight to our own interests."[54] Baron points out that impartiality should not be applied at the level of day-to-day activities. Like indirect rule utilitarians, who apply the principle of utility through rules, she believes that impartiality should select rules or principles that permit enjoying our friends' company, mourning their losses, or rejoicing in their happiness and successes.

Baron's position resembles Wolf's Moderate Impartialism, though Baron draws very different lines about how much one may do on behalf of one's friend. Baron does not believe that friendship justifies breaking moral rules that require concertgoers to purchase tickets. She disapproves of John Hardwig's outlook:

> If we are close and I know that you care for me and will keep my interests in mind, you don't have to obey the rules for impersonal relationships. You can, for example, invade my privacy by cross-examining me about my personal life, disrupt what I'm doing for no better reason than that you're at loose ends and want someone to talk to, or fail to respect my private property by taking $20 from my wallet, removing a book from my office, or borrowing my car without permission. All that is fine, so long as I am convinced that you care for me.
>
> In fact, it would be insulting or deeply troubling (if not ludicrous) if you *did* obey the rules for impersonal relationships, for freedom from those rules is one of the signs by which we show that we appreciate that the relationship is personal.[55] (emphasis in original)

Baron does not believe that friendship licenses greater latitude in disregarding moral prohibitions. In this regard, she is siding with Cicero and Aristotle against Hardwig.[56] Cicero does not believe that friendship changes the moral quality of actions, and Aristotle believes that goodwill friends try to treat each other in morally exemplary ways. Baron chooses an example in her article that closely resembles the "Jean Valjean" example from chapter 3. She asks about the ethics of pulling strings to get one's son cancer surgery earlier than the normally prescribed two- or three-month waiting period.[57] Baron emphasizes that it is unfair to pull strings, yet most parents would want their son to receive special treatment, and only parents with the strongest moral sense of duty would not try to pull strings if they could. Though Baron does not take a stand on what parents morally ought to do in this case, she thinks that impartiality implies that it would be morally permissible for anyone in the parents' situation to pull strings only if the procedures for scheduling surgery were quite poor. For Baron, fair scheduling procedures are the best resolution of this difficult-to-decide conflict.[58]

Not all forms of friendship create potential kinds of partialist conflicts with impartial morality, on which Wolf and Baron focus. The kinds of special preference shown between friends in Kant's intimacy or female same-sex friendships fail to create conflicts with impartiality. Exchanges of confidences, of private and personal information, and aiming at communion of beliefs are not actions required by impartial morality toward all persons equally. Nor do the demands of these friendships require friends to promote each other's well-being. Similarly, few conflicts with impartial morality arise from Lewis's shared interest friendships or same-sex male friendships where friends pursue their interests with those who share them. Nothing essential to these interest friendships requires well-being promoting actions. Conflicts with impartiality primarily arise from goodwill friendships where friends especially try to promote each other's well-being. Ideal Indian friendships and Aristotle's virtue, utility, and pleasure friendships are the kinds most likely to raise conflicts with impartiality.

It is these last forms of friendship, however, that contain the impersonal pull. Goodwill friendships that most conflict with impartiality and equality have been shown to contain additional reasons to promote the well-being of nonfriends. The pull of these friendships is not one-directional, always and only aimed at friends. Goodwill friendships try to promote and advance objective well-being. As I argued in the second section of chapter 3, where there is no scarcity of time, energy, or resources there is as good reason for promoting a nonfriend's well-being as there is for promoting a friend's. And while scarcity will always exist, there may be times when sufficient assets exist for treating a friend and a nonfriend equally well.

Baron's disagreement with Hardwig on the moral standards within friendship depends on which conception of friendship he has in mind. In Aristotle's ideal equal-virtue friendship, friends share all of their property in common. Hardwig's belief that all is fine in "taking $20 from my wallet, removing a book from my office, or borrowing my car without permission" is consistent with Aristotle's ideal that virtue friends share all property in common. For virtue friends, the car, wallet, and book are not mine but ours, so that no permission is required. Some of the Indian ideal friendships also permit friends to use each other's possessions without prior permission.[59] Most other forms of friendship, including Aristotle's utility- and pleasure-based ones, do not include common property in their objects of friendship. For those other forms, taking friend's property without permission would violate the friendship in addition to violating the morality of private property.

Wolf's Moderate Impartialism and Baron's application of impartiality to the level of rules rather than the level of actions demonstrate that there may be less conflict between friendship and equality than some might suppose. Gewirth's way of applying his universal egalitarian PGC to subprinciples that permit some special preference for friends also reduces possible conflicts. The weakness of all three attempts is the lack of specificity in drawing the line where preference for friends is justified and where it is not. Egalitarians and impartialists need to further refine their principles to better demarcate the areas of morally legitimate preference.

A second reason there may be less conflict between friendship and equality is that the objects of several forms of friendship require actions that do not conflict with universal, egalitarian, or impartial morality. Friendship, as understood by Kant and C. S. Lewis, as well as the same-sex friendships reported by Winstead, does not essentially involve actions that conflict with egalitarian morality. Of course, all friendships may stimulate affection between friends that can motivate preferential actions that possibly conflict with morality. But those conflicts, while real and morally salient, do not arise from the nature of the friendship, they arise as consequences of the friendships. Other relationships, such as teacher-student, that do not essentially involve affection also can sometimes generate affection that may motivate actions that conflict with morality. Nevertheless, the conflict is accidental, not essential. Impartialists and egalitarians who discuss conflicts with friendship need to be better aware of the many different conceptions of friendship.

Finally, goodwill friendships where there is the potential for greatest conflict contain an impersonal pull in addition to a personal pull. Were time and material resources less scarce, there would be good reasons for treating non-friends the same as friends.

WHAT IS SO GOOD ABOUT FRIENDSHIP?

Before examining utilitarian justifications of preference for friends, it will be useful to discuss the goods of friendship. It should not be assumed that what is so good about friendship is equivalent for all of the different conceptions. Each conception has its own goods that may be peculiar to it. Because utilitarian justifications depend on the amount of goods produced, and who it is produced for, utilitarian justifications are conditional on the goods of different conceptions.

Friendship can be valued either intrinsically, extrinsically, or both. What is so good about it? Does friendship benefit the friends primarily, or does it produce benefits for others than the friends themselves? What makes friendship so worthy of being desired?

To value friendship intrinsically is to value it for its own sake and not for anything produced by friendship. If friendship were only valued for its own sake, then there may be no answer to the question "What is so good about friendship?" except that people possess a natural desire to have friends and thus treasure having them.

Cicero tries to prove that people desire friendship for its own sake and not because of any "feebleness" and "inadequacy" or because friendship fulfills some need. As noted in chapter 3, Cicero, like Aristotle, understands friendship as mutual goodwill. Cicero notices that friends are often strongly inclined to do things for the sake of their friend that they would be unwilling to do for themselves. Friends often desire to do favors for each other that they would not have done for themselves.[60] Second, friends are willing to lower or humiliate themselves by asking others to help their friend in circumstances where they would never consider asking for their own help.[61] Cicero concludes that if friendship were only to have extrinsic value because friends valued friendship for what they got out of the friendship, then friends would be unlikely to perform either of these self-sacrificial acts that produce so much disvalue. He believes that the only explanation for friends' willingness to perform such actions is that the intrinsic value of friendship covers the cost, as it were, of performing acts that clearly cause great personal disvalue.

Aristotle also believes in the intrinsic value of friendship, though his two lesser forms based on utility or pleasure are not friendships valued intrinsically.[62] He begins chapter 8 of *Nicomachean Ethics* by arguing that no one would choose to live without friends even if he possessed all other goods. If his term *goods* is broadly interpreted to mean anything that has value, then Aristotle's argument would imply that friendship has intrinsic value. If someone literally possessed all other goods, then friendship could not be valued as a means of producing any other value besides its own. Although Aristotle might not have intended "goods" to carry this broad interpretation, he does believe that friendship has both extrinsic and intrinsic value, so much intrinsic value, perhaps, that no sum of other goods could make life worth living without friends.

Trying to demonstrate intrinsic value is not a difficulty unique to friendship. J. S. Mill confronts the problem of demonstrating intrinsic value in chapter 4 of *Utilitarianism*, where he tries to prove that happiness is the greatest intrinsic value.[63] What must be demonstrated in trying to prove that anything has intrinsic value is that the thing has value, or is valued, in itself and that instrumental reasons or values cannot enter the proof. In order to prove, for example, that knowledge has intrinsic value, the explanation of its value must only depend on knowledge and not on any other value that knowledge produces or causes in the world. Mill's argument for the intrinsic value of happiness reduces to the claim that everyone desires happiness or some component parts of happiness as an end in itself and not as a means to anything else. Just as there are component parts of happiness, according to Mill, there are component parts of friendship, such as trust, shared interest, communion, and reciprocal goodwill, that are desired for their own sake as part of the intrinsic value of friendship.

There are other tests for intrinsic value in addition to Cicero's and Mill's. Recently, T. M. Scanlon has rejected G. E. Moore's and W. D. Ross's famous test for intrinsic value: "that in order to decide whether a thing is intrinsically valuable or not we should imagine a world in which only that thing existed and ask ourselves whether we would judge its existence to be good."[64] Scanlon believes that asking about something's intrinsic value is not to ask, as Moore and Ross do, about what makes some "states of the universe" better than others.[65] Scanlon continues with his own suggestion:

> Now it may be true that the existence of friendship and the pleasures it brings make a world better, but it strikes me as odd to suggest that this is what is central to the value of friendship. . . . What I want to suggest, however, is that the claim that friendship is valuable is best understood as the claim that it is properly valued, that is to say, that the reasons recognized by someone who values friendship are in fact good reasons.[66]

For Scanlon to say that friendship has intrinsic value is to say that people who are capable of becoming friends have good reasons to become friends and to devote their lives to friendship. They have proper reasons to be good friends, to work hard at it, and to choose ways of being friends that are significant and not merely the easiest.[67] Nevertheless, if all of these arguments are correct and friendship has intrinsic value and only intrinsic value, then there would be little to be said about the value of friendship other than that people either have good reasons or strongly desire to have friends.

Friendship also can be valued extrinsically, that is, friendship can be valued because of what it produces or brings about. Friendship can produce good both for the friends themselves and for nonfriends whom the friendship affects. This also is true of the component parts of friendship. While the extrinsic values of friendship are emphasized in this section, nothing in the consideration of friendship's extrinsic value bars also considering friendship as having intrinsic value. Many things, such as knowledge and exercise, like swimming, can be valued both intrinsically because they are enjoyable in themselves and extrinsically because they are the means to something else, such as power or good health. Friendship is no different in this respect.

Philosophers such as R. M. Hare have maintained that friendship has extrinsic value and may produce social benefits for nonfriends that are at least as great as the benefits for the friends themselves.[68] The truth of his claim can adequately be assessed only after examining what the goods of friendship are.

In order to try to answer the question "What is so good about friendship?" the goods of friendship can be divided, perhaps in a not too arbitrary way, into internal and external goods. Internal goods are benefits that primarily obtain for the individuals who are friends. These include what might be called "agent-relative, prudential, or self-interested goods," but the term *internal goods* is preferable, because it does not seem to carry the selfish, egoistic, or self-centered connotations of the other terms. While it is certainly true that several of the internal goods of friendship, such as the ability to rely on one's friend for help in time of need, are self-interested, other internal goods of friendship, such as a feeling of identification with other people or improvement of friends' moral character, do not neatly fit into any self-interested category. Emphasizing this is crucial, because development of moral virtue is considered by both Aristotle and Kant to be among the most valued internal goods of friendship.

External goods are no more identical to moral values than internal goods are equated to the merely prudential or self-interested. External goods include advantages produced by friendship that benefit those other than the friends. Examples of external goods are kindnesses to others performed by someone who because of having a friend has learned to care for persons other than himself, cheerfulness to others exhibited by someone who has friends and is happier with herself, thus affecting how she treats others, or openness to others displayed by someone because friends have learned that other people can be trusted. None of the illustrated external goods should be considered moral values, because they are not morally required. Friendship may ultimately be seen as having value primarily because of the internal rather than the external goods, but that does not warrant concluding that the value of friendship is primarily self-interested rather than moral.

What the goods of friendship are depends on how friendship is conceived. Consider first Aristotle's conception of friendship as the virtue of promoting the good of a friend for the friend's sake in a shared life where friends identify with each other and judge what they possess to be common property.[69] Each friend's life can be enriched through friendship by expanding the domain of possible benefits that can accrue. For example, the goods of one's friend, her good experiences, and perhaps the good that she does are one's own good as well because of the identification between the two and the common property between them.[70] This category of personal enrichment through an expanded domain of benefits occurs without any additional costs beyond the ones involved in establishing and maintaining friendships (and these "costs" may be permeated with pleasure and enjoyment). A friend may, for example, devote a great deal of time and effort to researching and writing a book that is subsequently critically well received. Her well-deserved reward is a good that can be shared by her friend because of his identification with her well-being but without his having to undergo the cost of writing the book himself. It is possible that friendship, as Aristotle conceives of it, is an economically efficient way of advancing one's own well-being, if the investment in friendship is less than the benefits one receives because of the identification with the good of one's friend.

What does this imply about the evil or loss that befalls one's friend? Are they felt as strongly because of the smaller investment? If one's friend is to die, as was Pythias at the hand of an unjust tyrant, to die with him as his friend Damon chose is not to add to the loss, since if one's friend is to die in any case, the loss of his life is identical with losing one's own. If one of them must die, it is from their perspective as though there were two deaths.

It would be a mistake in considering the value of friendship to ignore the obvious internal benefit of friendships, that two are capable of accomplishing much more than one alone. These are clearly benefits of Aristotle's utility friendships, but there is no reason friendships based on equality of virtue cannot produce joint accomplishments as well if they are of the right kind, even though such accomplishments are not part of the object of virtue friendship. Many activities logically must be engaged in with others, for example, having a philosophical conversation, contributing in a liberal manner, or playing chess (doing so against a computer is only a recent phenomenon); other activities, such as building the Acropolis, are as a matter of fact possible only with the assistance of others. One of the greatest sources of good for friends is this ability to cooperate in activities that cannot be accomplished individually.

The goods of friendship provided by a friend are not at all limited to material goods. As one obvious illustration, shared philosophical conversations may not produce great material advantage. Nancy Sherman notes a second nonmaterial way that friends benefit from a shared life.[71] A component of friendship is that friends cooperate in planning the activities in which they jointly engage. Friends must learn what is needed to decide through cooperation what they will do together. This involves honing their reasoning skills, discovering how to compromise, and, in general, learning how to arrive at the jointly made decisions needed to direct their living together. As Aristotle says, " 'when two go together. . .', they are more capable of understanding and act-ing."[72] This resembles the benefits that Rousseau describes when citizens must consider each other in learning to act according to the General Will:

> Then only, when the voice of duty takes the place of physical impulses and right of appetite, does man, who so far had considered only himself finds that he is forced to act on different principles, and to consult his reason before lis-tening to his inclinations.[73]

Controlling inclinations through reason also may promote goods in non-friends, because they are regarded with greater moral respect.

According to Aristotle, the paramount way in which friends promote each others' good is by assisting each other in moral perfection. Friends are to help each other in becoming morally virtuous both by positive instruction and negative correction. This is why Aristotle believes that young people es-pecially need good friends.[74] Friends are uniquely situated to assist each other in virtue because of the more comprehensive (but not for Aristotle, intimate) knowledge that they have of each other and the greater care and concern that they possess for each other. Receiving correction and guidance from someone who is known to have one's best interests at heart is much easier and much more effective than from someone who is more distant and disinterested. In addition, Aristotle believes that each friend will be on good behavior in the presence of his friend because of the importance of his friend's opinion. Be-cause friends believe in each other's virtue and ability, they will give each other encouragement to try to expand and improve upon their abilities and strengths. This faith in a friend's virtue is based on comprehensive knowledge, not on any tenuous abstract assumption of human perfectibility. And, as far as friends know and trust each other, they can take risks that they might be less willing to take were they not able to count on each other's support: risks not only to gain material goods but, more important, risks to develop and grow in character and virtue.

Even though pleasure is not the basis of Aristotle's virtue friendship, virtue friendships are not without pleasure. Besides internal goods of moral enrichment and the perfection of virtue, each friend receives pleasure as a in-ternal good from two sources. The first is the pleasure each friend receives by performing virtuous actions that benefit the other. In this component are both pleasures of agent and pleasures of recipient. As agents, friends enjoy doing good for each other. They find pleasure and satisfaction both in contemplating and in performing actions that benefit their friend. As recipients, pleasure also is produced in one friend who receives good from the other. An act of kindness sometimes may be more pleasurable if received from a friend than from someone who is not; however, a "random act of kindness" may at other times bring great surprise and pleasure. The second source of pleasure is what friends jointly receive from being together, from planning and engaging in shared activities, from conversations, and from the special moments that spontaneously happen.

Augmented pleasure from shared activities may be produced, because some activities are more pleasurable if they are not engaged in individually. Obviously activities such as playing chess are not logically possible without another player. For these activities, partners are essential. Other activities for which the participation of others is not essential, such as watching a glorious sunset, seem, for many, to be more pleasurable if not done in isolation but with friends. The heightened pleasure need not arise from being able to discuss its beauty with a friend or to reminisce about it later, although those too may add to the pleasure. Merely watching it with someone one cares about can significantly augment one's own pleasure. A plausible explanation is that friends desire to share good things with each other, and thus knowing that one's friend is also experiencing this same good adds to one's own pleasure.

Kant's intimacy conception of friendship as a disposition is quite different from Aristotle's. Kant's friendship as a form of intimacy, of mutual sympathy and mutual understanding, need not manifest itself in promoting a friend's good through a shared life. Kant does not even believe that friends must have many common tastes or interests. Moral unity is essential for Kant in order to maintain friendships. As Kant says, friends need not share all or even many interests or professions; what friends must have in common is a moral principle or an outlook on life by which they can evaluate persons, events, and circumstances. This is similar to what Winstead claims about female same-sex friendships. Kantian friends must be concerned about each other and wish each other well, but, quite unlike Aristotle, Kantian friendship does not require that friends spend a great deal of time together or engage in many shared activities. The benefits of true friendship for Kant are first that "Friendship . . . is an aid in overcoming the constraint and the distrust man feels in his intercourse with others, by revealing himself without reserve,"[75] and second that "it is man's refuge in this world from his distrust of his fellows, in which he can reveal his disposition to another and enter into communion with him."[76]

Only through a unified moral outlook could there be a foundation for trust and communion.

The internal goods of friendship for Kant are quite different from the internal goods according to Aristotle. Kantian friendship does not require promoting a friend's good for a friend's sake, nor does Kant's conception of friendship require a shared life that Aristotle believes friendship demands. Because Kant's conception of friendship does not require that friends act to promote each others' good in a shared life, less conflict may be caused with the well-being of nonfriends. Where friends do act with preference toward each other, because of the kinds of actions that friends engage in (e.g., confiding intimate thoughts) their preferential actions will not cause material neglect or harm to nonfriends to the extent that this is possible, according to Aristotle's conception. Kant seems to think of the goods of friendship as a palliative against distrust and constraint. Kant must be assuming, first, that society is an impersonal and perhaps a hostile place where people cannot be trusting and open with each other and, second, that avoiding distress and constraint is a widely held desire.[77] Negatively, friendship removes these two evils, creating a more hospitable climate in which to live. If friendship has positive advantages beyond removing distress and constraint as sources of discomfort, then Kant must be assuming that people also possess positive desires for openness, self-disclosure, and intimacy. The openness and intimacy that constitute friendship, for Kant, permit each friend to "unburden" himself. This is one of the primary internal benefits of friendship, and one that is not likely to adversely affect nonfriends. For many people who have a strong desire or inclination to discuss their thoughts, especially their problems, insecurities, doubts, fears, anxieties, and so on, there may be a need not to live with and confront these on one's own. Young children often confide their problems to their parents (adolescents are another matter), and adults need someone on whom they can rely for this function. Friends are the obvious candidates.

Additional internal goods within friendship result from satisfying desires for openness and intimacy. Frankness and openness in friendship promote more accurate self-awareness. Because intimacy friends, for Kant, can be trusted to be open and frank about each other's actions, beliefs, motives, and attitudes, they give each other an honest evaluation and nonflattering self-image. In addition, friends can be trusted to correct or instruct in those circumstances where it is needed. Such honesty enables a friend to give warning against doing something self-destructive or immoral and to give encouragement to improve one's self-understanding and virtue.

Kant has an important point here about the value of friends. In a competitive world where people are too often concerned only with their own advantage and self-promotion, having someone who is open and honest to both confide in and be guided by is a valuable asset not merely to gain material goods or to act in accordance with duty but to become a person of genuine moral worth. As Kant stresses in *Grounding for the Metaphysics of Morals*, no one can be sure of his own goodwill, because motives of inclination or self-interest may secretly outweigh the motive of duty.[78] Someone may believe that he is acting from a motive of duty but may be deceived because one of the other two motives is actually stronger in the circumstance. A friend is especially capable of assisting in the examination of motives in an honest, a frank, and a sympathetic way that is invaluable in uncovering any heteronomy in the will, because friends are most privy to each other's thoughts and motives.

True intimacy friends, according to Kant, would not use each other as surrogate therapists or become a burden to each other. This is the point of Kant's remark, that friends should not make calls upon friendship or become a burden to each other. Few people are willing to listen to one who is constantly chattering about his insecurities or problems. The foundation of friendship, Kant believes, is knowing that one's friend is disposed to listen and to permit unburdening. Kant assumes that sparingly, only as needed, will a friend actually confide his thoughts about his problems or insecurities. He knows that his friend will be willing to listen, will be sympathetic and understanding, and will be in a special position to offer solace and, perhaps, advice. Friends understand each other well enough not to abuse the other's disposition to listen and assist so as to misuse the relationship. Each friend, in the normal course of the friendship, will not regard his disposition to listen and assist as a chore or burden but rather as something he is most willing and eager to perform as part of his friendship. In fact, a friend will feel hurt if his friend does not come to him with his problems, thinking that any hesitation is an indication of a failure in the friendship.

Consolation and contentment are the primary internal goods of being able to discuss one's problems. People feel relief simply through the activity of discussing fears and insecurities with another person quite independently of any resolution or removal of the problem. Francis Bacon makes a similar point: "A principal *fruit of friendship* is the ease and discharge of the fullness and swellings of the heart, which passions of all kinds do cause and induce."[79] The relief caused by discussion, however, is not the only dividend. A person can, through the activity of discussing his problems, achieve a degree of self-understanding or self-clarification that assists him in his own attempt to assess and resolve the problem. Friends sometimes do not actively contribute to any solution; they provide only an opportunity by listening. Bacon calls this a "second fruit of friendship":

> his wits and understanding do clarify and break up, in the communicating and discoursing with another: he tosseth his thoughts, more easily; He marshalleth them more orderly; He seeth how they look when they are turned into words; finally, he waxeth wiser than himself.[80]

Other times friends can make contributions to finding a solution. Friends are in a much better position than any others to offer clarification or to make suggestions to assist each other in working through problems. The intimate and perhaps comprehensive understanding that friends possess of each other's circumstances, personality, desires, and goals creates a most privileged position to help.

It is now appropriate to discuss the external goods of friendship (i.e., advantages that are produced by friendships for those other than the friends). Friendships are believed to promote what can be called an "anti-egoistic impulse" that propels friends to treat others, first their friends and then nonfriends, as equal human beings whose interests are identified with and given the same consideration as they give their own. People who have friends are more likely, it is alleged, to treat nonfriends better as a consequence of their habit, built out of the experiences learned through friendship, to regard other persons as having equal value and being worthy of equal respect. A person without friends would not have the same anti-egoistic impulse reinforced by many pleasurable experiences of regarding others as equals and deserving of respect. A friendless person might have even less of an impulse or a desire to consider others with the same concern that she considers herself. The shared life that Aristotelian friends experience is believed to reinforce ideas that other people have value and deserve respect, because friendship furnishes each friend with a comprehensive knowledge of the feelings, goals, aspirations, needs, reactions, hopes, fears, and details of another person's life, a person who is discovered to embody distinctively human characteristics. Such comprehensive knowledge is believed to create greater respect and compassion rather than contempt for others. Therefore, people with friends are believed to be willing to help and respect others, even nonfriends, more so than people without any friends.[81]

In an ideal Indian friendship, in contrast, where one friend serves as a mentor and the other is a pupil, equality between all persons may not be learned to the same extent as from an Aristotelian virtue friendship. Reasons may be imbedded in the caste-ridden, hierarchical Indian society to not encourage general equality of respect.

The anti-egoistic influence of friendship, assuming that it exists and is fairly strong, conflicts with the preference that friends feel for each other that disposes them to ignore or actually to harm nonfriends. One may decide to benefit a friend with some unneeded present rather than use those same assets to assist a needy nonfriend. Elizabeth Telfer has argued that benefits for others, which the anti-egoistic disposition produces, more than balance the harm caused by preferring one's friends.[82] R. M. Hare seems to believe that intuitive-level moral rules permitting the preferential treatment of friends will produce, if generally obeyed, optimific results for both friends and society as a whole.[83] Their arguments are examined in the next section.

Friendship's anti-egoistic influence differs from what I have called the "impersonal pull" of friendship. It is the anti-egoistic influence that causes a recognition of others as equal human beings. Telfer and Hare seem to understand its influence as psychological and motivational. Goodwill friendship's impersonal pull is a reason for promoting the good of nonfriends. It depends on recognizing others as relevantly similar humans. To this extent, the impersonal pull depends on recognizing others as human brought about by the anti-egoistic influence or by other means.

Aristotle's belief that friends occupy the same life promoting each other's good and virtue implies that friendships increase the number of virtuous people in the world. This would be of immense benefit to all nonfriends. Virtuous people do not knowingly commit immoral acts or harm others. This is a truism, but if friendship promotes virtue, as Aristotle believes, then nonfriends gain immeasurably from the reduction of vice.

The external goods of Kantian friendship are fewer than the external goods produced according to Aristotle's conception. One primary good for others, assuming Aristotle's conception, is the joint effort of friends to promote each other's virtue, which implies for Aristotle that friends will act more virtuously toward others. Less humanly caused evil would therefore exist in the world. In contrast, Kant's friends promote each other's virtue, not in the sense of promoting actions according to the requirements of duty but by promoting the right motive for action. Kant's discussion of intimacy friendship assumes that each friend will act according to the requirements of the categorical imperative (i.e., each of them will fulfill what Kant calls the "juridical duty" to act rightly). Fulfilling one's juridical duty is not morally virtuous for

Kant, because one need only act as is required by the categorical imperative; one is not required to act from the motive of duty.[84] Moral virtue in friends can be promoted, because they are privy to the kind of information about each other that can best assist them in examining their motives for action to ensure that they act from a sense of duty rather than from self-interest or inclination. Friends can thereby assist each other in being morally virtuous (i.e., to do their duty from a sense of duty), but no additional benefits will accrue to others, because the friends are only supporting each other in acting from the right motive and not in acting in the right way.

Because Kant presents so many arguments to separate the motives of duty from the probability that someone will act according to what duty requires, as well as arguments to separate morality from empirical or psychological evidence, there are good reasons for believing that the way in which friends enable each other to be more virtuous does not affect their conforming to the moral law. As Kant analyzes the relevance of motives in *Grounding*, actions that are contrary to duty are separated even before he considers the three motives to act consistently with the imperatives of duty.[85] Moreover, Kant insists in *The Metaphysical Elements of Justice* that a person can fulfill all of his juridical duties but still lack moral virtue.[86] Thus the moral virtue that friendship promotes is independent of actually acting according to duty and dependent on acting according to the morally right motive. Therefore, promoting the moral virtue of friends probably will not increase the external goods of friendship.

Though increased moral virtue may not affect external action, it is possible that people with friends, who can unburden themselves and avoid constraint or hostility, are less likely to violate juridical duties. Also, perhaps, the greater self-understanding and self-awareness that are outgrowths or fruits of Kantian friendship will reduce the likelihood that friends act contrary to duty. It is difficult to estimate how probable these conditional effects of friendship are, or how great the external benefits might be. In any case, both sets of effects need to be regarded as possible external goods of friendship.

The goods of Montaigne's fusion friendships primarily benefit the friends. It is difficult to generalize about any effects of fusion friendships on either friends or nonfriends, because the basis and objects of fusion friendships are so idiosyncratic. Insofar as fusion friends hold nothing back from each other, the benefits of friendship might resemble the goods of Kant's intimacy friendship and the communal goods of Aristotle's shared life friendship. For C. S. Lewis's shared interest friendship, the goods of friendship will primarily result from the common quest. A common interest in "dominoes or white mice" will have benefits different from a common interest in philosophy or literature.[87]

Utilitarianism, unlike the Golden Rule, impartiality, or the categorical imperative, does not presuppose a fundamental equal dignity of all persons. Henry Sidgwick expresses this idea well:

> For Utilitarianism is sometimes said to resolve all virtue into universal Benevolence: it does not, however, prescribe that we should love all men equally, but that we should aim at Happiness generally as our ultimate end, and so consider the happiness of any one individual as equally important with the equal happiness of any other, as an element of this total; and should distribute our kindness so as to make this total as great as possible, in whatever way this result may be attained.[88]

Equal treatment of people is only required if treating them equally results in the greatest total happiness; but if other distributions produce a greater total, then they would be morally preferable. It is morally legitimate to treat friends with preferential consideration, according to the utilitarian principle, whenever such treatment results in the greatest total possible happiness or, more generally, when preference for friends is optimific.

Sidgwick gives several credible reasons for believing that acting with special preference toward friends results in greater total happiness. First, friends expect to be treated with special preference and would perhaps suffer more acutely if they were not.[89] Also, because friends have better knowledge of each other and greater sympathy is felt between them, they are better able to promote happiness in each other than in people about whom they know less and care about less.[90] Finally, Sidgwick argues that greater total social happiness would result from special preference toward friends because humans are in fact psychologically constituted so that they are only capable of affection for a few other persons and, furthermore, that most people are "not in a position to do much good to more than a very small number of persons."[91]

Act-utilitarianism decides whom to save in the Classic Example by examining the consequences of each alternative and choosing the one that is optimific, producing the greatest total happiness. Which decision is morally right depends on what can be known about each of the two who are in danger. For example, if little or nothing is known about the nonfriend and the effects of her loss of life, it might be safely assumed that others—her friends, relatives, acquaintances, and colleagues—might miss her and feel pain over her loss. Similar reasons could be given about the loss of one's friend. Thus without specific knowledge to the contrary, one might have to assume that the consequences from saving either friend or nonfriend would be roughly equal.

There may be one relevant difference, however: the consequences of saving a friend might be better, causing less anticipated suffering than the consequences of saving a nonfriend. For example, one's own pain might be significantly greater knowing that it was possible to save a friend and that her loss was one's own choice because one saved a nonfriend instead. So where there is ignorance about the specifics of any nonfriend's life, this "rule of thumb" might function as a plausible guide for a utilitarian and permit choosing to save a friend.

Knowledge of important specifics of a nonfriend's life could radically alter any decision. If, as in Godwin's complication, the nonfriend were capable of greatly benefitting humankind and any potential benefits from saving a friend were far smaller, then the utilitarian decision clearly ought to be to save the nonfriend. One's pain over losing a friend plus any greater pain resulting from its being one's choice not to save her would be overwhelmed by the still greater happiness to the greater number of persons who would benefit by saving a nonfriend benefactor. In contrast, if saving a friend were to produce better overall consequences, then those better consequences, but not the friendship, would justify saving a friend.

Utilitarian explanations are felt to be unsatisfactory for the same reason the assumption of equal dignity and worth is: the utilitarian fails to take seriously personal attachments and relations. It is not friendships but the value of the consequences for the utilitarian that accounts for the rightness of these acts. Utilitarians may be guilty of underestimating the moral significance of friendship and of caring for another.

No special duties of friendship exist for act–utilitarians if the utilitarian principle is literally interpreted. Sometimes a greater total happiness results from helping those who are not friends, especially in circumstances where, like lowest-caste Indians, nonfriends are much less well off than are friends. Special duties to friends receive only conditional support from an act-utilitarian principle. Special beneficence to friends or special duties would only be justified in specific circumstances where acting specially, differentially, or preferentially to friends results in greatest total happiness or is optimific. In other circumstances where greater total happiness would result from no special, differential, or preferential beneficence, act–utilitarianism implies that no such special duties exist.

Sidgwick's reasons show why people are more likely to produce greater happiness by favoring their friends in many situations. Greater affection, greater knowledge, limited ability, and heightened expectations all support the production of greater happiness for friends in these situations. The mistake, however, is to consider these special duties. For an act-utilitarian, there are no special duties at all but merely an identifiable class of circumstances in which the preferential treatment of friends has a greater tendency to produce greater total happiness or total good. Act-utilitarianism does not imply a special duty to friends. For an act-utilitarian, there is only one duty—to produce the greatest happiness. Factors simply exist because of the relation of friendship. These factors have a tendency to augment the quantity of happiness or goodness in predictable ways.

Neera Kapur Badhwar argues that there is a deeper inconsistency between act-utilitarianism and special preference toward friends. For example, utilitarianism would not permit respecting a friend as an end in herself:

> In an end friendship, one loves the friend as an essential part of one's system of ends and not solely, or even primarily, as a means to an independent end—career advancement, amusement, philosophical illumination, or greater happiness in the universe. . . . Nor can she be replaced by a more efficient means to one's ends or abandoned on their achievement, for it is not as a means that one loves her.[92]

Badhwar is correct in thinking that friendship requires treating friends as ends in themselves. Nevertheless, her criticism of utilitarianism is mistaken, because it is based on an overly narrow understanding of valuation.

A utilitarian such as Sidgwick may believe that special preference for friends is justified because acting with preference for friends is generally a means to good consequences. But nothing in the logic of utilitarianism precludes utilitarians from valuing friends as ends in themselves. There is no internal inconsistency in valuing friends intrinsically and also valuing them instrumentally as a means of promoting other values. This point is ignored by Badhwar. She assumes that a contradiction or an inconsistency arises in valuing something for its own sake and in valuing it as a means to some other good. Both Aristotle and Mill, neither a neophyte in logic, argue that something may be desired both as a means to some other end and as an end in itself.

For example, someone may swim every day before work both because he values swimming as a means to good health and because he enjoys swimming for its own sake. In normal circumstances, both valuations are consistent, because swimming is normally a means of maintaining health. There may be exceptional circumstances where swimming is not a means to health, such as when the swimmer catches a cold or develops a ruptured spinal disk. In such circumstances, his valuing swimming as an end in itself conflicts with his valuing swimming as a means to health.

Two aspects of the logic of this conflict need to be carefully distinguished and not confused. The first aspect is that to value something intrinsically as an end in itself is not equivalent to valuing it as an overriding, a supreme, or an absolute value. The swimmer may value his family or friends more than swimming, even though he values swimming as an end in itself. There is nothing illogical in valuing swimming as an end in itself and valuing other things more than swimming. If, in exceptional circumstances, swimming is not a means to health, and as a result the swimmer prefers, over all and on balance, not to swim in order to regain or preserve his health, then it does not logically follow that he does not value swimming for its own sake. In the case of the cold, he may only temporarily have to give up swimming until the cold is cured. Even if a ruptured disk permanently prevented him from swimming, he could continue to value it in itself and wish he were still capable of swimming. That his valuing health may override his valuing swimming need not imply that he no longer values swimming for its own sake.

The second aspect concerns whether the decision to swim or not to swim is made within a single value system or a system containing plural values. A utilitarian such as G. E. Moore, who believes that there are many values, would weigh the intrinsic value of swimming along with other various competing and complementary values, both intrinsic and instrumental.[93] No logical inconsistency need arise in valuing swimming for its own sake and in possessing other different intrinsic values as well. In such a multi-value system, if the swimmer decides to forego swimming because of his health, then he may feel a loss and regret over the unrealized value, but he is not inconsistent.

That the two aspects of the conflict are logically distinct can be established by understanding that even a single-value consequentialism does not logically preclude valuing a number of things as ends in themselves. The theory of value, defined by David Gauthier's preference satisfaction as an illustration of a single-value system, need not imply that there can be only one thing that is valued for its own sake.[94] There does not seem to be any reason the intrinsic value of something such as swimming cannot be compared to other values, either intrinsic or instrumental, as they are located along a single scale of preference satisfaction value measurement. Because the swimmer may sometimes prefer not to swim when he has a cold so that he may quickly recover does not imply that he does not still value swimming for its own sake. There may be many, as good or better, means to health that he could choose but does not pursue as a result of the intrinsic value that he places on swimming. A single-value consequentialist need not adopt a position that denies that many things can be valued in themselves. Perhaps Bentham believed that pleasure is the single intrinsic value, but there is nothing in the logic of consequentialism that would necessitate such a narrow understanding of how humans place values on things.

An incompatibility between act utilitarianism and friendship similar to Badhwar's is proposed by Troy A. Jollimore in his book *Friendship and Agent-Relative Morality*. He argues that "the agent is often unable to act in accordance with the demands of particular personal relationships whose expression is essential to the existence of mutually recognized relationships such as friendships."[95] Jollimore believes that "in order for a friendship to exist the feelings [of affection] must be brought out into the open; they must, that is, be expressed through action."[96] Act utilitarianism, he contends, prevents friends from expressing their feelings of friendship for each other through their actions. One's feelings cannot play a significant role in determining actions for an act utilitarian, according to Jollimore, because acting to benefit a friend cannot be an expression of one's feelings but only one's belief that it is optimific.[97] Jollimore is making a mistake similar to Badhwar's by oversimplifying human motivation. For example, just as I can value something both as having value in itself and as a means to something else, my actions can express both my beliefs and my feelings. Suppose that some action required of me by act-utilitarianism does not benefit my friend. If I do what is morally required of me, that does not imply that my affectionate feelings of friendship played no significant role in my decision or action. I may greatly regret having to ignore my friend in this case where I am obligated to benefit others. My decision may have been painfully difficult. What is more, I can express my friendship feelings by acting in ways that clearly express my pain and regret over having to ignore my friend because of duty. This is just what friends would expect from each other in such circumstances. Jollimore overlooks the many ways that feelings of friendship can find expression.

Act-utilitarianism is therefore not incompatible with the special treatment of friends to the same extent as impartiality, the Golden Rule, or Kant's categorical imperative, but special treatment of friends does not constitute an independent special duty. Justifiable special preferential treatment is only an instance of an act-utilitarian duty to produce the greatest total happiness.

The effects on happiness produced by acts of preference for friends vary with the goods of friendship. Sidgwick's reasons for people being more likely to produce greater happiness by favoring their friends seem to presuppose Aristotle's reciprocal goodwill friendships. Goodwill friendships based on virtue, where the friends share their lives and goods in common, best fulfill Sidgwick's conditions that friends know each other well, care about each other, and expect each other's goodwill. Aristotle's virtue friends are in an excellent position to produce happiness for each other. To the extent that Aristotle's less-than-ideal goodwill friends also know each other well and care for each other, they too are in a favorable position to create happiness; but to the extent that pleasure-based friendships are short lived, or that utility-based friendships do not require comprehensive knowledge, then less happiness for the friends may result. Aristotelian virtue friends are less apt to cause happiness for themselves at the expense of nonfriends than are utility friends or pleasure friends who may lack the high moral character of some virtue friends. Only when preferring each other produces more happiness are friends justified by act-utilitarianism in favoring each other. If preferring nonfriends produces greater happiness, even taking into account the greater disappointment that friends will experience, then act-utilitarianism will not justify preference for friends.

The object of Kant's intimacy friendship has fewer effects on the happiness of friends and nonfriends. A disposition of self-revelation leading to communion has less of a tendency to produce unhappiness in nonfriends as a result of friends' preference for each other than does Aristotle's goodwill friendships. The ways in which Kant's intimacy friends express special preference for each other are unlikely to adversely affect the happiness of nonfriends, so that more acts of preferring friends may be justified than would be justified for Aristotle's goodwill friendships, where the adverse effects on nonfriends may be greater. Kant's friends are not likely to spend their resources on trivial presents for each other, while others who are in greater need can be helped. Still, act-utilitarianism implies that special preference for Kant's intimacy friends, however it is expressed, is justifiable only in circumstances where it is optimific.

Act-utilitarian justifications for preferring friends to nonfriends are thought to be too weak, because they fail to give appropriate justificatory weight to the "specialness" of friends. The consequences, not the relation, make preferring friends right when it is right. It is not the friendship relation in itself that possesses right-making characteristics. Additionally, utilitarian justifications are thought to be weak because preference for friends fails to get an absolute or unconditional justification. Preferring a friend is not right absolutely, but only on the condition that it produces the best overall consequences.

Though act-utilitarian justifications may be conditional and dependent on the consequences of preferring friends to nonfriends, they are not in conflict with special preference for friends to the degree that egalitarian, Kantian, and impartial justifications are. Preferring friends, according to an act-utilitarian, does not violate any presupposition of fundamental human equality, and as a result it does not stand in need of a special justification other than the type required for any (and all) actions. Act-utilitarian justifications also may be stronger than egalitarian, Kantian, or impartial justifications, inasmuch as preferring friends for act-utilitarians is right because of the good that it produces. As Sidgwick argues, special preference for friends frequently produces more good overall than acting without special preference. And, for Sidgwick, the special expectations of the friends themselves about each other's preferential goodwill explain some of the better consequences.

An act-utilitarian justification of preferring friends is not as open or apparently unrestricted as many libertarian justifications and so might appear weaker. For the libertarian, however, it is not the "specialness" of the friendship that justifies preferring friends to nonfriends but the "specialness" of each person's freedom to act for whatever reasons he or she prefers. Freedom, not friendship, is what justifies special preference. A libertarian deciding what to do in the Classic Example would be as justified in preferring persons with crimson hair to persons with flaxen hair as she would be in preferring friends to nonfriends. Libertarian justifications are no more focused on friendship than are act-utilitarian justifications. For the libertarian, freedom provides justification for choice; for the act-utilitarian, good consequences. Libertarian justifications are not necessarily more unrestricted than act-utilitarian justifications. Depending on the specifics of a libertarian's thesis, an individual's freedom to prefer her friends is limited to acts that do not interfere with the freedom of others, to acts and omissions that do not adversely affect the freedom of others, or to acts or omissions that do nothing to reduce freedom.[98] "Acts or omissions that do not adversely affect the freedom of others" define a more restricted range of permissible action than "acts that do not interfere." Act-utilitarian optimific consequences may or may not define a less restricted range of permissible preference for friends. It all depends on how libertarianism is interpreted, and on the peculiarities of the circumstances.

There is an additional way that friendship has good consequences for non-friends, which needs to be discussed. I have called it the "anti-egoistic" tendency of friendship. The anti-egoistic tendency of friendship, assuming it to exist and to be fairly strong, conflicts with the preference that friends feel for each other that disposes them to ignore or actually to harm nonfriends. While one may decide to benefit a friend with some unneeded present rather than use those same assets to assist a needy nonfriend, Telfer has argued that the good for others, which the anti-egoistic tendency produces, more than balances any harm caused by preferring one's friends. According to Telfer, friendship

> promotes the general happiness by providing a degree and kind of considera-
> tion for others' welfare which cannot exist outside it, and which compensates
> by its excellence for the "unfairness" of the unequal distribution of friendship.
> For even those who have no friends are (we may suppose) better off than they
> would be if there were no such thing as friendship, since the understanding de-
> veloped by it and the mutual criticism involved in it will improve the way
> friends deal with people outside the relationship.[99]

That friendship has "general serviceability to society" arises because friends learn to care for and identify with others besides themselves.[100] Telfer's idea is that people with friends identify with and care for others. Kantian friends, with their knowledge of each other's intimate lives, would similarly acquire compassion and respect for nonfriends. Kant, in *Lectures on Ethics*, does argue that friendship produces this anti-egoistic benefit for nonfriends.[101] People with friends are therefore believed to be willing to help and respect others, even nonfriends, more so than people without any friends.[102] Friendship's anti-egoistic tendency is weakest in C. S. Lewis's shared interest friendships and in same-sex male friendships, discussed by Winstead. Since the objects of these friendships are external interests and activities, little may be learned about the details of others' lives. There may be little reason to consider others human, or to compassionately identify with them.

Even with its anti-egoistic tendency and impersonal pull, any tendency to benefit nonfriends can be eroded by the strong desire of friends to benefit each other. Friendship, in its essence, is partial and not universal. A friend is someone who is treated with preference to others. Though goodwill friendships do pull friends toward helping nonfriends, in circumstances where nonfriends may need or deserve the assets more than friends do, the partiality inherent in friendship may result in nonfriends being harmed and not receiving what they deserve.

It is interesting to speculate in this context whether family or kinship bonds might have a stronger, anti-egoist tendency than does friendship. Only Lewis believes that the number of possible friends is large. Both Aristotle and Kant note that it is not likely that someone will have more than a few friends. For Montaigne, there can be only one friend. The number of others cared for and identified with as a result of friendship is quite small. In contrast, bonds of family and kinship, if those related not only by blood but also by marriage are considered, may extend care and identification to a much greater number of people. In addition to the relatives of one's spouse, there would arise many relatives gained through the marriage of one's children, grandchildren, siblings, cousins, nieces, and nephews who become part of an extended family with whom one identifies and feels concern. Because kinfolk are not voluntarily chosen to the same extent that friends are, kinship may teach greater tolerance for others who possess a variety of divergent characteristics.

Special preferences of friendship are believed to be explained more coherently by other forms of utilitarianism, sometimes called "rule," "indirect," or "conditional" utilitarianism. One plausible example is illustrated in R. M. Hare's *Moral Thinking*. Hare distinguishes between two levels of moral thinking. The intuitive level, which is the first level, involves using socially accepted prima facie principles to guide one's actions in ordinary situations. The second level, critical thinking, is the level of thinking where the correct prima facie principles are chosen by society for use and acceptance in intuitive moral thinking.[103] Hare's and Gewirth's arguments resemble each other in that the utilitarian principle justifies society's "subprinciples" for everyday intuitive moral thinking.[104] Without explaining the details of Hare's reasoning, suffice it to say that the critical level of thinking employs utilitarianism to select the prima facie principles for society (i.e., subprinciples that have the best consequences for society are selected for use at the intuitive level of moral thinking). Society would teach these prima facie principles to its members as the best principles by which to guide their actions and, importantly, members of the society would learn to follow such principles because they are believed to be the morally right ones. It is essential to Hare's argument that these prima facie principles are followed because they are believed to be right. Hare expects that members of society will be taught these principles as children and thus grow up to believe intuitively that these principles are the right ones to follow.

Hare actually cites the example of loyalty to family, which applies equally well to friends, as an illustration of how his two levels of moral thinking operate. His distinction shows how one should reason morally. Members of society would be taught that acting with special preference for friends is the right thing to do in most, but not all, situations. Hare argues that in our actual world, intuitions of preference for family and friends are a good thing, because they do, by and large, produce the best consequences.[105] For Sidgwick's reasons, discussed earlier, a great deal of pleasure and happiness is produced when friends (and family members) take special care of each other rather than trying to care for humanity as a whole. Intuitions of preference for friends will be taught and reinforced with their legitimacy sanctioned by society's moral principles. Members of society will believe that friendship (or family) justifies preferential treatment.

Hare considers possible counterinstances, where acting on prima facie principles of special preference for friends does not produce better consequences. He notes that society's prima facie principles have built-in exceptions that are understood as part of the principle. "Counterinstances" are not built-in exceptions but possible cases where following the principle (exceptions and all) has bad consequences. Hare argues that even when one suspects that one is in such an exceptional situation, on the intuitive level one still ought to follow the prima facie principles taught by society. These principles generally are good and wise to follow, even in suspected counterinstances, because one may not know before one acts all that one would need to know in order to reasonably judge that what one confronts is a legitimate counterinstance to the intuitive-level prima facie principles.[106] Further, one is also likely to be biased in one's own favor, even though one tries hard to be fair and objective. Hare believes that only in the rarest of circumstances should members of society resort to the critical level of thinking. Thus in the Classic Example, Hare would argue that one's friend ought to be saved. The socially taught prima facie moral principles that friends may be preferred to nonfriends would justify saving one's friend. The necessity of making a quick decision about who to save precludes "suspecting a counterinstance," because sufficient information may not be available for thinking that it is a "legitimate exception to the intuitive level prima facie principles." Godwin's complication that the nonfriend can benefit humanity would not be, for Hare, one of the legitimate exceptions that society recognizes to its prima facie principles. Society would not build in that exception at the critical level because of the difficulty of predicting with certainty good utilitarian consequences.[107] Were there sufficient time to discover who the nonfriend is (perhaps because it is obvious) and accurately assess information about his potential beneficence, then saving him would be justified, according to Hare, but these circumstances are so beyond one's experiences that it is difficult to know whether saving great benefactors would be one of society's built-in exceptions.

Hare's variant of utilitarianism avoids the conflict found between friendship and equal human dignity, because his utilitarianism is not grounded on fundamental human equality. Special preference for friends and duties to care for family rather than humanity as a whole is justified on Hare's critical level of moral thinking only if a society that teaches such prima facie duties of friendship to its members would produce greater overall good than would be produced by teaching some other prima facie moral principles. The difficulty in calculating the consequences of such teaching is, of course, one of the primary problems that Hare's arguments must confront.

Hare's arguments seem to be addressing Aristotelian conceptions of friendship. Activities that are the objects of Lewis's conceptions of friendship do not raise as great a potential conflict with utilitarianism. Pursuing common interests as the object of friendship, as Lewis understands friendship, does not supply friends with reasons for preferring each other's good to the good of nonfriends. Affection between friends may arise and cause feelings of preference, but affection between friends is not, for Lewis, an essential component of friendship.

For much the same reasons, Hare's arguments do not seem to be addressed to a Kantian intimacy conception of friendship. Intimacy friendship's objects are not activities that are likely to adversely affect the well-being of nonfriends. Kant's need friendship, in contrast, does contain the kind of preference for friends that Hare's moral theory explains. Prima facie social principles permitting friends to cooperate in procuring the necessities of life would have good consequences in the primitive conditions that Kant believes give rise to need friendship. Everyone might be better off if groups of friends worked together in providing necessities than they would were the rules to require everyone to work equally with everyone else. (Imagine trying to hunt with a huge mob.) Friends looking after each other produce better overall consequences than everyone looking after everyone, though, as Hare points out, exceptions may well exist.

The difficulty that Hare's justification of preference for friends confronts arises from calculating the consequences of such teaching. The calculations required by his theory are far more complex than calculations required by act-utilitarianism that themselves are not at all simple. Act-utilitarians must calculate the consequences into the foreseeable future of each possible alternative action for all who happen to be affected. Alan Donagan, with some humor, points out that "Utilitarians sometimes attempt to show that the calculations their theory calls for are neither as complex nor as difficult as their critics make out. Yet what ought to astonish readers of their work is neither the complexity nor the difficulty of utilitarian calculations, but their absence."[108]

Hare's theory requires calculations that are far more complex. To know that a particular prima facie rule permitting preference for friends is morally justified by having the best possible consequences requires comparing it, with its built-in exceptions, to all possible alternative rules permitting preference for friends with their different built-in exceptions. The consequences of most everyone following these rules somehow will have to be calculated. Also to be taken into account in the calculations will be the effects of prima facie friendship preference rules on the other prima facie moral rules of society, both actual and possible. Calculations are further complicated by a variety of different possible baselines for comparison.[109]

In the Classic Example, in order to apply Hare's theory, a number of possible built-in exceptions to preferring one's friend would have to be considered. A number of different possible prima facie rules might compete with each other by specifying different levels of potential beneficence to humankind on which to build in exceptions. The consequences of each of these rules would have to be calculated for society as a whole over some foreseeable future. It is doubtful that there ever could be confidence that just the right prima facie rule had been selected balancing the bonds of friendship with the benefits to society. And even if at some time it were believed that the right rule had been chosen, there could be little confidence that the rule still had optimific consequences, as societies continually change. Hare's calculations would be complicated, perhaps beyond the limits of possibility, because different conceptions of friendship have potentially different consequences.

Utilitarianism and libertarianism permit greater preference for friends than do external moral principles based on fundamental human equality. This should not be surprising. Human equality, as a foundation for moral principles, implies greater equal treatment for everyone than do the foundations of libertarianism and utilitarianism. Kant's categorical imperative seems to justify the least preference for friends in the sense of advancing friends' well-being ahead of nonfriends. Egalitarian and impartial attempts to reconcile preferring friends with presuppositions of human equality reach some accommodation through subprinciples, but their problem lies in working out the details of when preference is justified and when it is not. It is not at all clear how egalitarian or impartial subprinciples can be made sufficiently specific to guide decisions about legitimate preference. Utilitarians do not fare much better in providing subprinciples and giving guidance for when preferring friends is justified. Judging which utilitarian subprinciples permitting preference for friends have the best consequences confronts calculations of perhaps insurmountable complexity. Even trying to judge which particular act of preference has the best consequences frequently requires complex calculations.

Kant's intimacy friendship and Winstead's same-sex female friendships pose the least justificatory problem. The objects of these friendships, exchanging private thoughts and confidences, require actions that are much less likely to conflict with liberty, equality, or utility than are the objects of goodwill friendships. Goodwill friendships, where preference for friends requires promoting the other's well-being, sometimes can harm nonfriends, infringe upon their liberty, or disrespect their equality. Although goodwill friendships contain an impersonal pull, they also sometimes provide strong motives for ignoring nonfriends' legitimate moral claims. Aristotle's virtue friendship, where the object of friendship is living together and sharing all goods in common, has the greatest potential conflict with egalitarian and utilitarian principles. The shared external interests that Lewis believes are the objects of friendship also may create fewer conflicts with equality, though spending a lot of resources on "dominoes or white mice" may not advance utility. The degree of conflict and the difficulty of its resolution therefore depend on the various conceptions of friendship, in addition to the moral theories.

FIVE

CONCLUSIONS

_____

FRIENDSHIPS AND PREFERENCES

ON MORAL KNOWLEDGE

MORALLY JUSTIFYING preference for friends is complicated not only by the existence of a variety of different conceptions of friendship, each with its own internal expectations about how friends treat each other, but also by one's ignorance of which moral principle is the right one to use. Deciding when preference for friends is morally justifiable requires knowing which moral principle is the best one to use in making moral decisions. I am a foundationalist to this extent. In chapter 4, I examined how preference for friends is implied by, or is in contradiction to, various moral principles. I believe that valid inferences were drawn from these principles about preference for friends. An act–utilitarian, for example, believes that preferring friends to nonfriends is morally justified, if acts of preference produce more good than any other alternative. Other moral principles have different implications about when preference for friends is morally justifiable. Moral principles grounded on fundamental human equality permit less preference for friends than do libertarian or utilitarian moral principles. Because these and other principles arrive at different implications about preference for friends, some way of choosing between them eventually must be found.

Justifications for preferring friends can only be as firmly grounded as the moral principle on which they are based. Intuitions are not a sufficient moral justification. First, they are too culturally dependent. Second, it is difficult to explain why intuitions should have epistemic priority over good reasons or arguments: intuitions are merely strongly held beliefs for which one can give no reasons in support of their truth.

My own moral point of view is an amalgam for which, I sometimes fear, no possible coherent set of grounds may be possible. Kant's argument for fundamental human equality, what I call his "transcendental deduction of human dignity," leads me to believe that all humans are in some important way equal and should be so respected. But fundamental human equality also is compatible with several categories of unequal treatment. What they are exactly, and how they are justified, is beyond my knowledge at this moment.

I also believe that social practices such as friendship are justified by their socially good consequences. If having friends and sometimes acting with preference for them compared to nonfriends did not generally have good consequences, then friendship and preferring friends would not be morally right. Analogously to promising, friendship must produce benefits if it is to be morally justified. Were the consequences of friendship harmful to society overall, then friendship would be something society should do without.

Finally, I believe that one of the most important ways that fundamental human equality manifests itself is through individual autonomy. Rational adults should be free to determine their own good and be free to pursue that good in a way that is both compatible with others' equal rights to do the same and compatible with the overall good of society. Kant's transcendental deduction of human dignity is grounded on each person's presupposing her own intrinsic value as the only possible explanation for the value of satisfying her wants and desires. Human dignity is meaningless, unless each person is free to pursue her self-chosen value goals (within moral limits).

I cannot provide a coherent explanation of how these disparate, potentially conflicting moral criteria can fit together in one justificatory principle, nor have I found anyone else who has given them adequate justification. Until some rationally justified moral principle gains philosophical acceptance, the best that can be offered by understanding whether friendship and preference for friends is morally justifiable is to follow the procedure that I have undertaken here. A great deal can be known about the compatibility of different friendship conceptions with a variety of moral principles. Such knowledge is the finest possible, given our continuing disagreements over the foundations of morality.

ON VARIOUS CONCEPTIONS

A variety of different conceptions of friendship exists and has exerted influence, some stronger and others weaker, on philosophical discussions. Clearly no single, dominant conception captures something that might be considered the essence of friendship. Although there are similarities, overlaps, and family resemblances, important differences exist that have significant moral and nonmoral implications. At the extreme, there is no agreement whether friends should always treat each other better than nonfriends. Friends, according to John Hardwig, are expected to tolerate immoral behavior toward each other to a greater extent than they should tolerate immorality from nonfriends, while in contrast, Neera Kapur Badhwar argues that friends should act with ideal justice and benevolence toward each other.[1] Additional disagreement arises about whether friends should be more or less forgiving of each other when harm is caused.

I have shown that conceptions of friendship vary according to differences in their natures, objects, and bases. In addition to the three bases recognized since Aristotle, friendships can be based on other grounds such as need, affection, or common interests. While for Aristotle the common nature of friendship is reciprocal goodwill, intimacy and communion are additional examples of relationships understood as friendships. As objects of friendship, intimacy is a modern addition to Greek ideals of external virtuous action.

Questions remain to be answered about assessing the adequacy to one's experience of these diverse conceptions of friendship. Take Montaigne's ideal, that friends create so complete a union that all differences between them vanish. Modern feminist understandings of friendship, such as Marilyn Friedman's, contend that friends must maintain their own individuality within friendship and not lose it.[2] Or, as another illustration of the wide range of differences, consider Aristotle's ideal equal virtue friendship in contrast to the third Indian ideal friendship, which believes that inequality is needed to avoid the competition and envy inherent within friendship.[3]

The extent to which friendship requires any minimal morality that friends must fulfill toward each other remains unsettled. While Aristotle maintains that virtue friends have to be good (at least on some minimal level), he does not say that pleasure or utility friends must be good as well. C. S. Lewis also is silent on this goodness issue. Dean Cocking and Jeanette Kennett contend that a "true and good" friendship permits friends to engage in significantly immoral acts to benefit friends.[4] Utility friends must at least be sufficiently reliable to live up to their virtual agreement to be useful to each other, and Kant's intimacy friends must be sufficiently trustworthy to receive private, personal information without fear of disclosure.

Other variations exist between conceptions of friendship that complicate assessment by comparison of ideals of friendship to one's actual experiences or intuitions. While many philosophers who analyze friendship believe that ideal friendship only occurs between equals, unlike the third Indian ideal, these philosophers do not agree with each other about what constitutes equality between friends.[5] How to compare our experiences and intuitions of actual friendships with conceptions about equality in friendship is difficult to determine.

Conceptions of friendship also differ regarding the number of friends it is possible to have at any given time. Montaigne believes only one friend, Aristotle believes a few friends, and Lewis believes that many friends are not only possible but also desirable.

Intimacy, which plays such an important role in Kantian and same-sex female friendships receives no mention from Aristotle, and it almost seems banned from friendship, by C. S. Lewis. Philosophers such as Lawrence Blum include intimacy in a contemporary Aristotelian conception of shared-life friendship without mentioning that it never was a part of Aristotle's original conception.[6] It is not clear whether friendships, as Blum understands Aristotle, ever really exist. Trying to include too many requirements in an ideal of friendship, as I argued in chapter 2, makes ideal friendship too difficult to achieve and thus less relevant to one's actual life.

In addition to these disagreements, controversial issues about friendship exist that have not been discussed so far in this book. Some believe that true friendships (whatever they are) last forever, and that true friends never break or abandon their friendship. Little evidence is ever given in support of "true" friendship's astonishing permanence. Aelred of Rievaulx turns true friendship's permanence into a definition by agreeing with St. Jerome, who claims, "A friendship which can cease to be was never true friendship."[7] Still, the absence of evidence and the lack of any plausible methods for verifying these extravagant permanence claims have not stopped them from remaining widely accepted.

College students (at least in my classes) are perennially concerned about whether it is possible to be friends with a person after having sex (or living) with him or her. They rarely are satisfied with the answer—that it all depends on how the friendship is conceived. C. S. Lewis believes that erotic lovers also can become friends.[8] Though he does not say anything about the friendship lasting if the erotic love fades or fails, there might be reason to think that if some shared interests constituting the object of friendship were to remain strong, then friendship could survive. Aristotle's pleasure-based friendships are least likely to survive if sex comprises a large part of the pleasure in the lovers' friendship.

Canvassing my own experience with friendship, it is possible to observe elements from most of the different conceptions of friendships that I have had. Not all of my relationships might qualify as a friendship by all ideal conceptions, because some element is absent. Try as I might to free myself from my own cultural biases, I know how difficult it is to shed social upbringing and cultural indoctrination. Friendship is understood differently in cultures uninfluenced by my own, and I can see no reason to judge my culture's conception to be more true than another's, simply because it is mine.

Cultural variation does not argue against making comparisons or evaluations. Chapters 3 and 4 discuss many interconnections between moral principles and conceptions of friendship. From the moral point of view, some conceptions of friendship present more potential conflict, while other conceptions of friendship present less. Moral principles need not view all cultures' forms of friendship as having the same moral worth.

Criteria other than moral principles may be applied to evaluate or assess conceptions of friendship. Aristotle uses as his principal criterion stability and potential for permanence in friendships. He judges virtue or character friendship as being better, for the simple reason that it is more likely to permanently endure than a utility or pleasure friendship. Montaigne's fusion friendship is likely to be permanent, because each gives himself so completely to the other that there is nothing left by which to destabilize the friendship. Montaigne, however, seems to value fusion friendship more highly than other relationships, not only because of its potential permanence but because of the intrinsic value of completely fusing with another.[9] He would likely consider Lewis's shared interest friendships shallow, because their value is derivative from external shared interests. Lewis's shared interest friendships also might possess a high degree of stability if shared external interests remained unchanged. A third possible nonmoral criterion for valuing friendships might be the degree to which friendships have as their object the friends' private mental lives. By this criterion, Kant's and Montaigne's conceptions of friendship would rank higher than any of Aristotle's three conceptions.

Two additional nonmoral criteria for evaluating friendship conceptions were mentioned earlier. Conceptions of friendship differ from each other according to the number of friends it is possible to have, and they differ according to whether it is possible to predict who will become friends. If experience shows that, indeed, it frequently is possible to predict who will become friends with whom, then conceptions such as Aristotle's virtue friendship will be more relevant than Kant's intimacy conception or Montaigne's fusion conception, where no predictions are possible. If experience shows that only one friend, or at most two friends, could be possible at a time, then Montaigne's fusion friendship will have more relevance than would Lewis's. I do not know whether there is any evidence supporting the possibility of predicting who will become friends. Empirically testing whether friendships can be predicted or whether more than one friend or a few friends could be possible is difficult, because people use the concept "friendship" in so many different ways. Too many diverse relations might be counted as friendships, so that no clear-cut results would emerge, either for the question regarding the number of friends or the possibility of predicting friendships.

Permanence stands out as a plausible, nonmoral criterion to evaluate friendships. Since most people value their friends and find value in friendships, they naturally have reasons to keep their friendships alive. For some forms of friendships, such as Kant's intimacy friendship, sizable costs are involved in initiating friendships. For other forms, such as Aristotle's virtue friendship, maintaining friendship has its costs. Thus friendships that fail to survive might be considered "squandering" these costs. When affection develops between friends, friends come to like each other and to feel pleasure in each other's company. Ending an affection-based friendship thus becomes a source of sadness and pain. Nevertheless, some friendships should end if the bases of the friendship change, or if the friend's situation or character is altered. It might be a mistake to use permanence as the overriding value of friendship.

No compelling reasons exist to adopt a subjectivist position concerning friendship. That a variety of different conceptions of friendship has been uncovered, and that a variety of different nonmoral criteria is available by which to evaluate them, does not imply that objectivity is impossible. Rationally convincing arguments might be found that provide a rough ranking of friendships. As long as any value presuppositions are made manifest, explicit comparisons are possible. Ultimately, it may turn out that several forms of friendship are considered more valuable on the basis of nonmoral as well as moral criteria. While cultural differences certainly do exist, some nonmoral criterion, such as permanence, could conceivably emerge as winning widespread, cross-cultural acceptance.

ON FRIENDSHIP'S PULLS

Friends are pulled in two directions. As friends, they prefer each other to non-friends. Each conception of friendship has as its own object activities that express preference within friendship. Friendship, by its nature, is partial, particular, and individual. I have argued that some conceptions of friendship additionally contain an impersonal pull to treat nonfriends in ways resembling friends.

Elizabeth Telfer and R. M. Hare believe that friendship has an anti-egoistic tendency, because one of the consequences of having friends is learning to care for other persons besides oneself.[10] They believe that this tendency compensates for acts of preference between friends, possibly causing harm to nonfriends. The strength of any anti-egoistic tendency in friendship, and its good consequences for nonfriends, is an empirical issue that is not easy to measure. It may not be possible to isolate friendship as a cause of goodwill for nonfriends.

The impersonal pull that I have identified in friendship differs from friendship's anti-egoistic tendency. It is not an external, empirical consequence of friendship. The impersonal pull is internal to several forms of friendship, and it supplies a reason for promoting the well-being of nonfriends in addition to promoting the well-being of friends. Friends are pulled to promote similar goods in similar nonfriends, because they want to promote each other's good or objective well-being. As Jennifer Whiting argues, our reason for promoting our friend's well-being is that it is good for her and not merely that she is our friend.[11] It is this objective goodness, and not the individual relationship, that functions as a grounding reason. Thus reason exists in goodwill friendships to promote nonfriends' good. If nonfriends are the kind of persons who also would benefit, there is a prima facie reason for acting toward them in that equivalently beneficial way.

The impersonal pull also differs from the kind of care for others practiced by enlightened egoists who are concerned with others' well-being only because of the advantages to themselves. Enlightened egoists (or constrained maximizers) believe that they benefit in the long run from assisting others, because others will respond in kind. They do not have goodwill for other persons, and they expect to be repaid. Friendship's impersonal pull is grounded on a genuine goodwill that logically extends to relevantly similar nonfriends, without any thought of repayment.

Friendship's impersonal pull explains why having goodwill for nonfriends is not an imposition forced upon friends by external moral principles, or by a "view from nowhere."[12] Friendship does not demand goodwill for friends only. Where friendship contains goodwill for friends, it also demands similar consideration of nonfriends' well-being. In conditions without scarcity of time and resources, nonfriends' well-being should be respected equally to that of friends'. Where scarcity exists, and this is just about everywhere, friendship still contains a prima facie reason for the similar treatment of nonfriends, though a balancing of reasons will be required to weigh the benefits between friend and nonfriend.

Friendship, to this extent, is analogous to justice, as conceived by Hobbes, Hume, and Rawls. Neither friendship nor justice requires equal treatment for all persons all of the time. Both permit dissimilar treatment if there are justifying reasons, at least in conditions of scarcity. But justifying reasons must exist for, like justice, friendship contains a prima facie reason for treating friend and nonfriend similarly. This is an internal ramification of friendship's impersonal pull, not an external moral imposition.

Friendship's impersonal pull softens the partiality inherent in friendship. While it is not possible to be friends with everyone, according to most conceptions, friendship's partiality nevertheless requires consideration of nonfriends' well-being.

Not all conceptions of friendship contain an impersonal pull. It exists only in friendships where goodwill exists between friends, in the sense of their desire to promote each other's well-being for its own sake. In friendships that resemble C. S. Lewis's shared interest friendship or same-sex male friendships, there may be no impersonal pull. Many of the other friendships, however, do contain an impersonal pull.

A FRIEND IN NEED IS A FRIEND INDEED

Aristotle's less-than-ideal utility friendship is undervalued as a form of friendship, because it has been so misunderstood. If utility friendship is properly understood, there are a number of good reasons for valuing utility friendship and for believing that it is almost as worthwhile as Aristotle's ideal virtue friendship. Utility friendship probably is closer to what many people think a "good" friendship is. A great deal can be said in vindication of utility friendship.

"A friend is someone you can count on," "friends are there to help you," "friends care about each other," and "a friend in need is a friend indeed" are commonly voiced expressions characterizing friendships. Utility friends do not help, look after, protect, and promote friends' well-being solely out of narrow self-interest or cost-benefit calculations. As I argued at the end of chapter 2, utility friends are capable of valuing each other intrinsically, thereby caring about each other and wanting to promote each other's good for its own sake. There need be no difference between utility and virtue friendships in friends valuing each other intrinsically. There is no contradiction in valuing something both intrinsically and as a means to some other valuable end. Utility, as a basis of friendship, therefore permits friends to value each other intrinsically in addition to valuing friendship because it is beneficial in the broad sense of the term, which can include finding the friendship pleasant.[13]

Utility friends also can benefit from disclosing intimate information to each other. There is nothing in utility as a basis of friendship that prevents friends from being intimate. Advantages to friends can arise from their intimacy. As I pointed out in the fourth section in chapter 4, intimacy friendship creates psychological benefits for friends, in addition to the intrinsic value of communion. Francis Bacon describes one of these benefits as "the ease and discharge of the fullness and swellings of the heart, which passions of all kinds do cause and induce."[14] A second benefit noted by Bacon is the self-clarification that intimacy with another can sometimes produce. Intimacy is useful in examining motives of action to determine whether duty, rather than inclination or self-interest, is the strongest motive in particular situations. Intimate utility friends are in a good position to offer all of these kinds of benefits.

Including intimacy in a conception of utility friendship does not render utility friendship impossibly difficult to achieve. Earlier I argued against combining Aristotle's ideal virtue friendship with Kant's intimacy friendship because it would make ideal friendship too demanding and difficult to achieve. Unlike Aristotle's virtue friends, utility friends need not desire to spend all of their time together, nor to share all of their goods in common. Utility friends have more separate lives to live than do virtue friends. Further, they need not resemble each other as closely as virtue friends, so that there is a larger pool of potential friends. Utility friendships are therefore much more easily entered into and maintained, so they can more effortlessly be combined with intimacy.

It also is a mistake to undervalue utility friendship because of Aristotle's belief that utility friends have little need to be virtuous. Utility friends need more than a minimal degree of virtue. They must be sufficiently virtuous to have goodwill for each other and to be trusted to look after each other's well-being. To receive benefits from utility friendship, friends may place themselves in potentially vulnerable positions where immoral persons could easily take advantage of them. They need to rely on each other's trustworthiness while engaging in mutually advantageous joint activities and long-range projects. Immoral, narrowly self-interested people cannot predictably reap the benefits of utility friendships.

While utility friends must maintain a minimal degree of morality toward the other, there is always the possibility that they will act to benefit themselves at the other's expense. Cocking's and Kennett's example of moving the body illustrates how utility friends may engage in immoralities to benefit the other.[15] To the extent that utility friends behave immorally toward nonfriends, their friendship is not as morally good as a utility friendship, in which friends benefit from each other without any immoral behavior. The value of utility friendships depends on the behaviors that constitute the object of those friendships. There is no reason to suppose that all utility friendships have equivalent value. Some may be better than others.

Utility friendships do not limit the number of possible friends to the same small extent as do Aristotle's virtue friendships. The idea that it is possible to have only one friend or two friends is presently thought to be counterintuitive (or counterexperiential). Few reasons exist within utility friendships to limit friendships to only one friend or two friends. Several mutually beneficial friendships are possible, where friends desire to promote the other's well-being for its own sake. While utility friendship augmented by intimacy makes fewer friends possible, actual limits on the number of friends depend on the degree or depth of intimacy. Utility friendships avoid C. S. Lewis's interest friendship's extreme, where a great number of friends is not only possible but desirable. Not enough time and resources exist for a large number of utility friendships, and if, again, intimacy is added, still fewer friendships are possible.

Utility friendships measure up well against the nonmoral criterion of permanence. Aristotle's arguments about why utility friendships lack stability are misleading. Many of his arguments for the lack of stability depend on an understanding of utility friendships as being short range and narrowly self-interested. In the fourth section in chapter 2, I explained how utility friendships can be distinguished from self-interested or merely exploitative relationships. Properly understood, utility friendships need not produce numerous conflicts about how each person benefits by comparison to the other, Aristotle's primary reason for believing that utility friendships become destabilized. Stability can be maintained, in part, because friends can value each other intrinsically and not merely extrinsically.

Furthermore, benefits that ground utility friendship need not be so fragile or temporary, as Aristotle suggests. Utility friendships can be grounded in mutually beneficial circumstances that are almost as stable as character is in virtue friendships. Conditions that make friendship beneficial can be both comparatively unchanging and productive of long-term benefits. Formed at work, for example, utility friendships can remain stable over many years or decades. The benefits of friendship can last as long as the employment continues. Adding intimacy to utility friendships might make them even more permanent, because the utility that grounds those friendships could be based on character and therefore less dependent on causes external to the friends themselves.

Like ideal virtue friendships, utility friendships contain goodwill's impersonal pull. Because utility friends desire to advance each other's well-being, they have a reason to promote similar well-being in similar nonfriends. In this respect, utility friendships have the same social value as Aristotle's virtue friendships. There also is little appreciable difference in external moral evaluation between utility friendships containing intimacy and Aristotle's ideal friendship. The conflicts with egalitarian, impersonal, and impartial moral principles that exist for virtue friendship also exist for utility friendship. The social benefits that utilitarians believe are produced by preference between virtue friends would be produced by utility friendships, except for the slender difference that ideally just virtue friends might harm nonfriends less. From the libertarian perspective, no difference exists between utility friendship and Aristotle's ideal friendship. Utility friends may not benefit each other at the moral expense of nonfriends to any greater extent than would other kinds of friends. Utility friendships can have the same extrinsic value as virtue friendships. No compelling reason exists to hold utility friendships in low esteem, as Montaigne does, solely because benefits are produced as part of friendship. Thus I see little reason to regard utility friendship, properly conceived, as a significantly less valuable ideal than virtue friendship.

On the positive side, utility friendships with intimacy are consistent with my amalgamated moral point of view grounded in equality, good consequences, and autonomy. Utility friendships constituted by goodwill are consistent with fundamental human equality and dignity. Utility friends are capable of valuing each other intrinsically and respecting each other's human dignity. That utility friendship produces benefits for friends need not imply that friends value each other only instrumentally.

Utility friendships also produce beneficial consequences for society. Social good is promoted by friends' looking out for other friends' well-being. Friends who know each other well and care for each other are most likely to act in ways that produce good results. People who do not know each other as well or who do not care as much as friends are not likely to achieve similarly valuable outcomes. Thus social well-being is advanced by networks of friends assisting each other. Social harm from friends' ignoring others may not be prominent in relatively affluent societies. Utility friends are capable of acting morally and of not sacrificing nonfriends' well-being in order to produce trivial goods for the other. There is nothing in the nature of utility friendships that would lead utility friends to greater immorality than other members of society. Utility friends who pursue their own goals within moral limits can advance their overall good.

Utility friendship, where friends promote each other's well-being, also is consistent with the criterion of autonomy. Unlike Aristotle's virtue friendship, with its perfectionist (illiberal) overtones, utility friends' own values should be decisive in determining their well-being. Because utility friends not only value each other as means to some benefits but also value each other as ends in themselves, they can respect each other's autonomy in deciding on a conception of the good and how to pursue that good. Utility friends need not fuse into one indistinguishable unit. They can maintain their own individuality, because they respect each other's autonomy. It is the intrinsic value of friends that explains why it is valuable to promote friends' well-being as they conceive of it.

As I noted at the beginning of this chapter, I cannot provide justification for this comprehensive moral point of view. Still, to the extent that this point of view is cogent, as I believe it is, the value of utility-based conceptions of goodwill friendship is demonstrated. Montaigne simply is biased in downgrading friendships that produce benefits for friends. Properly understood, utility friendships have many of the same valuable elements, both moral and nonmoral, as do Aristotle's virtue friendship and Kant's intimacy friendship. Utility friendships are easier to originate and maintain, and thus they are a more accessible, yet an equivalently valuable, form of human friendship.

NOTES

CHAPTER ONE
PREFERENCE FOR FRIENDS

1. I use the term *nonfriend* throughout to refer to persons who are not friends. For some reason, there is no single elegant English word to capture the idea that persons are not friends. The term *stranger* is not right, for people can know each other and still not be friends. *Acquaintance* is not right either, because it leaves out strangers. Sometimes I will use the term *others* to convey the same idea, that the persons are not friends.

2. See Michael Stocker, *Plural and Conflicting Values* (Oxford: Clarendon Press, 1990); Martha Nussbaum, *The Fragility of Goodness* (Cambridge: Cambridge University Press, 1986); Lawrence A. Blum, *Friendship, Altruism, and Morality* (London: Routledge and Kegan Paul, 1980); Jacques Derrida, *Politics of Friendship*, trans. George Collins (London: Verso, 1997).

3. See Bernard Williams, *Ethics and the Limits of Philosophy* (Cambridge: Harvard University Press, 1985), 14, and his *Moral Luck* (Cambridge: Cambridge University Press, 1981), 18.

4. Neera Kapur Badhwar, "Why It Is Wrong to Be Always Guided by the Best: Consequentialism and Friendship," *Ethics*, 101:3 (April 1991): 499.

5. Troy A. Jollimore, *Friendship and Agent-Relative Morality* (New York: Garland, 2001), 9.

6. Again, I have in mind here Bernard Williams. But see Peter Railton, "Alienation, Consequentialism, and the Demands of Morality," in *Consequentialism and its Critics*, ed. Samuel Scheffler (Oxford: Oxford University Press, 1988), pp. 95–96, and Adrian M. S. Piper, "Moral Theory and Moral Alienation," *Journal of Philosophy* 84:2 (February 1987): 102–118.

7. W. D. Ross, *The Right and The Good* (Oxford: Clarendon Press, 1930), 28.

8. See John Hardwig, "In Search of an Ethics of Personal Relationships," in *Person to Person*, ed. George Graham and Hugh LaFollette (Philadelphia: Temple University

Press, 1989), p. 17. Quoted in Marcia Baron, "Impartiality and Friendship," *Ethics* 101:4 (July 1991): 846.

9. Legal obligations would be undertaken by the rule-constituted social institution of contracting.

10. This does not contradict the point made by Laurence Thomas, that friendships are minimally structured. See Laurence Thomas, "Friendship and Other Loves," in *Friendship: A Philosophical Reader,* ed. Neera Kapur Badhwar (Ithaca: Cornell University Press, 1993), p. 50.

11. The basis, object, and nature of friendship are fully explained in chapter 2.

12. Nancy Sherman, "Aristotle on the Shared Life," in *Friendship: A Philosophical Reader,* ed. Neera Kapur Badhwar (Ithaca: Cornell University Press, 1993), p. 91. She also cites John Cooper's article, "Aristotle on Friendship," in *Essays on Aristotle's Ethics,* ed. A. O. Rorty (Berkeley: University of California Press, 1980), p. 308.

13. Aristotle, *Complete Works of Aristotle,* ed. Jonathan Barnes (Princeton: Princeton University Press, 1984), 1156a3.

14. Aristotle, *Complete Works,* 1166a30 and 1159b25.

15. Ibid., 1171b29.

16. Sherman, "Aristotle," 99.

17. Less-than-ideal friendships are more fully discussed in chapter 2.

18. More later about intimacy in Aristotle's friendships.

19. Lara Denis, "From Friendship to Marriage: Revising Kant," *Philosophy and Phenomenological Research* 63:1 (July 2001): 5–8.

20. See C. S. Lewis, "Friendship—The Least Necessary Love," in *Friendship: A Philosophical Reader,* ed. Neera Kapur Badhwar (Ithaca: Cornell University Press, 1993), p. 42.

21. As an example, see Ferdinand Schoeman, "Aristotle on the Good of Friendship," *Australasian Journal of Philosophy* 63:3 (September 1985): 280.

22. David Konstan, *Friendship in the Classical World* (Cambridge: Cambridge University Press, 1997), 15.

23. From here on, I will use either the word "virtue" or "character" interchangeably to refer to what I have been calling Aristotle's "ideal character" or "virtue friendship."

24. Aristotle, *Complete Works,* 1160a1.

25. Ibid., 1172a18.

26. Ibid., 1177a21.

27. Cicero, "*De Amicitia,*" in *Other Selves: Philosophers on Friendship,* ed. Michael Pakaluk (Indianapolis: Hackett, 1991), p. 95.

28. Aristotle, *Complete Works,* 1159a8.

29. Immanuel Kant, *The Metaphysics of Morals,* trans. Mary Gregor (Cambridge: Cambridge University Press, 1991), 261.

30. Kant, *Metaphysics,* 261.

31. Ibid., 244.

32. Ibid., 244.

33. Ibid., 249.

34. Neera Badhwar Kapur [sic], "Why It Is Wrong to Be Always Guided by the Best: Consequentialism and Friendship," *Ethics* 101:3 (April 1991): 499, and see Christine M. Korsgaard, "Creating the Kingdom of Ends: Reciprocity and Responsibility in Personal Relations," in *Philosophical Perspectives, 6 Ethics, 1992*, ed. James E. Tomberlin (Atascadero, Calif.: Ridgeview, 1992), p. 305.

35. Kant, *Metaphysics*, 263.

36. Immanuel Kant, *Lectures on Ethics*, trans. Louis Infield (New York: Harper Torchbooks, 1963), 205. All references to Kant's *Lectures on Ethics* are to this edition, unless explicitly stated otherwise.

37. Kant, *Metaphysics*, 263.

38. Kant, *Lectures*, 206.

39. Kant, *Metaphysics*, 263.

40. Kant, *Lectures*, 206.

41. Ibid., 203.

42. Dean Cocking and Jeanette Kennett, "Friendship and the Self," *Ethics* 108:3 (April 1998): 516.

43. Cocking and Kennett, "Friendship," 519.

44. Laurence Thomas, "Friendship and Other Loves," in *Friendship: A Philsophical Reader*, ed. Neera Kapur Badhwar (Ithaca: Cornell University Press, 1993), p. 55. Thomas also illustrates the failure of distinguishing Kant's and Aristotle's conceptions of friendship. Thomas says that his analysis of friendship is inspired by Aristotle's account, while the emphasis on revealing private information is much closer to Kant's.

45. Thomas seems to realize that there is a significant cultural component.

46. Kant, *Lectures*, 203.

47. Ibid., 206.

48. Ibid., 207.

49. Ibid.

50. Immanuel Kant, *Lectures on Ethics*, trans. Peter Heath (Cambridge: Cambridge University Press, 1997), 414.

51. Hanna Arendt, *Men in Dark Times* (New York: Harcourt, Brace & World, 1968), 24.

52. See the Peter Heath edition of Kant's *Lectures on Ethics*, 415.

53. Kant, *Lectures*, 206. See also the Heath edition, 412.

54. C. S. Lewis, "Friendship—The Least Necessary Love," in *Friendship: A Philosophical Reader*, ed. Neera Kapur Badhwar (Ithaca: Cornell University Press, 1993), p. 42.

55. Lewis, "Friendship," 42.

56. Ibid., 41.

57. Ibid., 44.

58. Montaigne, "Of Friendship," in *Other Selves: Philosophers on Friendship*, ed. Michael Pakaluk (Indianapolis: Hackett, 1991), 191. For Cicero, see *"De Amicitia,"* p. 87.

59. Cicero, "*De Amicitia*," 85.

60. Ibid., 87.

61. Montaigne, "Of Friendship," 194.

62. Ibid., 192.

63. Ibid., 193.

64. Ibid., 188.

65. Ibid., 194.

66. Ibid., 192.

67. Ibid., 195.

68. Ibid., 194.

69. Bhikhu Parekh, "An Indian View of Friendship," in *The Changing Face of Friendship*, ed. Leroy S. Rouner (Notre Dame: University of Notre Dame Press, 1994), p. 105. Of course, India is a widely diverse country, and the three ideals discussed should not be considered an exhaustive enumeration of Indian friendships.

70. Parekh, "An Indian View," 108.

71. Ibid., 100.

72. Ibid.

73. Ibid.

74. Ibid., 101.

75. Ibid.

76. Ibid., 102.

77. Ibid., 104.

78. Khushwant Singh, *Train to Pakistan* (Delhi: Ravi Dayal, 1988), 54.

79. Cicero, "*De Amicitia*," 95.

80. Parekh, "An Indian View," 104.

81. Ibid., 105.

82. Ibid., 106.

83. See Rabindranath Tagore, *Gora* (Madras: Macmillan India, 1989).

84. Parekh, "An Indian View," 106.

85. Ibid., 107.

86. Ibid.

87. Ibid., 109.

88. Ibid., 99.

CHAPTER TWO
THE STRUCTURE OF FRIENDSHIP

1. Cf. Neera Kapur Badhwar, "Friends as Ends in Themselves," in *Sex, Love, and Friendship*, ed. Alan Soble (Amsterdam: Rodopi, 1997), p. 334. She uses "object or focus"

of friendship in the way I use basis. Martha C. Nussbaum, *The Fragility of Goodness* (Cambridge: Cambridge University Press, 1986), 355, uses "goal" and "end" to refer to what I call the "object of friendship." I prefer to use the object of friendship because "goal" and "end" may connote more of an instrumental value to friendship than many writers would permit.

2. See Badhwar, "Friends," 334; Nussbaum, *The Fragility of Goodness*, 355.

3. Aristotle, *The Complete Works of Aristotle*, ed. Jonathan Barnes (Princeton: Princeton University Press, 1984), 1156a5.

4. Bhikhu Parekh, "An Indian View of Friendship," in *The Changing Face of Friendship*, ed. Leroy S. Rouner (Notre Dame: University of Notre Dame Press, 1994), p. 100.

5. Cf. Richard Kraut, *Aristotle on the Human Good* (Princeton: Princeton University Press, 1989), 137.

6. Immanuel Kant, *The Metaphysics of Morals*, trans. Mary Gregor (Cambridge: Cambridge University Press, 1991), 261.

7. Immanuel Kant, *Lectures on Ethics,* trans. Louis Infield (New York: Harper Torchbooks, 1963), 205. Unless otherwise stated, all citations to Kant's *Lectures on Ethics* are to this edition.

8. Immanuel Kant, *Lectures on Ethics,* trans. Peter Heath (Cambridge: Cambridge University Press, 1997), 414.

9. See C. S. Lewis, "Friendship—The Least Necessary Love," in *Friendship: A Philosophical Reader*, ed. Neera Kapur Badhwar (Ithaca: Cornell University Press, 1993), p. 42.

10. See, for example, Carol Gilligan, *In a Different Voice: Psychological Theory and Women's Development* (Cambridge: Harvard University Press, 1982); Nel Noddings, *Caring: A Feminine Approach to Ethics and Moral Education* (Berkeley: University of California Press, 1984).

11. Kim-Chong Chong, "Egoism, Desires, and Friendship," *American Philosophical Quarterly* 21:4 (October 1984): 353.

12. Marilyn Friedman, *What Are Friends For?* (Ithaca: Cornell University Press, 1993), 174.

13. Aristotle, *Complete Works*, 1208b27.

14. Ibid., 1155b30.

15. Ibid., 1126b12.

16. Elizabeth Telfer, "Friendship," in *Other Selves: Philosophers on Friendship*, ed. Michael Pakluk (Indianapolis: Hackett, 1991), p. 251.

17. Ferdinand Schoeman, "Aristotle on the Good of Friendship," *Australasian Journal of Philosophy* 63:3 (September 1985): 275.

18. Nussbaum, *The Fragility of Goodness*, 355.

19. Aristotle, *Complete Works*, 1156a6.

20. Douglas Den Uyl and Charles Griswold Jr., "Adam Smith on Friendship and Love," *Review of Metaphysics* 49 (March 1996): 626.

21. Jennifer E. Whiting, "Impersonal Friends," *The Monist* 74 (January 1991): 12.

22. David O. Brink, "Eudaimonism, Love, and Friendship, and Political Community," *Social Philosophy and Policy* 16:1 (Winter 1999): 268.

23. Aristotle, *Complete Works*, 1106b5.

24. John M. Cooper, "Aristotle on Friendship," in *Essays on Aristotle's Ethics*, ed. Amelie Oksenberg Rorty (Berkeley: University of California Press, 1980), p. 312.

25. Aristotle, *Complete Works*, 1277b23.

26. Lewis, "Friendship," 41.

27. Ibid., 42.

28. Ibid.

29. Ibid., 41.

30. Kant, *Lectures on Ethics*, 206.

31. Kant, *Lectures on Ethics*, 197; *The Metaphysics of Morals*, 262.

32. Montaigne, "Of Friendship," in *Other Selves: Philosophers on Friendship*, ed. Michael Pakaluk (Indianapolis: Hackett, 1991), p. 192.

33. Whiting, "Impersonal Friends," 12.

34. Ferdinand Schoeman, "Aristotle on the Good of Friendship," *Australasian Journal of Philosophy* 63:3 (September 1985): 276.

35. Aristotle, *Complete Works*, 1166a6.

36. Kant, *Lectures on Ethics*, 203.

37. Ibid.

38. Aristotle, *Complete Works*, 1156a22.

39. Gordon C. Roadarmel, "Cultural Cues and Clues for the American in India," in *Fulbright to India* (New Delhi: United States Educational Foundation in India, 1995), p. 108.

40. Barbara A. Winstead, "Sex Differences in Same-Sex Friendships," in *Friendship and Social Interaction*, ed. Valerian J. Derlega and Barbara A. Winstead (New York: Springer-Verlag, 1986), p. 81.

41. Winstead, "Sex Differences," 81.

42. Ibid., 82.

43. Ibid.

44. Ibid.

45. Ibid., 83.

46. Parekh, "An Indian View," 99.

47. Lewis, "Friendship," 44.

48. Nancy Sherman, "Aristotle on the Shared Life," in *Friendship: A Philosophical Reader*, ed. Neera Kapur Badhwar (Ithaca: Cornell University Press, 1993), p. 91.

49. John Carbonara, in a private conversation.

50. Nussbaum, *The Fragility of Goodness*, 304, and Friedman, *What Are Friends For?*, 191, also make this point.

51. See Alan Gewirth, *Self-Fulfillment* (Princeton: Princeton University Press, 1998), 147–48.

52. See Friedman, *What Are Friends For?*, 248, and Lawrence A. Blum, *Friendship, Altruism, and Morality* (London: Routledge and Kegan Paul, 1980), 68–70. The difference between Aristotle's and Kant's conceptions also is understated by Christine M. Korsgaard, "Creating the Kingdom of Ends: Reciprocity and Responsibility in Personal Relations," in *Philosophical Perspectives, 6 Ethics, 1992*, ed. James E. Tomberlin (Atascadero, Calif.: Ridgeview, 1992), p. 305.

53. Kant, *Lectures on Ethics*, 207.

54. In addition to Schoeman and Whiting, see, for example, Bernard Williams, *Ethics and the Limits of Philosophy* (Cambridge: Harvard University Press, 1985), 14.

55. Aristotle, *Complete Works*, 1156a3.

56. Ibid., 1380b34.

57. Ibid., 1156a6-25.

58. Ibid., 1237b10.

59. Ibid., 1157a13.

60. Ibid., 1167a12.

61. Ibid., 1162b22.

62. Ibid., 1157b1.

63. Ibid., 1156a22, 1157a26.

64. Immanuel Kant, *Grounding for the Metaphysics of Morals*, trans. James W. Ellington (Indianapolis: Hackett, 1981), 10.

65. Kant, *Grounding*, 19.

66. See Aristotle, *Complete Works*, 1156b13, 1157a1.

67. Ibid., 1157a13.

68. Ibid., 1241a3.

69. Nussbaum, *The Fragility of Goodness*, 355.

70. Ibid.

71. Michael Slote, *Beyond Optimizing* (Cambridge: Harvard University Press, 1989), 12.

72. Aristotle, *Complete Works*, 1244a20.

73. Ibid., 1169b6.

74. Ibid., 1156a27.

75. Ibid., 1171b32. (Note the resemblance to C. S. Lewis.)

76. Ibid., 1156a30.

77. Ibid., 1156a22.

78. Ibid.

79. Kant, *Lectures on Ethics*, trans. Louis Infield (New York: Harper Tourchbooks, 1963), 203.

80. Kant, *The Metaphysics of Morals*, 261.

81. Kant, *Lectures on Ethics*, 203.

82. Ibid., 205.

83. Kant, *Lectures on Ethics*, trans. Peter Heath, 187.

84. Manfred Kuehn, *Kant: A Biography* (Cambridge: Cambridge University Press, 2001), 154.

CHAPTER THREE
INTERNAL JUSTIFICATIONS

1. Aristotle, *Complete Works of Aristotle*, ed. Jonathan Barnes (Princeton: Princeton University Press, 1984), 1156b8.

2. See, for example, Marilyn Friedman, *What Are Friends For?* (Ithaca: Cornell University Press, 1993), 59.

3. This point is made by Christine M. Korsgaard, "Creating the Kingdom of Ends: Reciprocity and Responsibility in Personal Relations," in *Philosophical Perspectives, 6 Ethics, 1992*, ed. James E. Tomberlin (Atascadero, Calif.: Ridgeview, 1992), p. 306.

4. See, for example, Elizabeth Telfer, "Friendship," in *Other Selves: Philosophers on Friendship*, ed. Michael Pakaluk (Indianapolis: Hackett, 1991), p. 264.

5. Telfer, "Friendship," 267.

6. Cicero, *"De Amicitia,"* in *Other Selves: Philosophers on Friendship*, ed. Michael Pakaluk (Indianapolis: Hackett, 1991), p. 95.

7. See Alan Donagan, *The Theory of Morality* (Chicago: University of Chicago Press, 1977), 173.

8. See R. M. Hare, *Moral Thinking* (Oxford: Oxford University Press, 1981), 130.

9. Cicero, *"De Amicitia,"* 92.

10. Ibid., 100.

11. Dean Cocking and Jeanette Kennett, "Friendship and Moral Danger," *Journal of Philosophy* 97:5 (May 2000): 278.

12. Cocking and Kennett, "Friendship," 280.

13. Ibid., 279.

14. Ibid., 284–85.

15. Ibid., 287.

16. Ibid.

17. Neera Kapur Badhwar, "Why It Is Wrong to Be Always Guided by the Best: Consequentialism and Friendship," *Ethics* 101:3 (April 1991): 499.

18. Immanuel Kant, *The Metaphysics of Morals*, trans. Mary Gregor (Cambridge: Cambridge University Press, 1991), 261.

19. Badhwar, "Why It Is Wrong," 499.

20. Ibid., 500. Badhwar thinks the relevant virtues in these examples are courage and honor, but the difference is not relevant to my point about the difficulty in calculating the differential weights in making any decision.

21. Badhwar, "Why It Is Wrong," 500.

22. See the third section of chapter 2 for a more detailed discussion.

23. Badhwar, "Why It Is Wrong," 483.

24. Martha C. Nussbaum, *Love's Knowledge* (Oxford: Oxford University Press, 1990), 60.

25. H. A. Paton, *The Moral Law* (New York: Barnes & Noble, 1967), 91.

26. Even Bentham, who believes that pleasure alone has intrinsic value, must presuppose that pleasure is something that people want and desire. (I owe this insight to Lansing Pollock.)

27. Jennifer E. Whiting, "Impersonal Friends," *The Monist* (January 1991): 10.

28. I am using "out of friendship" in Michael Stocker's sense. See Michael Stocker, "Values and Purposes: The Limits of Teleology and the Ends of Friendship," *Journal of Philosophy* 78:12 (December 1981): 750.

29. How confining that material assets are will, of course, depend on the moral demands of assistance for each moral theory. Act-utilitarian demands will be stronger and more difficult to fulfill than the demands of some libertarians. Bill Gates, owner of Microsoft, may have an easier time meeting the moral demands of material assistance than I do (at least as of March 7, 2002).

30. See Thomas Hobbes, *Leviathan* (New York: E. P. Dutton and Company, 1950), 102; David Hume, *Treatise of Human Nature*, ed. L. A. Selby-Biggs (Oxford: Oxford University Press, 1964), 494; John Rawls, *A Theory of Justice* (Cambridge: Harvard University Press, 1971), 127.

31. Kim-Chong Chong, "Egoism, Desires, and Friendship," *American Philosophical Quarterly* 21:4 (October 1984): 353.

32. Montaigne, "Of Friendship," in *Other Selves: Philosophers on Friendship* ed. Michael Pakaluk (Indianapolis: Hackett, 1991), p. 195.

33. C. S. Lewis, "Friendship—The Least Necessary Love," in *Friendship: A Philosophical Reader*, ed. Neera Kapur Badhwar (Ithaca: Cornell University Press, 1993), p. 43.

34. My point here differs from Jennifer E. Whiting, who views objective similarities in character as reasons for treating others similarly to friends where I am considering the similarities in the good to be produced by friendship as a reason for treating others similarly. See Whiting, "Impersonal Friends," 8.

35. Aristotle, *Complete Works*, 1160a6.

36. Paul Schollmeier, *Other Selves: Aristotle on Personal and Political Friendship* (Albany: State University of New York Press, 1994), 38.

37. Schollmeier, *Other Selves*, 39.

38. Ibid., 38.

39. Montaigne, "Of Friendship," 192.

40. Ibid., 195.

41. David Konstan, *Friendship in the Classical World* (Cambridge: Cambridge University Press, 1997), 59.

42. Bhikhu Parekh, "An Indian View of Friendship," in *The Changing Face of Friendship*, ed. Leroy S. Rouner (Notre Dame: University of Notre Dame Press, 1994), p. 104.

43. Immanuel Kant, *Lectures on Ethics*, trans. Louis Infield (New York: Harper Torchbooks, 1963), 203. See also Kant, *The Metaphysical Principles of Virtue* (Indianapolis: Bobbs-Merrill, 1964), 135–40.

44. Kant, *Lectures*, 205.

45. Ibid., 203.

46. See John Hunter, "Sex and Personal Intimacy," in *Moral Issues*, ed. Jan Narveson (Oxford: Oxford University Press, 1983), p. 283.

47. Kant, *Lectures*, 204.

48. Ibid., 205.

49. Kant, *The Metaphysical Principles*, 119–20. Kant makes the same point in his *Lectures on Ethics*, 204.

50. Kant, *Lectures*, 206.

51. Ibid., 207.

52. Aristotle, *Complete Works*, 1163b29.

53. John Cottingham, "The Ethics of Self-Concern," *Ethics* 101:4 (July 1991): 801.

CHAPTER FOUR
EXTERNAL JUSTIFICATIONS

1. Reference to the Stoics comes from Alan Donagan, *The Theory of Morality* (Chicago: University of Chicago Press, 1977), 174; William Godwin, *Enquiry Concerning Political Justice*, ed. Isaac Kramnick (Harmondsworth: Pelican Books, 1976), 170; Bernard Williams, *Moral Luck* (Cambridge: Cambridge University Press, 1981), 18.

2. They may receive pleasure, which Aristotle would consider different from utility. We, today, might not see as much of a difference.

3. Lawrence A. Blum, *Friendship, Altruism, and Morality* (London: Routledge and Kegan Paul, 1980), 44.

4. Blum, *Friendship*, 44. For a similar point about Kant see Andrew Oldenquist, "Loyalties," *Journal of Philosophy* 79:4 (April 1982): 173.

5. See, for example, John Stuart Mill, *Utilitarianism* (Indianapolis: Bobbs-Merrill, 1957), 26.

6. Lansing Pollock, *The Free Society* (Boulder: Westview Press, 1996), 10.

7. Pollock, *The Free Society*, 11.

8. Ibid., 15.

9. Jan Narveson, *The Libertarian Idea* (Philadelphia: Temple University Press, 1988), 7.

10. Narveson, *The Libertarian Idea*, 30–33.

11. See my discussion of Nozick in James O. Grunebaum, *Private Ownership* (London: Routledge and Kegan Paul, 1987), 78.

12. See Narveson, *The Libertarian Idea*, 62–98; Robert Nozick, *Anarchy, State, and Utopia* (New York: Basic Books, 1974), 167–83.

13. This is Pollock's view.

14. I am assuming that, in this case, the moral duty is not enforceable by threat of punishment.

15. See the second section of chapter 3 for a more detailed discussion.

16. The issue also arises for male-only or white-only clubs.

17. See Alan Gewirth, *Reason and Morality* (Chicago: University of Chicago Press, 1978); "Ethical Universalism and Particularism," *Journal of Philosophy* 85:6 (June 1988); *Self-Fulfillment* (Princeton: Princeton University Press, 1998).

18. Narveson and Pollock are exceptions. Jan Narveson is one of the few libertarians who tries to supply a rational justification for his libertarian rights, but Narveson's justification is not grounded on any assumption of human equality. Pollock appeals to equal moral standing.

19. Søren Kierkegaard, "You Shall Love Your Neighbor," in *Other Selves: Philosophers on Friendship*, ed. Michael Pakaluk (Indianapolis: Hackett, 1991), p. 240.

20. Kierkegaard, "You Shall Love," 243.

21. See the first section of chapter 3 for a more detailed discussion.

22. H. A. Paton, *The Moral Law* (New York: Barnes & Noble, 1967), 86.

23. Blum, *Friendship*, 44.

24. Ibid.

25. Michael Stocker, *Plural and Conflicting Values* (Oxford: Clarendon Press, 1990), 88.

26. See Paton, *The Moral Law*, 71–72.

27. Blum, *Friendship*, 44.

28. Gewirth, "Ethical Universalism and Particularism," 283.

29. Ibid., 288–89.

30. Ibid., 289.

31. Ibid., 292.

32. See the third section of chapter 1 for a more detailed discussion.

33. Gewirth, "Ethical Universlism and Particularism," 292.

34. See the second section of this chapter.

35. Gewirth, *Self-Fulfillment*, 140.

36. Ibid., 108.

37. Ibid., 109.

38. Ibid., 112.

39. Ibid., 141.

40. Ibid.

41. Ibid., 146.

42. Gewirth, *Self-Fulfillment*, 145, explicitly uses parents and children, but nothing of substance hangs on it being parents and children rather than friends.

43. Gewirth, *Self-fulfillment*, 144.

44. See the first section of this chapter.

45. Gewirth, *Self-fulfillment*, 144.

46. Susan Wolf, "Morality and Partiality," in *Philosophical Perspectives, 6, Ethics, 1992*, ed. James E. Tomberlin (Atascadero, Calif.: Ridgeview, 1992), p. 243.

47. Wolf, "Morality and Partiality," 246.

48. Ibid., 244.

49. Ibid., 245.

50. Ibid.

51. Ibid.

52. Ibid., 252.

53. Marcia Baron, "Impartiality and Friendship," *Ethics* 101:4 (July 1991): 838.

54. Baron, "Impartiality and Friendship," 843.

55. John Hardwig, "In Search of an Ethics of Personal Relationships," in *Person to Person*, ed. George Graham and Hugh LaFollette (Philadelphia: Temple University Press, 1989), p. 17. Quoted in Baron, "Impartiality and Friendship," 846.

56. See chapter 3.

57. Baron, "Impartiality and Friendship," 855.

58. Ibid., 856.

59. See Gordon C. Roadarmel, "Cultural Cues and Clues for the American in India," in *Fulbright to India* (New Delhi: United States Educational Foundation in India, 1995), p. 108.

60. Cicero, "*De Amicitia,*" in *Other Selves: Philosophers on Friendship*, ed. Michael Pakaluk (Indianapolis: Hackett, 1991), p. 92.

61. Cicero, "*De Amicitia,*" 100.

62. Friends' well-being may be valued for the friends' own sake, even if the friendship has instrumental value. See my discussion of Aristotle's and Kant's less-than-ideal friendships in chapter 2. Similarly, depending on the senses of "care for the person," friends may care for the person even if the friendship is not valued intrinsically.

63. J. S. Mill, *Utilitarianism* (Indianapolis: Bobbs Merrill, 1957), 44–52.

64. T. M. Scanlon, *What We Owe to Each Other* (Cambridge: Harvard University Press, 1999), 88.

65. Scanlon, *What We Owe*, 88.

66. Ibid., 89.

67. Ibid., 90. Scanlon uses the example of science, but what he says about science applies equally well to friendship.

68. See R. M. Hare, *Moral Thinking* (Oxford: Oxford University Press, 1981), 130–46.

69. Aristotle, *The Basic Works of Aristotle*, ed. Richard McKeon (New York: Random House, 1941), 1166a, 1160a.

70. Aristotle, *The Basic Works*, 1159b.

71. Nancy Sherman, "Aristotle on the Shared Life," in *Friendship: A Philosophical Reader*, ed. Neera Kapur Badhwar (Ithaca: Cornell University Press, 1993), p. 99.

72. Aristotle, *The Basic Works*, 1155a.

73. Jean Jacques Rousseau, *The Social Contract and Discourses*, trans. G. D. H. Cole (London: Everyman's Library, 1913), 15.

74. Aristotle, *The Basic Works*, 1155a.

75. Immanuel Kant, *Lectures on Ethics*, trans. Louis Infield (New York: Harper Torchbooks, 1963), 206.

76. Kant, *Lectures on Ethics*, trans. Louis Infield, 207.

77. Kant is, of course, writing after Hobbes, so he is much less likely than Aristotle to believe that humans naturally live together with trust and peace. There may be little reason today to accept Aristotle's view rather than Kant's. It certainly would be naive to think that people in general can be trusted to the same degree that friends can.

78. Immanuel Kant, *Grounding for the Metaphysics of Morals*, trans. James W. Ellington (Indianapolis: Hackett, 1981), 19.

79. Francis Bacon, "Of Friendship XXVII," in *Other Selves: Philosophers on Friendship*, ed. Michael Pakaluk (Indianapolis: Hackett, 1991), p. 203.

80. Bacon, "Of Friendship," 205.

81. See William A. Galston, "Cosmopolitan Altruism," *Social Philosophy and Policy* 10:1 (Winter 1993): 128, who offers a similar argument.

82. Elizabeth Telfer, "Friendship," in *Other Selves: Philosophers on Friendship*, ed. Michael Pakaluk (Indianapolis: Hackett, 1991), p. 264.

83. Hare, *Moral Thinking*, 130–46.

84. Immanuel Kant, *The Metaphysical Elements of Justice*, trans. John Ladd (Indianapolis: Bobbs-Merrill, 1965), 19.

85. Kant, *Grounding for the Metaphysics of Morals*, 10.

86. Kant, *The Metaphysical Elements of Justice*, 19.

87. See the second section of chapter 2 for a more detailed discussion.

88. Henry Sidgwick, *Methods of Ethics* (New York: Dover, 1966), 241.

89. Sidgwick, *Methods*, 258.

90. Ibid., 432.

91. Ibid., 434.

92. Neera Kapur Badhwar, "Why It Is Wrong to Be Always Guided by the Best: Consequentialism and Friendship," *Ethics* 101:3 (April 1991): 483.

93. G. E. Moore, *Principia Ethica* (Cambridge: Cambridge University Press, 1962), 192.

94. David Gauthier, *Morals by Agreement* (Oxford: Oxford University Press, 1986), 46.

95. Troy A. Jollimore, *Friendship and Agent-Relative Morality* (New York: Garland, 2001), 16.

96. Jollimore, *Friendship*, 16.

97. Ibid., 20.

98. See the second section of this chapter, where different interpretations of libertarianism are discussed. The third option is deliberately left vague.

99. Telfer, "Friendship," 264.

100. Ibid., 265.

101. Kant, *Lectures on Ethics*, trans. Louis Infield, 201.

102. Galston, "Cosmopolitan Altruism," 128.

103. Hare, *Moral Thinking*, 40–49.

104. See the third section of this chapter, where the application of Gewirth's principle of generic consistency to self-fulfillment and friendship is discussed.

105. Hare, *Moral Thinking*, 130.

106. Ibid., 130–46.

107. Ibid., 138.

108. Donagan, *The Theory of Morality*, 203.

109. For a much more complete discussion of the difficulties in performing utilitarian calculations, see Donagan, *The Theory of Morality*, 192–209.

CHAPTER FIVE
CONCLUSIONS: FRIENDSHIPS AND PREFERENCES

1. John Hardwig, "In Search of an Ethics of Personal Relationships," in *Person to Person*, ed. George Graham and Hugh LaFollette (Philadelphia: Temple University Press, 1989), p. 17, quoted in Marcia Baron, "Impartiality and Friendship," *Ethics* 101:4 (July 1991): 846; Neera Kapur Badhwar, "Why It Is Wrong to Be Always Guided by the Best: Consequentialism and Friendship," *Ethics* 101:3 (April 1991): 499.

2. See, for example, Marilyn Friedman, *What Are Friends For?* (Ithaca: Cornell University Press, 1993), 191.

3. Bhikhu Parekh, "An Indian View of Friendship," in *The Changing Face of Friendship*, ed. Leroy S. Rouner (Notre Dame: University of Notre Dame Press, 1994), p. 100.

4. Dean Cocking and Jeanette Kennett, "Friendship and Moral Danger," *Journal of Philosophy* 97:5 (May 2000): 278–96.

5. As an example, see Friedman, *What Are Friends For?*, 188.

6. Lawrence A. Blum, *Friendship, Altruism, and Morality* (London: Routledge and Kegan Paul, 1980), 68–70.

7. Quoted in *Other Selves: Philosophers on Friendship*, ed. Michael Pakaluk (Indianapolis: Hackett, 1991), p. 135.

8. C. S. Lewis, "Friendship—The Least Necessary Love," in *Friendship: A Philosophical Reader*, ed. Neera Kapur Badhwar (Ithaca: Cornell University Press, 1993), p. 43.

9. See the fifth section in chapter 1 for a more detailed discussion.

10. Elizabeth Telfer, "Friendship," in *Other Selves: Philosophers on Friendship*, ed. Michael Pakaluk (Indianapolis: Hackett, 1991), p. 264; R. M. Hare, *Moral Thinking* (Oxford: Oxford University Press, 1981), 130–46.

11. Jennifer E. Whiting, "Impersonal Friends," *The Monist* 74 (January 1991): 10.

12. See, for example, Thomas Nagel, *The View from Nowhere* (Oxford: Oxford University Press, 1986).

13. In this discussion of utility friendships, I want to blur Aristotle's distinction between pleasure and utility as a basis of friendship.

14. See Francis Bacon, "Of Friendship XXVII," in *Other Selves: Philosophers on Friendship*, ed., Michael Pakaluk, (Indianapolis: Hackett, 1991), p. 203.

15. Cocking and Kennett, "Friendship," 279.

SELECTED BIBLIOGRAPHY

BOOKS

Anderson, Elizabeth. *Value in Ethics and Economics.* Cambridge: Harvard University Press, 1993.

Annas, Julia. *The Morality of Happiness.* Oxford: Oxford University Press, 1993.

Aristotle. *Complete Works of Aristotle.* Edited by Jonathan Barnes. Princeton: Princeton University Press, 1984.

Badhwar, Neera Kapur, ed. *Friendship: A Philosophical Reader.* Ithaca: Cornell University Press, 1993.

Baron, Marcia W. *Kantian Ethics Almost without Apology.* Ithaca: Cornell University Press, 1995.

Beiner, Ronald. *Political Judgment.* Chicago: University of Chicago Press, 1983.

Bloom, Allan. *Love and Friendship.* New York: Simon and Schuster, 1993.

Blosser, Philip, and Marshall Carl Bradley, eds. *Friendship: Philosophic Reflections on a Perennial Concern.* Lanham, Md.: University Press of America, 1997.

Blum, Lawrence A. *Friendship, Altruism, and Morality.* London: Routledge and Kegan Paul, 1980.

————. *Moral Perception and Particularity.* Cambridge: Cambridge University Press, 1994.

Cates, Diana Fritz. *Choosing to Feel.* Notre Dame: Notre Dame University Press, 1997.

Comte-Sponville, Andre. *A Small Treatise on the Great Virtues.* Translated by Catherine Temerson. New York: Metropolitan Books, 2001.

Crisp, Roger. *How Should One Live?* Oxford: Oxford University Press, 1996.

Derrida, Jacques. *Politics of Friendship.* Translated by George Collins. London: Verso, 1997.

Fletcher, George. *Loyalty.* Oxford: Oxford University Press, 1993.

Friedman, Marilyn. *What Are Friends For?* Ithaca: Cornell University Press, 1993.

Gewirth, Alan. *Self-Fulfillment*. Princeton: Princeton University Press, 1998.

Graham, George, and Hugh LaFollette, eds. *Person to Person*. Philadelphia: Temple University Press, 1989.

Hare, R. M. *Moral Thinking*. Oxford: Oxford University Press, 1981.

Jollimore, Troy A. *Friendship and Agent-Relative Morality*. New York: Garland, 2001.

Kant, Immanuel. *Lectures on Ethics*. Translated by L. Infield. New York: Harper Torchbooks, 1963.

————. *The Metaphysics of Morals*. Translated by M. Gregor. Cambridge: Cambridge University Press, 1991.

————. *Lectures on Ethics*. Translated by Peter Heath. Cambridge: Cambridge University Press, 1997.

Konstan, David. *Friendship in the Classical World*. Cambridge: Cambridge University Press, 1997.

Korsgaard, Christine. *The Sources of Normativity*. Cambridge: Cambridge University Press, 1996.

Kraut, Richard. *Aristotle on the Human Good*. Princeton: Princeton University Press, 1989.

Lomansky, Loren. *Persons, Rights, and the Moral Community*. Oxford: Oxford University Press, 1987.

Louden, Robert. *Morality and Moral Theory*. Oxford: Oxford University Press, 1992.

Nagel, Thomas. *Equality and Partiality*. New York: Oxford University Press, 1991.

Nerlich, Graham. *Values and Valuing*. Oxford: Clarendon Press, 1989.

Nussbaum, Martha. *The Fragility of Goodness*. Cambridge: Cambridge University Press, 1986.

————. *The Therapy of Desire*. Princeton: Princeton University Press, 1994.

Okin, Susan Moller. *Justice, Gender, and the Family*. New York: Basic Books, 1989.

Pakaluk, Michael, ed. *Other Selves: Philosophers on Friendship*. Indianapolis: Hackett, 1991.

Price, A. W. *Love and Friendship in Plato and Aristotle*. Oxford: Clarendon Press, 1989.

Raz, Joseph. *The Authority of the Law*. Oxford: Clarendon Press, 1979.

Ross, Jacob. *The Virtues of the Family*. New York: Free Press, 1994.

Rothleder, Dianne. *The Work of Friendship*. Albany: State University of New York Press, 1999.

Rouner, Leroy, ed. *The Changing Face of Friendship*. Notre Dame: University of Notre Dame Press, 1994.

Scanlon, T. M. *What We Owe to Each Other*. Cambridge: Harvard University Press, 1999.

Schollmeir, Paul. *Other Selves: Aristotle on Personal and Political Friendship*. Albany: State University of New York Press, 1994.

Sidgwick, Henry. *Methods of Ethics*. New York: Dover, 1966.

Slote, Michael. *Morals From Motives*. Oxford: Oxford University Press, 2001.

Soble, Alan. *Sex, Love, and Friendship*. Amsterdam: Value Inquiry Book Series, Rodopi, 1997.

Stern-Gillet, Suzanne. *Aristotle's Philosophy of Friendship*. Albany: State University of New York Press, 1995.

Stocker, Michael. *Plural and Conflicting Values*. Oxford: Clarendon Press, 1990.

Swanson, Judith A. *The Public and the Private in Aristotle's Political Philosophy*. Ithaca: Cornell University Press, 1992.

Wadell, Paul J. C. P. *Friendship and the Moral Life*. Notre Dame: University of Notre Dame Press, 1989.

White, Alan. *Rights*. Oxford: Oxford University Press, 1984.

Williams, Bernard. *Moral Luck*. Cambridge: Cambridge University Press, 1981.

———. *Ethics and the Limits of Philosophy*. Cambridge: Harvard University Press, 1985.

Williams, Clifford. *On Love and Friendship*. Boston: Jones and Bartlett, 1995.

Yang, Mayfair Mei-hui. *Gifts, Favors, and Banquets: The Art of Social Relationships in China*. Ithaca: Cornell University Press, 1994.

ARTICLES

Adams, Don. "A Socratic Theory of Friendship." *International Philosophical Quarterly* 35:3, issue 139 (September 1995): 269–82.

Annis, David B. "The Meaning, Value, and Duties of Friendship." *American Philosophical Quarterly* 24:4 (October 1987): 349–56.

Ashford, Elizabeth. "Utilitarianism, Integrity, and Partiality." *Journal of Philosophy* 97:8 (August 2000): 421–39.

Badhwar, Neera Kapur. "Friendship, Justice, and Supererogation." *American Philosophical Quarterly* 22:2 (April 1985): 123–31.

———. "Why It Is Wrong to Be Always Guided by the Best: Consequentialism and Friendship." *Ethics* 101:3 (April 1991): 483–94.

Baron, Marcia. "Impartiality and Friendship." *Ethics* 101:4 (July 1991): 836–57.

Brink, David O. "Utilitarian Morality and the Personal Point of View." *Journal of Philosophy* 83:8 (August 1986): 417–38.

———. "Eudaimonism, Love and Friendship, and Political Community." *Social Philosophy and Policy* 16:1 (Winter 1999): 252–89.

Chong, Kim-Chong. "Egoism, Desires, and Friendship." *American Philosophical Quarterly* 21:4 (October 1984): 349–57.

Cocking, Dean, and Jeanette Kennett. "Friendship and the Self." *Ethics* 108:3 (April 1998): 502–27.

———. "Friendship and Moral Danger." *Journal of Philosophy* 97:5 (May 2000): 278–96.

Cocking, Dean, and Justin Oakley. "Indirect Consequentialism, Friendship, and the Problem of Alienation." *Ethics* 106:1 (October 1995): 86–111.

Cooper, John M. "Aristotle on Friendship." In *Essays on Aristotle's Ethics*, edited by Amelie Oksenberg Rorty, 301–40. Berkeley: University of California Press, 1980.

Cottingham, John. "The Ethics of Self-Concern." *Ethics* 101:4 (July 1991): 798–817.

Denis, Lara. "From Friendship to Marriage: Revising Kant." *Philosophy and Phenomenological Research* 63:1 (July 2001): 1–28.

Dziob, Anne Marie. "Aristotelian Friendship: Self-Love and Moral Rivalry." *Review of Metaphysics* 46 (June 1993): 781–801.

Fox, Ellen L. "Paternalism and Friendship." *Canadian Journal of Philosophy* 23:4 (December 1993): 575–94.

Friedman, Marilyn. "The Practice of Partiality." *Ethics* 101:4 (July 1991): 818–35.

Galston, William A. "Cosmopolitan Altruism." *Social Philosophy and Policy* 10:1 (Winter 1993): 118–34.

Gewirth, Alan. "Ethical Universalism and Particularism." *Journal of Philosophy* 85:6 (June 1988): 283–302.

Gilbert, Paul. "Friendship and the Will." *Philosophy* 61 (January 1986): 61–70.

Gomberg, Paul. "Friendship in the Context of a Consequentialist Life." *Ethics* 102:3 (April 1992): 552–54.

Griswold, Charles, and Douglas Den Uyl. "Adam Smith on Friendship and Love." *Review of Metaphysics* 49 (March 1996): 609–37.

Grunebaum, James O. "Friendship, Morality, and Special Obligation." *American Philosophical Quarterly* 30:1 (January 1993): 51–61.

———. "On Becoming Friends." *Cithara* 38:1 (November 1998): 44–59.

Herman, Barbara. "Agency, Attachment, and Difference." *Ethics* 101:4 (July 1991): 775–97.

Jackson, Frank. "Decision-Theoretic Consequentialism and the Nearest and Dearest Objection." *Ethics* 101:3 (April 1991): 461–82.

Jeske, Diane. "Friendship, Virtue, and Impartiality." *Philosophy and Phenomenological Research* 57:1 (March 1997): 51–72.

———. "Families, Friends, and Special Obligations." *Canadian Journal of Philosophy* 28:4 (December 1998): 527–55.

Korsgaard, Christine M. "Aristotle and Kant on the Source of Value." *Ethics* 96:3 (April 1986): 486–505.

———. "Creating the Kingdom of Ends: Reciprocity and Responsibility in Personal Relations." In *Philosophical Perspectives, 6 Ethics, 1992*, edited by James E. Tomberlin, 305–32. Atascadero, Calif.: Ridgeview, 1992.

Kupfer, Joseph. "Can Parents and Children Be Friends?" *American Philosophical Quarterly* 27:1 (January 1990): 15–26.

Langton, Rae. "Duty and Desolation." *Philosophy* 67 (October 1992): 481–505.

Mason, Elinor. "Can an Indirect Consequentialist Be a Real Friend?" *Ethics* 108:2 (January 1998): 386–93.

Oldenquist, Andrew. "Loyalties." *Journal of Philosophy* 79:4 (April 1982): 173–93.

Passell, Dan. "Duties to Friends." *Journal of Value Inquiry* 25 (1991): 161–65.

Pettit, Philip, and Robert Goodin. "The Possibility of Special Duties." *Canadian Journal of Philosophy* 16:4 (1986): 651–76.

Piper, Adrian M. S. "Moral Theory and Moral Alienation." *Journal of Philosophy* 84:2 (February 1987): 102–18.

———. "Impartiality, Compassion, and Modal Imagination." *Ethics* 101:4 (July 1991): 726–57.

Schall, James V. "Friendship and Political Philosophy." *Review of Metaphysics* 50 (September 1996): 121–41.

Scheffler, Samuel. "Individual Responsibility in a Global Age." In *Contemporary Political and Social Philosophy*, edited by Ellen Frankel Paul et al., 219–36. Cambridge: Cambridge University Press, 1995.

———. "Relationships and Responsibilities." *Philosophy and Public Affairs* 26:3 (Summer 1997): 189–209.

Schoeman, Ferdinand. "Aristotle on the Good of Friendship." *Australasian Journal of Philosophy* 63:3 (September 1985): 269–82.

Schwartzenbach, Sibyl A. "On Civic Friendship." *Ethics* 107:1 (October 1996): 97–128.

Stocker, Michael. "Values and Purposes: The Limits of Teleology and the Ends of Friendship." *Journal of Philosophy* 78:12 (December 1981): 747–65.

Swanton, Christine. "Profiles of the Virtues." *Pacific Philosophical Quarterly* 76 (1995): 47–71.

Whiting, Jennifer. "Friends and Future Selves." *Philosophical Review* 95:4 (October 1986): 547–80.

———. "Impersonal Friends." *The Monist* 74 (January 1991): 3–29.

Winstead, Barbara A. "Sex Differences in Same-Sex Friendships." In *Friendship and Social Interaction*, edited by Valerian J. Derlega and Barbara A. Winstead, 81. New York: Springer-Verlag, 1986.

Wolf, Susan. "Morality and Partiality." In *Philosophical Perspectives, 6, Ethics, 1992*, edited by James E. Tomberlin, 243–59. Atascadero, Calif.: Ridgeview, 1992.

INDEX

191